BACKROADS & BYWAYS OF

MINNESOTA

BACKROADS & BYWAYS OF

MINNESOTA

Drives, Day Trips &
Weekend Excursions

SECOND EDITION

AMY C. REA

THE COUNTRYMAN PRESS
A division of W. W. Norton & Company
Independent Publishers Since 1923

We welcome your comments and suggestions.
Please contact:
Editor
The Countryman Press
500 Fifth Avenue
New York, NY 10110
or e-mail countrymanpress@wwnorton.com.

Photo page 168: © Shutterstock.com/John Brueske
Maps by Michael Borop (sitesatlas.com)

For information about special discounts for bulk purchases, please contact
W. W. Norton Special Sales at specialsales@wwnorton.com or 800-233-4830

The Countryman Press
www.countrymanpress.com

A division of W. W. Norton & Company, Inc.
500 Fifth Avenue, New York, NY 10110
www.wwnorton.com

978-1-68268-297-5 (pbk.)

10 9 8 7 6 5 4 3 2 1

In memory of my father, Ernie Crippen, who loved the state of Minnesota, helped build a good many roads across it, and was thrilled that his daughter had the opportunity to explore and write about this wonderful state.

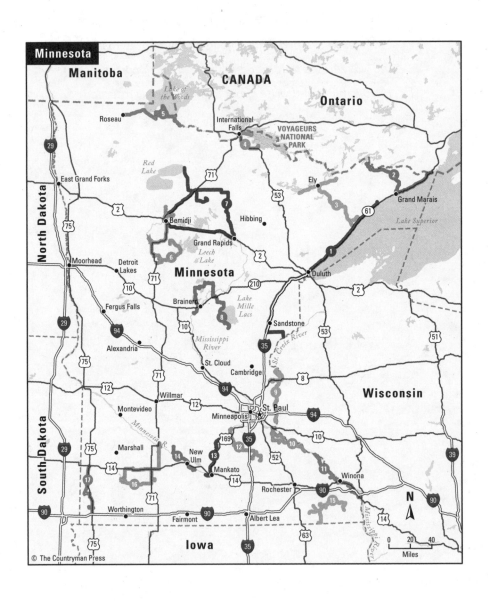

Contents

Acknowledgments

Where to even begin? So many people, directly and indirectly, helped me with this project, and in some cases I don't even know their names. For example: the blond woman at the International Falls Visitor Center who took one look at me—when I'd been on the road for hours on a hot day and had just emerged from the detour from hell—wagged her finger, and said, "You look like you could use a view and a drink." Truer words were never spoken, and her recommendation that I head east out of International Falls and make my way to Sha Sha Resort was spot on. An hour later, I was on a sunny deck overlooking Rainy Lake, enjoying a walleye salad and a Summit beer, and the stress of the day was melting away. Whoever you are, friendly woman in International Falls—thank you.

Staff at visitor centers and chambers of commerce, servers in restaurants, clerks in stores and gas stations, other tourists on hiking trails, employees and volunteers at county and state historical society branches and sites, DNR personnel at state parks and online, my friends on Twitter—who not only encouraged me, but gave me tips and leads: these are just a few of the people who offered me insight and help when I most needed it.

And, of course, thanks to Jim and Mitchell and Michael, my very own family, who have put up with absences and long-winded dinnertime conversations about arcane Minnesota subjects. I love you all!

Introduction

The word Minnesota comes from a Dakota word meaning "sky-tinted water," an appropriate name for the land of 10,000 lakes—or more accurately, 15,000 lakes. With the Mississippi headwaters here, and the Minnesota and St. Croix Rivers flowing through its countryside, Minnesota is also a state of rushing rivers. The state's terrain varies wildly: from rolling, swooping roads and bluffs along the rivers to the expansive prairies in the south and west to the dramatic, hilly vistas along the North Shore of Lake Superior, and the dense forests and wetlands of the northern part of the state. Most of the state's lakes and rivers were formed from glacial drift thousands of years ago. The southeastern corner of the state, known as the Driftless Zone, is the one exception.

The state's first inhabitants were the Anishinaabe and Dakota tribes. Later, the Sioux made their way into the state, as did the European traders known as voyageurs. Violence arising from tensions between Europeans and Native Americans is an ugly part of the state's history, with its culmination in the Dakota War of 1862, which led to the largest mass execution of indigenous people in Minnesota history, along with the deaths of hundreds more. The War is remembered and documented throughout south-central Minnesota.

Logging and farming were the two primary occupations in the early settler years, followed closely by mining in the northeastern part of the state and tourism around the Brainerd Lakes area. Industrialization increased in Minnesota after World War II and resulted in population growth in larger city centers. Some rural towns, however, disappeared altogether, while others have found a way to, if not grow, remain stable enough to thrive.

This book takes you to many of those towns. These are villages and hamlets where you can find all manner of history preserved in small museums and community centers. Still, the biggest motivator for traveling outside the Twin Cities metropolitan area is, to put it mildly, to enjoy the view. Lakes and rivers, bogs and wetlands, dense old-growth forests, rolling hills full of trees and wildflowers, and wide-open prairies are all to be found within the state's borders. Opportunities for outdoor recreation seem nearly endless: hiking, biking, canoeing, swimming, fishing, hunting, camping, geocaching, backpacking, snowshoeing, sledding, skating, downhill and cross-country skiing, skijoring, dogsledding, snowmobiling, ice fishing. Whatever the season, there's a way to enjoy the beauty Minnesota has to offer.

I truly loved researching this book. While the project was often exhausting, it was never dull. Every corner I turned, I seemed to find something new and exciting. Until you've spent time in greater Minnesota (as the area beyond the Twin Cities is known), you really haven't begun to experience what the state has to offer.

YEAR-ROUND TRAVELS

As already noted, you can travel the state year-round and find plenty of things to do. However, winter outstate is a different beast than winter in the metro area. There's no disputing how beautiful it can be—miles of untouched snow, trees covered in hoarfrost, brilliant blue skies, and exhilaratingly intense sunsets over frozen lakes. But if you're planning on traveling outstate, especially to the western part of the state, keep a close watch on the weather: in areas where there are wide-open spaces, particularly in the southwest, snowstorms can be windswept into zero visibility, and highways can sometimes be closed. Always travel with a winter safety kit in your car, which should include a fully charged cell phone, a flashlight and spare batteries, blankets (yes, multiple), a shovel, extra clothes in case you need to turn your car off, nonperishable snacks and bottled water, flares, rope, a knife of some sort, waterproof matches and candles, and a first-aid kit.

I don't mean to make traveling in winter in Minnesota sound like an especially dangerous or foolish thing to do. But use common sense—if the weather forecaster is sounding apocalyptic, it might be a good idea to postpone your trip.

That said, summer is the peak time to visit many of these places, as travelers are drawn to warm, sunny days outdoors. In most areas, you'll find some of the visitor attractions (museums, restaurants) have limited or seasonal hours. When planning your trip in the winter months, be sure to confirm which sites are open and when to avoid being disappointed.

One thing you can nearly always find open is a state park. Most of Minnesota's 70-plus state parks are open for at least some of the winter. And for good reason: winter recreation enthusiasts appreciate the opportunities to get out their cross-country skis or snowshoes and take in the natural beauty

found in these parks. Many parks offer special winter activities and events, sometimes highlighting the area's history as viewed through a wintry lens.

FINDING YOUR WAY

A good state map is essential, but if you really want to explore the back roads and byways, you're going to need more than that. Most of the county routes (designated throughout as CR) don't appear on state maps for lack of room. One solution is, of course, GPS; however, that's not 100 percent reliable either. On my journeys, I was sometimes frustrated to be told I was on a road in a different county, and on one memorable trip, the GPS informed me that I wasn't on a road at all, although the view out the front windshield convinced me otherwise.

The best thing I did to prepare for these trips was to purchase county road maps from the Minnesota Department of Transportation (call 651-366-3017 for more information, or visit the website www.dot.state.mn.us/mapsales). These were inexpensive and incredibly detailed, and they kept me from getting lost on many occasions. They may be a bit bulky to carry around, but if you're wandering around a part of the state that has a bewildering number of county routes that don't show up on your state map, and your GPS has given up trying, these maps are invaluable.

SPEAKING OF ROADS . . .

The annual summer joke is that road construction is Minnesota's fifth season. While technology has improved to the point that some construction jobs can be done year-round, summer remains the prime time for roadwork (if for no other reason than to fix the potholes created by winter turning into spring). Minnesota's Department of Transportation does an admirable job of updating their website (www.dot.state.mn.us) with roadwork around the state, and I'd strongly advise checking with them when planning specific routes and dates. There's nothing more dispiriting than coming on an unexpected, lengthy detour.

That said, I wouldn't necessarily recommend trying to avoid detours; you never know what you might discover by going off the main route. However, it's more enjoyable if you know it's coming and you're not scrambling to reach your bed-and-breakfast before the sun goes down on the very dark Gunflint Trail.

You'll find some roads are paved and in good condition. Others may be in need of work, so it makes sense to take things a bit more slowly. You'll also end up on some gravel roads, which do not make for the most comfortable drive but are always worth the trouble to get to your final destination.

ROUTES AND TIMING

At the beginning of each chapter, I've included an estimated distance for the described drive and the travel time required to complete it. Take the word "estimated" very seriously. Estimated times are of the "as the crow flies" variety, and they assume a moderate speed with only a few stops. If you want to visit most of the sites along each route, your trip time will increase, especially if you decide to enjoy some of the outdoor recreational opportunities. How much extra time? That's not for me to say—how long will you need to linger over works of art at the Minnesota Marine Art Museum in Winona? How much time will you spend climbing the Mount Rose Trail in Grand Portage, or browsing the fun shops in Nisswa, or biking the Heartland Trail, or touring the Ellsworth Rock Gardens by boat tour on Kabetogama Lake? Anything is possible.

Finally, remember to be respectful of the places you visit. Signs in various state parks ask that you leave only footprints and take only pictures. If you're visiting a small historical museum, consider making a small donation to help them continue to operate and grow their collections. Thank your bed-and-breakfast proprietor and the staff at the local café who made you an amazing batch of pancakes with local maple syrup. These gems are all valuable, and we want them around for years to come.

1

THE NORTH SHORE, PART 1
Hinckley to Lutsen

ESTIMATED DISTANCE: 165 miles

ESTIMATED TIME: 2 hours 45 minutes

GETTING THERE: From the Twin Cities, take I-35W north to Duluth, then follow old MN 61 north to Lutsen.

HIGHLIGHTS: The view overlooking Lake Superior; small shipping towns like Two Harbors; historic sites including Split Rock Lighthouse; and numerous points of natural beauty, including Gooseberry Falls and Palisade Head. This route can be extended by adding the Gunflint Trail, Grand Marais, and Grand Portage (see Chapter 2).

In a state that has lakes small and large, prairies, and rolling countryside, it's hard to pick one area as the most scenic, but the North Shore has arguably some of the loveliest vistas in the state, and the region is one of the state's most popular for visitors.

The eastern edge of the Arrowhead runs along the shores of Lake Superior. Much of the Lake Superior area was inhabited by the Ojibwe before the arrival of the Europeans. The French were prominent explorers and settlers in this region, looking for furs and other goods for trade, and their influence is seen in towns with names like Grand Marais and Grand Portage. Fur trading remained a central activity until about 1840, when most of the traders and trappers moved elsewhere. The arrival of railroads in 1869, combined with increased ship traffic on Lake Superior, however, led to a population boom. The growth of commercial fishing, the development of the iron ore industry, sophisticated new infrastructure and shipping methods further helped to establish communities and also led to the beginning of the tourism

LEFT: SPLIT ROCK LIGHTHOUSE

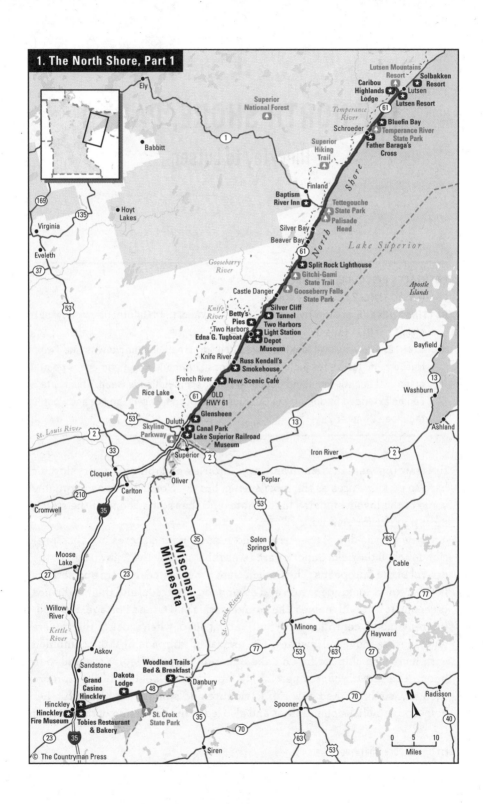

1. The North Shore, Part 1

Ely

Superior National Forest

Lutsen Mountains Resort
Solbakken Resort
Caribou Highlands Lodge
Lutsen
Lutsen Resort
61
Temperance River
Bluefin Bay
Schroeder
Temperance River State Park
Father Baraga's Cross

Babbitt

1

Superior Hiking Trail

Finland

North Shore

169

135

Hoyt Lakes

Baptism River Inn

Tettegouche State Park
Palisade Head

Virginia

Eveleth

37

Silver Bay
Beaver Bay
61

Lake Superior

53

Gooseberry River

Split Rock Lighthouse
Gitchi-Gami State Trail
Gooseberry Falls State Park

Apostle Islands

Castle Danger

Knife River

Betty's Pies
Silver Cliff Tunnel
Two Harbors Light Station
Edna G. Tugboat
Two Harbors
Depot Museum

Bayfield

Knife River

Russ Kendall's Smokehouse

13

Washburn

French River
New Scenic Café

Rice Lake

61
OLD HWY 61
Glensheen

Ashland

53

St. Louis River

2

Duluth
Skyline Parkway
Canal Park
Lake Superior Railroad Museum

13

Superior

2

Iron River

2

33

Oliver

Poplar

Cloquet

Carlton

210

53

Cromwell

35

Solon Springs

63

Cable

Moose Lake

35

Willow River

Wisconsin
Minnesota

23

27

77

Kettle River

St. Croix River

Minong

Hayward

Askov

77

53

63

27

Sandstone

Woodland Trails Bed & Breakfast

Dakota Lodge

Danbury

70

Radisson

Grand Casino Hinckley

48

N

Hinckley
Hinckley Fire Museum

St. Croix State Park

35

Spooner

40

Tobies Restaurant & Bakery

23

35

70

Siren

70

63

53

0   5   10
Miles

© The Countryman Press

industry. During the region's heyday, the lumber and agricultural industries also boomed but suffered later on during the Depression when competition in other parts of the country reduced their prominence.

Today's North Shore still sees considerable commercial fishing and mining activity, but tourism has come to play an ever-increasing role in the local economy. Whereas visitors used to arrive only in the summer for fishing and hiking, they now come year-round, taking advantage of the area's winter landscape for activities like skiing, snowmobiling, snowshoeing, and even dogsledding.

If you're traveling north from the Twin Cities via I-35W, it's worth a brief stop in Hinckley to visit the **Hinckley Fire Museum**. On September 1, 1894, a historic event occurred in this quiet logging town. A fire started, and while any fire that burns out of control in the wilderness can be considered a wildfire and therefore devastating, the fire that consumed Hinckley was worse. Its technical name is firestorm; flames shot up 4 miles into the air, and 20 square miles of land were destroyed in less than four hours. The firestorm evolved much like a natural disaster, with cyclones of fire advancing and wreaking havoc. The only other comparable firestorms in the twentieth century were related to the launching of atomic bombs in Hiroshima.

The Hinckley Fire Museum is housed in a small building that previously served as the town's railroad depot (built to replace the one destroyed by the firestorm). Though small, it has a sizable collection of fire artifacts, as well as a brief documentary movie on view, and several Native American pieces. The friendly staff knows the history of the firestorm well and is happy to answer questions or provide information on the individual artifacts.

Also worth a visit is **St. Croix State Park**, the largest of Minnesota's state parks at just over 34,000 acres. Hiking, biking, canoeing, horseback riding, and camping are all popular warm-weather activities, especially along trails that explore the Kettle River and St. Croix River. Winter finds the park attractive to cross-country skiers, snowshoeing enthusiasts, and snowmobilers.

You can also take a break from driving and visit the legendary **Tobies Restaurant & Bakery**, conveniently located right on the interstate. Tobies' claim to fame is its cinnamon and caramel rolls. Having grown from its location on a prominent tourist route, this self-nicknamed Halfway Stop now serves breakfast, lunch, and dinner 24 hours a day. The nearby **Grand Casino Hinckley** also offers several dining options.

Hinckley is a good place to stop for the night if you've left the Twin Cities late in the afternoon. Consider planning ahead and reserving a room at either of these two fine lodging choices. **Dakota Lodge** offers a wide variety of accommodations: four bed-and-breakfast lodge rooms, all with private bath and fireplaces; cabins; and a two-bedroom guesthouse. The bed-and-breakfast rooms come with a full breakfast daily. The property is a naturalist's haven, with easy access to nearby St. Croix State Park.

Woodland Trails Bed & Breakfast is a country charmer situated on 500 acres of woodland. The property includes 4 miles of trails for hiking as well as access to Grace Lake for bird-watching, paddleboating, or catch-and-release fishing. The five guest rooms are each equipped with private baths and electric fireplaces. A full breakfast is included.

Back on I-35W, enjoy the sweeping vista that greets you when you arrive in Duluth. You'll witness the city sloping down to the harbor, ore boats proceeding slowly through the canal as sailboats large and small dot the waters around them, and the famous Aerial Lift Bridge that connects Duluth with neighboring Wisconsin. Originally settled by Sioux and Ojibwe tribe members, Duluth established itself as a central port for shipping in the United States in the mid-1800s. Besides being the only US port to have access to both the Atlantic and the Pacific, Duluth was on the edge of large-scale lumber, grain, and mining operations that kept the city growing. In the early twentieth century, steel production further boosted Duluth's prominence. In the second half of the twentieth century, however, foreign competition in the steel industry had a severe impact on the city. Refocused efforts on promoting Duluth as a tourist destination, along with renovation of waterfront areas, brought new life to the area.

Duluth's shipping history is on display at the **S.S. William A. Irvin**, which for over 40 years not only delivered coal and iron ore but also transported dignitaries around the Great Lakes region. Today the ship is available for tours during the summer, and in October she becomes the "Ship of Ghouls."

Another facet of Duluth's history is available for exploration at the **Lake Superior Railroad Museum**. Devoted to Duluth's locomotive history, the museum has on display vintage wood-burning steam engines (including the largest one ever built), railroad snowplows, and an operating model train exhibition. Between Memorial Day and Labor Day, visitors can ride a vintage electric trolley around the museum or sign up to take a ride on the **North Shore Scenic Railroad**, which has a number of options. Visitors who purchase a ride on the North Shore Scenic Railroad are eligible for discounts on museum admission.

A different aspect of Duluth's history can be found at **Glensheen**. Just north of downtown Duluth, on a stretch of Lake Superior shoreline, sits the 39-room Glensheen mansion. Built in the early 1900s by the prosperous Congdon family, Glensheen is now open to the public as a historical site. There are three tours available to suit different levels of interest and time commitment: the house's exterior and grounds; the exterior, grounds, and first and second floors; or all of these plus the third floor, attic, and basement. In addition, there are several seasonal specialty tours as well. The comprehensive tour, while long (and toasty in warmer weather because central air conditioning was not available when the mansion was built), is worth the extra time, if you can manage it. The docents are well trained and full of interesting tidbits about the mansion's history and construction, and the home is still filled with original furniture, decorations, and artwork. The grounds, set on a wide expanse of shoreline, include a rocky beach, a boat-house, a carriage house, and a gardener's home, as well as extensive, lavish gardens.

One event that goes unmentioned during the tour is the murder of Elisa-beth Congdon and her nurse at Glensheen in 1977. In the past, docents were not allowed to talk about it. This is no longer the case, but you will have to inquire at the end of the tour. For some, this is reason enough to visit Glen-sheen. For others, visiting Glensheen provides an unusually detailed and carefully preserved view of a lost way of life.

A great place to spend a sunny afternoon is **Canal Park**. This area, which surrounds the Minnesota side of the **Aerial Lift Bridge**, is full of small shops and restaurants, both for dine-in or to carry out and enjoy on a walk along the bridge's pier. You can also wander down the **Lakewalk**, a 3-mile board-walk that hugs the Lake Superior shoreline and runs the distance of down-town. Periodic stairways and paths provide access to additional shops and restaurants, and there are plenty of benches where you can rest and watch the boats going by.

Canal Park is home to several browse-worthy shops: **The Dewitt-Seitz Marketplace**, itself listed on the National Register of Historic Places, houses **Blue Heron Trading Co.**, a gift and cookware store; **Northern Waters**

Sights along the Parkway

Skyline Parkway is a short scenic byway that provides impressive views of Duluth and the harbor as it winds through residential and rural areas along the ridges above downtown. The parkway can be maddening to follow. It's not terribly well marked, although the city is working to remedy that, but taking this route is worth the effort for spectacular views of Lake Superior, the city of Duluth, and western Wisconsin. Take a detailed Duluth map with you, and be aware that parts of the road are closed during the winter months. Along the way, you can visit **Enger Park**, a small but lush picnic area with a stone tower open for climbing and shaded picnic tables spread generously throughout the grounds. During the summer months, the floral display here is breathtaking. A large park set along Lake Superior, **Leif Erikson Park** offers strolls along the lakeside, an open-air amphithe-ater that hosts live performances during the summer months, and a lovely, fragrant rose garden.

Smokehaus, a gourmet food shop; **J. Skylark Company**, a toy store; and **Art Dock**, featuring artworks and craft items by local artists.

There are also several good dining options in Canal Park. You can stop by **Grandma's Saloon and Grill**, **Lake Avenue Café**, **Little Angie's Cantina**, **Canal Park Brewery**, or **Bellisio's**. Not far from the lakefront are **Fitger's Brewhouse and Grill** (part of a larger complex that includes shopping and lodging), **Pizza Luce**, **Burrito Union**, **Zeitgeist Arts Café**, **OMC Smokehouse**, and **JJ Astor Restaurant**, situated at the top of the **Radisson Hotel**, with a revolving dining room for aerial viewing. **The Boat Club**, located in the historic **Fitger's Inn**, has upscale American food. The **Duluth Grill** serves three hearty meals a day. **Endion Station** is close to the Lakewalk and specializes in fun takes on bar foods. Not far from downtown is **At Sara's Table**, near the University of Minnesota campus and renowned for its locally sourced foods. **Tavern on the Hill** offers new twists on classic items like sandwiches and pizzas. **Silos Restaurant** offers gourmet versions of American classics, including steak and seafood. **Sound Duluth** has creative fusion food. You will also find **Amazing Grace Bakery & Café,** offering casual food and baked goods. **Black Woods Grill & Bar** has locally sourced flatbreads, soups, salads, and sandwiches, while **Pickwick** has steaks and ribs in a charming old pub-style building. Finally, just outside Duluth on Old MN 61 is the **New Scenic Café**, one of the area's best restaurants, so it's a good idea to make reservations. The menu changes frequently and incorporates what's available locally for the season.

Lodging is also plentiful, but it's best to plan ahead for weekends, even in winter. Just south of Duluth is **Mountain Villas on Spirit Mountain**, 14 unique cottages open year-round. In Canal Park, try the **Canal Park Lodge**, the **Inn on Lake Superior** (the rooftop outdoor pool is open year-round), **Captain's Canal Park**, **The Suites Hotel at Waterfront Plaza**, or the **South Pier Inn**. Close to Canal Park is the **Park Point Marina Inn** and **Pier B Resort Hotel**. Near the harbor and the lake is the **Beacon Pointe Resort**. Across the harbor from Canal Park is **Cottage on the Point**, a bed-and-breakfast in a historic home. On Duluth's east end, there are a number of turn-of-the-century bed-and-breakfasts (see the sidebar on the next page), as well as the **A. Charles Weiss Inn**, a historic home built by the former editor and publisher of the *Duluth Herald*. Constructed in 1895, the inn offers five rooms with private bath, and it is available as a whole-house rental only. On Park Point Beach, **Solglimt** is a bed-and-breakfast with five suites and 120 feet of shoreline. A bit further up the shore is **North Shore Lighthouse Suites**, built as a model of a Michigan lighthouse and offering two units with two bedrooms each. Nearby is **The Inn on Gitche Gumee**, a delightful property that was once a motel but has been refurbished into charming cottages. Near the lake, **Dodges Log Lodges** is, as its name implies, a resort with log lodging.

When it's time to move on from Duluth, find MN 61. While many people think of this direction as heading north, it's actually northeast, and you might sometimes hear this route referred to as heading east. Note: there are actually two MN 61 routes. The official route runs parallel to old MN 61, but old MN 61 is a better choice, because it's closer to the shoreline of Lake Superior and offers a better view of the lakefront along the way. You'll see all manner of lakeshore lifestyle, from elaborate houses and resorts to decades-old fishing cabins and family-owned motels. There are several small towns in the early stretch of the drive, including French River and Knife River, towns built during the mining glory days and still alive today thanks to fishing and tourism. In Knife River, stop at the highly regarded **Russ Kendall's Smokehouse**, the oldest smokehouse on the North Shore, for some topnotch herring, smoked whitefish, or salmon.

A few miles north of Knife River is Two Harbors, an iron ore and fishing port. Staying on MN 61 doesn't take you to the scenic, historic heart of the town, so turn right on Waterfront Drive and continue a few blocks to the shore, where you'll find a more typical harborside small town. From Two

Bed & Breakfasts

At Duluth's east end, not on Lake Superior but within a short drive or walk, is a stretch of historical houses (including the Congdon mansion, Glensheen). Here you'll find a cluster of bed-and-breakfasts, most from the nineteenth or early twentieth centuries and often built by prominent citizens of the time.

Built in 1909 by architect Edwin H. Hewitt, the **A. G. Thomson House** has four rooms with private baths in the main house as well as three rooms with private baths in the adjacent carriage house.

The Cotton Mansion, a 16,000-square-foot 1908 Italianate mansion, offers seven rooms and suites, all sumptuously appointed. A full breakfast is served each morning by candlelight, and an afternoon wine and cheese service is provided daily.

The Ellery House's four elegant suites all have private baths, robes, and feather beds; one suite has a private sun porch, while another has a separate sitting area.

The Firelight Inn on Oregon Creek was built in 1910 and offers five suites with private baths, robes, and in-room breakfast. Public areas include a glassed-in porch, a second-floor deck, and a sitting room with fireplace.

The Olcott House's luxurious accommodations include five suites with private baths, as well as a separate carriage house suite. Several suites have fireplaces and whirlpool tubs; all have air conditioning, LCD TVs, and either a four-poster or canopy bed.

TWO HARBORS LIGHT STATION

Harbors, the view to the lake is focused on an enormous ore dock, still used today for taconite from the Iron Range. Dwarfed by the dock is the **Edna G.**, the last coal-fired, steam-powered tugboat, permanently anchored and available for tours seasonally. Nearby is the **Duluth and Iron Range Depot**, formerly the headquarters for that company, today home to the **Depot Museum** and a testament to the importance of railroads to the area.

From the Depot Museum, travel on South Avenue as it winds shoreward until you reach the **Two Harbors Light Station**. First lit in 1892, the Light Station is still illuminated today, although automation has replaced the lighthouse keeper. The site today is a historic museum, open seasonally for visitors, and part of the lighthouse serves as the **Lighthouse Bed & Breakfast**, for guests who want to experience its history more intimately.

The grounds and adjacent shoreline are worthy of exploration. A trail from the lighthouse leads you out to the rocky outcroppings, which are easy hiking (but use caution when the rocks are slippery), or you can take a walk along the water break into Lake Superior and get a better view of the shoreline and the iron ore dock.

Another unique lodging option is the **Northern Rail Traincar Bed & Breakfast**, which is exactly as described—a bed-and-breakfast built out of train cars. Unusual for a B&B, this establishment welcomes children. If you'd like more traditional lodging, the Superior Shores Resort has everything you'll need, including a prime location on the lakefront.

For meals, it's hard to beat the menu at the **Rustic Inn Café**, open for breakfast, lunch, and dinner, and **Betty's Pies** has been famous for years for its pastries. Pizza aficionados will appreciate the made-from-scratch offerings at **Do North Pizza**. **Black Woods** is an offshoot of the Duluth restaurant with classic bar food, including soups, salads, and sandwiches. If you're looking for a coffee shop with breakfast and lunch options, try **Vanilla Bean**, or **Judy's Café**, for a home-cooked diner feel.

Returning to MN 61, a few miles northeast of Two Harbors, you'll pass through a massive tunnel carved into Silver Cliff. Beyond being an impressive sight, the tunnel serves as the gateway to the "true" North Shore.

NORTHERN RAIL TRAINCAR BED & BREAKFAST

From this point forward, the drive will become more hilly and the scenery more dramatic as rock cliffs tower over the narrow road, which passes over fast-flowing rivers and through thick forests of ash, birch, aspen, and evergreens.

Shortly after you pass through the town Castle Danger (which, in spite of its evocative name, doesn't appear to have a dangerous castle), you'll reach **Gooseberry Falls State Park**. This waterfall is by no means the largest in the United States, but the park is friendly and easy to navigate, with a sizable visitor center and extensive trails and walkways. Pets are allowed, and there are "doggie bags" strategically placed to encourage dog owners to clean up after their pets. The park twists and turns around the base of the falls, allowing access on both sides. Be sure to wear sturdy shoes; crossing wet rocks is a tricky proposition even in the best footgear, and flip-flops could be downright dangerous. Many visitors stay in the falls area, but if you have the time, take the River View Trail to Agate Beach, where the Gooseberry River flows into Lake Superior. The trail will take you high onto the cliffs overlooking the river, then onto the beautiful stony beach.

Just a few miles north of Gooseberry Falls, you'll find another state park worth visiting: **Split Rock Lighthouse State Park**. This small safety beacon for passing ships is situated on a dramatic, steep cliff, where it proved its worth for decades. Now the lighthouse is open for tourists to visit. The large visitor center holds a gift shop and video presentation. If you're feeling fit, take the trail that leads down the side of the cliff to the beach below (171 steps each way) for amazing views of the lighthouse and the surrounding

GOOSEBERRY FALLS AT GOOSEBERRY FALLS STATE PARK

shorelines. The park's grounds are connected to the **Gitchi-Gami State Trail**, which is available for use by bikers or inline skaters. The lighthouse itself is rarely lit anymore, but every year on the anniversary of the sinking of the *Edmund Fitzgerald* (November 10), a ceremony and lighting take place.

As you drive northeast on MN 61, you'll arrive in Silver Bay. A stop at the

BEARGREASE TRAIL

Chamber of Commerce (located on MN 61) will get you the directions you need to find the cemetery where John Beargrease is buried. Beargrease was a legendary mail carrier on the North Shore in the early 1900s, employing sled dogs and canoes to bring the mail to the remote edges of the state. Duluth's famous John Beargrease Sled Dog Marathon, held each January, commemorates his accomplishments.

PALISADE HEAD

About 4 miles north of Silver Bay, look for signs on the right directing you to **Palisade Head**. Off MN 61, the gravel road is short and narrow, leading you to a parking lot and scenic overlook off a 200-foot rock cliff formed by lava over a billion years ago. Palisade Head is technically part of **Tettegouche State Park**, although it's not physically part of the park itself. This is a popular spot for rock climbers, but even if you don't climb, you'll be rewarded with the views afforded from the parking lot. On a good weather day, you can see Split Rock Lighthouse in the distance and

Hiking on the North Shore

The North Shore is a hiker's (and biker's) paradise. There are trails looping up and down the shore, sometimes intersecting with one another, in and out of state parks and **Superior National Forest**. Many are short and meant for easy day hikes, but others offer opportunities for longer and more ambitious treks. **The Superior Hiking Trail** is a collection of hiking byways and trails covering 277 miles along the Lake Superior shoreline from Jay Cooke State Park south of Duluth to the Canadian border west of Grand Portage. Loop trails allow hikers to complete a circle in a short period of time, and frequent campsites and parking lots allow visitors to choose between short day hikes and extended. Contact the Superior Hiking Trail Association for information on its Lodge-to-Lodge Hiking Programs, which allow non-camping hikers to reserve lodging along the trail and have routes plotted accordingly by the association.

The **Gitchi-Gami State Trail** is a work in progress, but final plans include 86 miles of nonmotorized trails extending from Two Harbors to Grand Marais. At press time, various portions of the trail were complete, some in unconnected chunks, the longest finished section located between Gooseberry Falls State Park and Beaver Bay, with a satellite trail leading to Split Rock Lighthouse State Park. Check the Gitchi-Gami Trail Association for updated information on completed sections and parking information.

the Sawtooth Mountains to the northeast, as well as Wisconsin's Apostle Islands directly east. If you're traveling with young children, hang on to them—Palisade Head does not have safety fences. For overnight arrangements, look no further than the **Baptism River Inn**, a beautiful log cabin bed-and-breakfast.

Tettegouche State Park is also well worth a visit. The park has nearly every kind of natural feature—Lake Superior shoreline, waterfalls and rivers (including the 60-foot High Falls), mountainous hiking terrain, six inland lakes, and dense forests. There are 23 miles of hiking trails; in winter, cross-country skiers have access to 15 miles of trails. Snowmobilers and ATV users have limited trails to use as well.

Near Schroeder you'll see a sign pointing the way to **Father Baraga's Cross,** a historic site with a lovely vista. Father Baraga was a Slovenian priest who took on the arduous task of ministering to a number of Ojibwe settlements in Minnesota, Wisconsin, and Michigan, often traveling by snowshoe or canoe. After surviving a devastating storm in which his canoe was tossed by the wind into the mouth of the Cross River, Father Baraga erected a wooden cross in gratitude, which was later replaced with the granite cross

TRAIL AT TETTEGOUCHE STATE PARK

that stands there today. A visit to the site in inclement weather could give you some idea what Father Baraga faced and why he was so thankful to have survived.

Not far from Father Baraga's Cross is the heavily wooded **Temperance River State Park**, good for camping, hiking, rock climbing, cross-country skiing, and snowmobiling. To gain one of the best vantage points in the park, take the trail that winds upstream from the parking lot until you reach the Temperance River Gorge, a trail that is incredibly narrow and leads to many spectacular waterfalls.

FATHER BARAGA'S CROSS, TOFTE

At first glance, the township of **Lutsen** appears to be nothing more than a wide spot in the road with a coffee shop and convenience store (where you can buy fish bait and yarn). But Lutsen is Minnesota's largest ski area, boasting 90 runs of varying difficulty across four mountains. Downhill skiers, snowboarders, and cross-country skiers have 1,000 acres of land at their disposal, along with an Alpine Slide and a mountain tram for prime sightseeing, and there's also the option of learning to dogsled through **Stoney Creek Kennels**. Lutsen isn't just popular in the winter, although that is its prime season; the area's lush greenery attracts numerous visitors in summer who enjoy hiking, horseback riding, mountain biking, rock climbing, kayaking, and canoeing. What Lutsen lacks in "town" amenities, it more than makes up for in natural beauty and outdoor recreation. For lodging, there are many resorts that cater to skiers and hikers, including **Lutsen Resort**, **Bluefin Bay** (which also has a great restaurant, the **Bluefin Grille**), **Solbakken Resort**, and **Caribou Highlands Lodge**. Nearly all the resorts in the area offer some kind of dining option, or you can cook your own meals if you've booked a condo or townhouse.

IN THE AREA

Accommodations

A. CHARLES WEISS INN, 1615 East Superior Street, Duluth. Call 888-640-7927. Website: www.vrbo.com/433553.

A.G. THOMSON HOUSE, 2617 East 3rd Street, Duluth. Call 218-724-3464; 877-807-8077. Website: www.thomsonhouse.biz.

BAPTISM RIVER INN, 6125 MN 1, Silver Bay. Call 218-353-0707; 877-353-0707. Website: www.baptismriverinn.com.

BEACON POINTE RESORT, 2100 Water Street, Duluth. Call 218-724-1100; 877-462-3226. Website: www.beaconpointeduluth.com.

BLUEFIN BAY ON LAKE SUPERIOR, 7192 MN 1, Tofte. Call 218-663-7296; 800-258-3346. Website: www.bluefinbay.com.

CANAL PARK LODGE, 250 Canal Park Drive, Duluth. Call 218-279-6000; 800-777-8560. Website: www.canalparklodge.com.

CAPTAIN'S CANAL PARK, 325 South Lake Avenue, Duluth. Call 218-663-7971; 800-950-4361. Website: www.cascadevacationrentals.com.

CARIBOU HIGHLANDS LODGE, 371 Ski Hill Road, Lutsen. Call 218-663-7241; 800-642-6036. Website: www.caribouhighlands.com.

COTTAGE ON THE POINT, 3332 Minnesota Avenue, Duluth. Call 218-727-3738. Website: www.cottageonthepoint.com.

COTTON MANSION, 2309 East 1st Street, Duluth. Call 218-724-6405; 800-228-1997. Website: www.cottonmansion.com.

DAKOTA LODGE, 40497 MN 48, Hinckley. Call 320-384-6052. Website: www.dakotalodge.com.

DODGES LOG LODGES, 5852 North Shore Drive, Duluth. Call 218-525-4088; 855-236-3437. Website: www.dodgeslog.com.

THE ELLERY HOUSE, 28 South 21st Avenue, Duluth. Call 218-724-7639; 800-355-3794. Website: www.elleryhouse.com.

FIRELIGHT INN ON OREGON CREEK, 2211 East 3rd Street, Duluth. Call 218-724-0272; 888-724-0273. Website: www.firelightinn.com.

THE INN ON GITCHE GUMEE, 8517 Congdon Boulevard, Duluth. Call 218-525-4979; 800-317-4979. Website: www.innongitchegumee.com.

THE INN ON LAKE SUPERIOR, 350 Canal Park Drive, Duluth. Call 218-726-1111; 888-668-4352. Website: www.theinnonlakesuperior.com.

LIGHTHOUSE BED & BREAKFAST, 1 Lighthouse Point, Two Harbors. Call 888-832-5606. Website: www.lighthousebb.org.

LUTSEN RESORT, 5700 West MN 61, Lutsen. Call 218-206-8157; 800-258-8736. Website: www.lutsenresort.com.

MOUNTAIN VILLAS, 9525 West Skyline Parkway, Duluth. Call 218-624-5784; 866-688-4552. Website: www.mtvillas.com.

NORTH SHORE LIGHTHOUSE SUITES, 5730 Homestead Road, Duluth. Call 218-349-2910. Website: www.northshorelighthousesuites.com.

NORTHERN RAIL TRAINCAR BED & BREAKFAST, 1730 County Route 3 (CR 3), Two Harbors. Call 218-834-0955; 877-834-0955. Website: www.northernrail.net.

THE OLCOTT HOUSE, 2316 East 1st Street, Duluth. Call 218-728-1339; 800-715-1339. Website: www.olcotthouse.com.

PARK POINT MARINA INN, 1033 Minnesota Avenue, Duluth. Call 218-491-7111; 888-746-2673. Website: www.parkpointmarinainn.com.

PIER B RESORT, 800 West Railroad Street, Duluth. Call 218-481-8888. Website: www.pierbresort.com.

SOLBAKKEN RESORT, 4874 West MN 61, Lutsen. Call 218-663-7566; 800-435-3950. Website: www.solbakkenresort.com.

SOLGLIMT, 828 South Lake Avenue, Duluth. Call 218-216-8954. Website: www.solglimt.com.

SOUTH PIER INN, 701 South Lake Avenue, Duluth. Call 218-786-9007; 800-430-7437. Website: www.southpierinn.com.

SUPERIOR SHORES RESORT & CONFERENCE CENTER, 1521 Superior Shores Drive, Two Harbors. Call 800-242-1988. Website: www.superior shores.com.

THE SUITES HOTEL AT WATERFRONT PLAZA, 325 South Lake Avenue, Duluth. Call 218-727-4663; 800-794-4663. Website: thesuitesduluth.com.

WOODLAND TRAILS BED & BREAKFAST, 40361 Grace Lake Road, Hinckley. Call 320-655-3901. Website: www.woodlandtrails.net.

Attractions and Recreation

DEPOT MUSEUM, 520 South Avenue, Two Harbors. Call 218-834-4898. Website: lakecountyhistoricalsociety.org/museums/view/depot-museum.

DEWITT-SEITZ MARKETPLACE, 394 South Lake Avenue, Duluth. Call 218-722-0047. Website: dewittseitz.com.

EDNA G. TUGBOAT, Two Harbors. Call 218-834-4898. Website: www .lakecountyhistoricalsociety.org/museums/view/edna-g.-tugboat.

ENGER PARK, 16th Avenue West and Skyline Parkway, Duluth. Website: www.duluthmn.gov/parks/parks-listing/enger-park.

GITCHI-GAMI STATE TRAIL. Website: www.ggta.org.

GLENSHEEN, 3300 London Road, Duluth. Call 218-726-8910. Website: glensheen.org.

GOOSEBERRY FALLS STATE PARK, 3206 MN 61 East, Two Harbors. Call 218-834-3855. Website: www.dnr.state.mn.us/state_parks/gooseberry_falls /index.html.

HINCKLEY FIRE MUSEUM, 106 Old Highway 61 South, Hinckley. Call 320-384-7338. Website: hinckleyfiremuseum.com.

JAY COOKE STATE PARK, 780 MN 210, Carlton. Call 218-673-7000. Website: www.dnr.state.mn.us/state_parks/jay_cooke/index.html.

LAKE SUPERIOR RAILROAD MUSEUM, 506 West Michigan Street, Duluth. Call 218-727-8025. Website: www.lsrm.org.

LEIF ERIKSON PARK, 1301 London Road, Duluth. Call 218-730-4300. Website: www.duluthmn.gov/parks/parks-listing/leif-erikson-park.

LUTSEN MOUNTAINS, 445 Ski Hill Road (CR 5), Lutsen. Call 218-663-7281. Website: www.lutsen.com.

NORTH SHORE COMMERCIAL FISHING MUSEUM, 7136 MN 61, Tofte. Call 218-663-7050. Website: www.commercialfishingmuseum.org.

RUSS KENDALL'S SMOKEHOUSE, 149 Scenic Drive, Knife River. Call 218-834-5995. Website: www.facebook.com/RussKendalls.

S.S. WILLIAM A. IRVIN, 301 Harbor Drive, Duluth. Call 218-722-5573. Website: decc.org/william-a-irvin.

SPLIT ROCK LIGHTHOUSE, 3713 Split Rock Lighthouse Road, Two Harbors. Call 218-226-6372. Website: www.mnhs.org/splitrock.

ST. CROIX STATE PARK, 30065 St. Croix Park Road, Hinckley. Call 320-384-6591. Website: www.dnr.state.mn.us/state_parks/st_croix/index.html.

STONEY CREEK KENNELS, 142 Sawbill Trail, Tofte. Call 218-663-0143. Website: www.stoneycreeksleddogs.com.

SUPERIOR HIKING TRAIL. Call 218-834-2700. Website: www.shta.org.

TEMPERANCE RIVER STATE PARK, 7620 West MN 61, Schroeder. Call 218-663-3100. Website: www.dnr.state.mn.us/state_parks/temperance_river/index.html.

TETTEGOUCHE STATE PARK, 5702 MN 61, Silver Bay. Call 218-353-8800. Website: www.dnr.state.mn.us/state_parks/tettegouche/index.html.

TWO HARBORS LIGHT STATION, 1 Lighthouse Point, Two Harbors. Call 218-834-4898. Website: www.lakecountyhistoricalsociety.org/museums/view/two-harbors-light-station.

Dining

AMAZING GRACE BAKERY & CAFÉ, 394 South Lake Avenue, Duluth. Call 218-723-0075. Serving three meals a day along with fresh-baked treats. Website: www.amazinggracebakeryandcafe.com.

AT SARA'S TABLE, 1902 East 8th Street, Duluth. Call 218-724-6811. American cuisine, locally sourced. Website: www.astccc.net.

BELLISIO'S, 405 South Lake Avenue, Duluth. Call 218-727-4921. Italian in a bistro setting. Website: www.bellisios.com.

BETTY'S PIES, 1633 MN 61, Two Harbors. Call 877-269-7494. Serving all three meals, but the pie is the main draw. Website: www.bettyspies.com.

BLACK WOODS GRILL & BAR, 2525 London Road, Duluth. Call 218-724-1612. Locally sourced American foods. Website: www.blackwoods.com.

BLACK WOODS TWO HARBORS, 612 7th Avenue, Two Harbors. Call 218-834-3846. Locally sourced American foods. Website: www.blackwoods.com.

BLUEFIN GRILLE, 7192 West MN 61, Tofte. Call 218-663-6200. American food with an emphasis on local Lake Superior seafood when available. Website: www.bluefinbay.com.

BOAT CLUB, 600 East Superior Street, Duluth. Call 218-727-4880. Upscale American food in the historic Fitger's Inn. Website: www.boatclubrestaurant.com.

BURRITO UNION, 1332 East 4th Street, Duluth. Call 218-728-4414. Mexican food, including breakfast. Website: www.burritounion.com.

CANAL PARK BREWERY, 300 Canal Park Drive, Duluth. Call 218-464-4790. Brewery and upscale bar food. Website: www.canalparkbrewery.com.

DO NORTH PIZZA, 15 Waterfront Drive, Two Harbors. Call 218-834-3555. Upscale pizza with dough and sauces made in-house. Website: www.donorthpizza.com.

DULUTH GRILL, I-35 and 27th Avenue West, Duluth. Call 218-726-1150. Hearty breakfasts, extensive lunch and dinner options. Website: duluthgrill.com.

ENDION STATION, 200 Lake Place Drive, Duluth. Call 218-722-4251. Craft beer, cider, and bar food. Website: www.endionstation.com.

FITGER'S BREWHOUSE AND GRILL, 600 East Superior Street, Duluth. Call 218-279-2739. Open daily for lunch and dinner. Hearty sandwiches, burgers, and quesadillas, all available with your choice of brew. Website: www.fitgeresbrewhouse.com.

GRANDMA'S SALOON & GRILL, Canal Park: 522 South Lake Avenue, Duluth. Call 218-727-4192. Miller Hill: 2202 Maple Grove Road, Duluth. Call 218-727-4192. American cuisine. Website: www.grandmasrestaurants.com.

J.J. ASTOR RESTAURANT, 505 West Superior Street (in the Radisson Hotel), Duluth. Call 218-727-8439. Upscale American cuisine. Website: jjastorsrestaurant.com.

JUDY'S CAFÉ, 623 7th Avenue, Two Harbors. Call 218-834-4802. Homemade comfort food. Website: www.facebook.com/judyscafemn.

LAKE AVENUE CAFÉ, 394 South Lake Avenue, Duluth. Call 218-722-2355. Upscale American. Website: lakeaveduluth.com.

LITTLE ANGIE'S CANTINA, 11 East Buchanan Street, Duluth. Call 218-727-6117. Website: www.littleangies.com.

NEW SCENIC CAFÉ, 5461 North Shore Scenic Drive, Duluth. Call 218-525-6274. Contemporary American. Website: www.newsceniccafe.com.

OMC SMOKEHOUSE, 1909 West Superior Street, Duluth. Call 218-606-1611. Barbecue and sandwiches. Website: omcsmokehouse.com.

PICKWICK, 508 East Superior Street, Duluth. Call 218-623-7425. American steakhouse. Website: www.pickwickduluth.com.

PIZZA LUCE, 11 East Superior Street, Duluth. Call 218-727-7400. Excellent pizza, including gluten-free and vegan options. Website: www.pizzaluce .com.

RUSTIC INN CAFÉ, 2773 MN 61, Two Harbors. Call 218-834-2488. Seasonally changing menu highlighting Minnesota items, including walleye. Website: rusticinn.cafe.

SILOS RESTAURANT, 800 West Railroad Street, Duluth. Call 218-336-3430. Upscale American food. Website: www.pierbresort.com/food-drink /the-silos.

SOUND, 132 East Superior Street, Duluth. Call 218-464-1972. Upscale American food and raw bar. Website: www.soundduluth.com.

TAVERN ON THE HILL, 1102 Woodland Avenue, Duluth. Call 218-724-0010. Hearty bar foods. Website: www.tavernduluth.com.

TOBIES, 404 Fire Monument Road, Hinckley. Call 320-384-6174. Hearty American food and famous cinnamon rolls. Website: www.tobies.com.

VANILLA BEAN RESTAURANT, 812 7th Avenue, Two Harbors. Call 218-834-3714. Website: www.thevanillabean.com.

ZEITGEIST ART CAFÉ, 222 East Superior Street, Duluth. Call 218-722-9100. Part of a larger arts building, serving gourmet American food. Website: www.zeitgeistarts.com/cafe.

Other Contacts

GITCHI-GAMI TRAIL ASSOCIATION, Silver Bay. Website: www.ggta.org.

HINCKLEY CONVENTION AND VISITOR BUREAU, P.O. Box 197, Hinckley. Call 320-384-0126; 800-952-4282. Website: www.hinckleymn.com.

LUTSEN TOFTE TOURISM ASSOCIATION, 7136 West MN 61, Tofte. Call 888-922-5000. Website: www.visitcookcounty.com.

SUPERIOR HIKING TRAIL, 731 7th Avenue, Suite 2, Two Harbors. Call 218-834-2700. Website: www.shta.org.

TWO HARBORS CHAMBER OF COMMERCE, 1331 MN 61, Two Harbors. Call 218-834-6200. Website: www.twoharborschamber.com.

VISIT DULUTH, 225 West Superior Street, Suite 110, Duluth. Call 800-438-5884. Website: www.visitduluth.com.

2

THE NORTH SHORE, PART 2
Grand Marais, Grand Portage, and the Gunflint Trail

ESTIMATED DISTANCE: 100 miles

ESTIMATED TIME: 2 hours

GETTING THERE: From the Twin Cities, take I-35W north to Duluth. From Duluth, take MN 61 along the North Shore to Grand Marais and Grand Portage. From Grand Marais, take County Route 12 (CR 12, also known as the Gunflint Trail) to Trail's End.

HIGHLIGHTS: The lakeshore town of Grand Marais, with its shops, art galleries, and excellent restaurants; the Devil's Kettle Waterfall at Judge C.R. Magney State Park; Grand Portage National Monument and the view of the monument from the Mount Rose Trail; a leisurely drive along the Gunflint Trail with a stop at the Chik-Wauk Museum and Nature Center. Enjoy the sights while listening to the local radio station, WTIP, which does an excellent job of covering local events and history in rotation with an eclectic selection of music.

The terrain on the approach to Grand Marais on MN 61 is some of the most beautiful and dramatic in the state. The road offers periodic pull-offs with scenic overlooks, and there's much to see: rivers flowing into Lake Superior, massive stone bluffs with towering pine trees and hardwoods, and the Sawtooth Mountains in the distance. The remnants of the state's ancient geological history are on full display here: the magnificent stony cliffs were formed by volcanic activity millions of years ago. Fishing, fur trading, lumber, and mining have contributed to the development of the area, but there are nevertheless miles and miles of untouched wilderness in the Arrowhead portion of the state.

Summer in this part of the state is generally temperate, and it's not

LEFT: HIKING TRAIL AT THE CHIK-WAUK MUSEUM AND NATURE CENTER

uncommon to find lodgings that don't have air-conditioning, simply because it isn't necessary. On the other hand, winter can be very cold, with heavy snowfall. But that doesn't deter outdoor enthusiasts from exploring the Arrowhead in winter; there are stores in Grand Marais that can properly and safely outfit you for the cold, and the region is full of cross-country skiing, snowshoeing, and snowmobiling opportunities.

For the first-time visitor to Grand Marais, he or she may be surprised to find the town more civilized than expected, given its remote location. Not merely a great destination for outdoor recreation, Grand Marais has a reputation as an arts community. Many artists live here year-round, and more arrive in the warmer months. The support of the arts has extended to a wider definition of art, including culinary and folk art skills. These factors, combined with the easy-living harbor location, make Grand Marais a favorite in the state.

North House Folk School is a nonprofit organization working to rekindle interest and develop skills in old-style crafts and survival techniques. Over 200 courses are offered each year, some as short as a day, some taking several days. Courses include knitting, papermaking, jewelry, and ancient Native American techniques for basket weaving, and kayak and canoe construction. You can also learn how to build a yurt or a facsimile of Thoreau's cabin, how to cook and bake in an outdoor brick oven, or how to build the oven itself. Students come from all over the United States to learn these ancient skills and enjoy the harborside lifestyle.

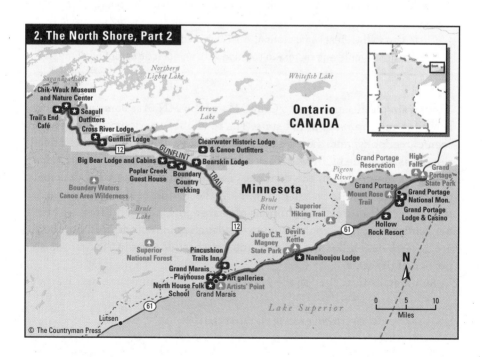

THE HARBOR AT GRAND MARAIS

More traditional art studies can be found at the **Grand Marais Art Colony**. Like North House, the Grand Marais Art Colony offers classes year-round in visual arts, book arts, ceramics, glass, and printmaking. Classes are available for children and adults.

The **Grand Marais Playhouse** is a 40-year-old theater group that offers performances just about every month of the year, with a range of drama to comedy to musicals. The Playhouse also offers summer theater workshops.

One of the most scenic overlooks in town is **Artists' Point**, a short walk along the harbor to the Coast Guard parking lot, where a trail takes you a ½-mile over lava rock and through a forest with breathtaking views of the harbor and the coastline. Its name references the number of artists—visual, literary, and musical—who have come here again and again for inspiration.

Art galleries are plentiful too. The **Betsy Bowen Studio and Gallery**, the **Blue Moose**, and the **Sivertson Gallery** are just a few of the venues showcasing local (as well as regional and some national) artists. These galleries are just steps from one another in the easily walkable downtown of Grand Marais. You can also find local art at the **Johnson Heritage Post Art Gallery**, which has revolving exhibitions as well as a permanent collection of works by early twentieth-century artist Anna Johnson. **Joy and Company** also carries local artists' work, as well as jewelry, antiques, and art supplies. Note: many galleries are closed during winter months, so call ahead if you're planning a winter visit.

Other stores can help you with the more practical aspects of your stay. Part souvenir shop, part outfitter for wilderness experiences, the **Lake Superior Trading Post** is staffed with friendly people who know their stock. The log cabin construction gives the store a north woods feel, and Lake Superior is right outside the door. The **Gunflint Mercantile** is a food store for backpackers and general visitors alike. Come in for the free fudge sample, view the extensive supply of lightweight foods for the trail, and stay for the coffee and soup. **Drury Lane Books** is possibly one of the most charming bookstores you'll ever find, and **Wilderness Waters** is one-stop shopping for outdoor survival, from books and maps to clothing and gear. The store also provides canoe-outfitting services.

There are plenty of casual choices in Grand Marais too. **My Sister's Place** isn't much to look at on the outside, but it has friendly service and solid soups and sandwiches that will satisfy any taste and appetite (including some vegetarian options, such as the "Fungi" mushroom sandwich). The house specialty is burgers, and there are 24 variations to choose from. **Sven and Ole's** is the quintessential Grand Marais experience. Contrary to the name, this is no bland Scandinavian fare, but a local pizza haunt with hearty, flavorful pies with Scandinavian names: uffda Zah, anyone? The menu does include an option for a lutefisk pizza, but unless you have the $1 million in cash, better to order one of the other offerings. **Blue Water Café** is a diner with a view of the harbor serving three meals a day. **The Wunderbar Eatery** has a small but tasty menu of sandwiches and "tidbits" (appetizers), along with soup, salad, and cinnamon-sugar cashews. **Hughie's Taco House** serves Mexican food and makes its tortillas made from scratch.

Fine Dining in Grand Marais: Local, Sustainable, Organic

The food scene in Grand Marais is impressive, especially given the town's size and location. Talented chefs are increasingly exploring the more remote outposts in the northeast, and they're bringing creativity and a willingness to work with locally sourced foods for their inventive menus. **The Angry Trout Café** has a strong focus on local ingredients and sustainability, and offers indoor and outdoor dining. Be sure to check out the artsy bathrooms. **The Dockside Fish Market & Deli** is a retail market and a deli with a limited but delicious menu, including several varieties of fish caught in Lake Superior. **The Gunflint Tavern** has a innovative menu that uses organic ingredients when possible. Presenting dress-up food in a casual atmosphere, **The Crooked Spoon** offers contemporary American cuisine, while **Harbor House Grille** has steakhouse offerings along with pizzas baked in a wood-fired oven.

Sate your sweet tooth with a trip to the **Pie Place**, a pie shop that gives Betty's Pies in Two Harbors serious competition. Their flaky crusts and traditional and innovative fillings will leave you wanting more. Or venture over to **World's Best Donuts**. While the name is certainly self-congratulatory, the doughnuts are truly wonderful. The walk-up window opens at 4:30 a.m.

Lodging choices vary from traditional hotels and motels to condos to bed-and-breakfasts. Right on the harbor is **East Bay Suites**, all of which have decks or patios overlooking the lake as well as full kitchens, fireplaces, washers and dryers, and WiFi. Accommodations vary in size from studios to three bedrooms, with some suites offering bunk beds. Nearby is **Cobblestone Cove Villas**, a newer townhouse property with upscale accommodations within easy walking distance of the shops and restaurants of Grand Marais.

Opel's Lakeside Cabins are just north of Grand Marais on Croftville Road. Opel's has five rustic but charming cabins, all directly on the Lake Superior shoreline. The views and location are hard to beat.

Bed-and-breakfasts are available too. In Grand Marais proper is **Bally House Bed & Breakfast**, built in 1912 and offering four rooms with private bath. **MacArthur House B&B** has five rooms with private bath, and a common-area fireplace and hot tub. A bit further east is the **Art House B&B**, just 200 feet from the Lake Superior shore, featuring four rooms with private baths and a common area with wood stove and deck.

Another option is glamping at the **Wunderbar Eatery & Glampground**, where you'll have your choice of revamped campers or Lotus Belle tents.

East and north of Grand Marais are an abundance of state parks and wildlife areas. Be sure to check local conditions before visiting—nearly annual droughts have brought severe fire restrictions in parks and campsites in recent years, and some park access is limited during wildfires. Check with individual parks for up-to-the-minute information.

Depart Grand Marais on MN 61 heading east to find **Judge C.R. Magney State Park**, located between Grand Marais and Grand Portage and home to the Brule River. The Brule leads to **Devil's Kettle**, a unique 50-foot waterfall rumored to have a bottomless cauldron. Nine miles of hiking trails, including an ascent to Devil's Kettle, are open during season, as well as several fishing sites. Campsites are available, but advance reservations are recommended.

The naturalists on hand during the summer months at **Grand Portage State Park**, the only Minnesota state park managed jointly with a Native American tribe, are tribe members who can speak about local Ojibwe history. The park's northern boundary is the Pigeon River, which is also the international boundary with Canada. The park's 120-foot High Falls can be viewed by hiking the Falls Trail, which includes a 700-foot boardwalk and three overlooks. Camping is not available, but the falls are easily accessible for day visitors via the ½-mile trail and boardwalk.

Not far from the monument is **Grand Portage Lodge & Casino**. Located just south of the Canadian border, the Grand Portage Lodge has spacious rooms and a friendly staff ready to help with anything you need. The hotel offers an indoor pool and sauna, a full-service restaurant overlooking Lake Superior, and a seasonal (mid-May to mid-October) RV park. The casino takes the north woods theme and runs with it: a northern lights display adorns the carefully designed ceiling. Open 24/7, the casino offers a shuttle to Thunder Bay, Ontario (US citizens will need passports to cross the border).

If you're looking for lodging that's a bit quieter, reserve a room at the

Naniboujou Lodge

Even in an area with eclectic lodging options (see, for example, the yurt on the Gunflint Trail), **Naniboujou Lodge** stands apart both for its physical structure and for its history. Listed on the National Register of Historic Places, its colorful past matches its bright interior. The lodge was built in the 1920s as a private club for founding members who included Babe Ruth and Jack Dempsey, but it never reached its potential as the country soon tumbled into the Great Depression. Eventually reborn as a hotel and lodge, Naniboujou has a beautifully decorated Great Hall, painted in vivid primary and jewel

colors with designs reflective of Cree Indian culture. The hall also boasts the state's largest native rock fireplace. Rooms are tastefully and comfortably appointed, but they lack TVs and telephones (in order to preserve the sense of getting away from it all). The dining room, open in the summer, serves hearty home-cooked food. Although the lodge is close to a state park with excellent hiking trails, you might find yourself tempted to just relax on the extensive, peaceful lawns, soaking in the Lake Superior views from your Adirondack chair.

THE GREAT HALL AT NANIBOUJOU LODGE

Hollow Rock Resort, just a few miles south of the casino. Hollow Rock has five cottages, all with lake views and some with decks on the lake.

Returning to Grand Marais, it's time to travel inland from the lake and explore the route known as the **Gunflint Trail**. A 57-mile paved road leading from Grand Marais to Saganaga Lake near the Canadian border, the Gunflint Trail is hands down one of the most beautiful drives in the region. With acres of forest interrupted by only the occasional café or shop, the Trail is also home to numerous lodging options nestled within the trees. Watch your speed as you drive; it's not unusual for a deer, wolf, or even a moose to appear on the road, and all of these animals can do as much harm to you and your vehicle as you can do to them. The area has enjoyed some growth in year-round tourism, thanks to the increased popularity of winter sports, which have joined the ranks of favored pastimes such as birding, mountain biking, fall foliage viewing, canoeing and kayaking, camping, fishing, and even mushroom and berry picking.

DEVIL'S KETTLE FALLS AT JUDGE C. R. MAGNEY STATE PARK

The Gunflint Trail is also the gateway to the eastern edge of the **Boundary Waters Canoe Area Wilderness**. The Boundary Waters is an amazing natural preserve, encompassing over a million acres of woods (all contained within the Superior National Forest) and at least 2,500 of Minnesota's famed lakes, teeming with wildlife. It is still best discovered while traveling as the explorers of old did: by canoe, with backpack and tent. While a few areas have opened up to motorized vehicles, the beauty of this area is the peacefulness the absence of motors brings. Visitors can hear the myriad bird calls and wolf howls, and the sound of water and wind.

It is possible to day-trip in the Boundary Waters, or at least along the edges, by starting from Ely or the Gunflint Trail (see Chapter 3 for the former). More ambitious travelers may want to portage in with canoes and set up camp. Experienced canoers and campers can plot their routes, but if you're fairly new to this type of adventure, you might consider working with an outfitter, who can also reserve a permit for you. Permits for camping visitors are required in order to limit the number of entrances into the BWCAW

THE GUNFLINT TRAIL

each day, in an effort to keep the wilderness, well, wild. See the sidebar for details.

If you're planning on venturing into the **Boundary Waters**, it's strongly recommended that you purchase the Superior National Forest Visitor Map. Published by the USDA in conjunction with Superior National Forest, it is an incredibly detailed map of the Boundary Waters Canoe Area Wilderness (BWCAW). (It wouldn't hurt to buy a magnifying glass to use with it.) The BWCAW is full of trails and portages, rivers and streams, that don't appear on most state maps and can get you lost unless you're very familiar with the area. Many local gas stations and convenience stores sell the map, as do BWCAW permit offices, or you can contact the Superior National Forest headquarters in Duluth (218-626-4300) for information on ordering one.

You can drive for miles down the Gunflint Trail and see few, if any, other cars or people. It might look like miles and miles of forest and wilderness, but there are plenty of recreational stops to make. You can take advantage of several hiking options available, including the local portion of the **Superior Hiking Trail**, the longest hiking trail in the Midwest at over 200 miles. But there are many other trails to choose from, some of which overlap or intersect the Superior Trail. Stop at any of the lodges along the Gunflint Trail (or check with the visitor center in Grand Marais) to pick up a Gunflint Trail hiking map that details each route, how long and how difficult it is, and what you're likely to find there.

Grand Portage National Monument

Continuing east on MN 61 will bring you to the **Grand Portage National Monument**, one of only two national monuments in the state (the other, Pipestone National Monument, is in the opposite southwest corner of the state; see Chapter 17). This monument is really a don't-miss for visitors to the area. An extensive re-creation of the life of traders and Native Americans before there was a United States or Canada, this National Monument has a traditional Ojibwe village, a reconstruction of the Northwest Company's stockade (including a great hall and kitchen), a fur trade canoe under construction, and historic gardens that represent the crops once grown in trading villages. Kids' programs are offered in the summer, and costumed historical guides are available to answer questions. Trails outside the stockade take visitors deep into the northern wilderness, and there are snowshoe trails available during the winter. The National Monument also serves as the departure point for the ferry to Isle Royale, the largest island in Lake Superior (and technically part of Michigan). One of the best views of the monument is provided by hiking the trail across the street from the entrance: the **Mount Rose Trail**. This short (½-mile) but very steep trail leads hikers to an overlook that provides stunning views of the monument, the Sawtooth Mountains, and Lake Superior. Keep an eye out as you drive along the water for areas where wild rice is growing.

GRAND PORTAGE NATIONAL MONUMENT

A couple of miles from the end of the 57-mile trail, you'll reach CR 81. Turn right, and you'll shortly be at the entrance to the **Chik-Wauk Museum and Nature Center**. Housed in a lodge built in 1934, Chik-Wauk opened in its new capacity in 2010. It's small but packed with displays about the history of the Gunflint Trail, including artifacts, interactive and hands-on exhibitions, and video and written histories of local pioneers. The grounds of Chik-Wauk surround a bay of Saganaka Lake and offer five short hiking trails of varying difficulty (including one ADA trail).

At the very end of the Gunflint Trail is **Trail's End Café**. The knotty pine interior fits well with the wooded wonderland outside, and the Trail's End serves basic but hearty meals, including burgers, sandwiches, and pizzas.

Camping sites are plentiful, but if you'd prefer a building over a tent, there are many options hidden away along the trail, including bed-and-breakfasts. **Poplar Creek Guest House** is tucked into a peaceful wooded area and has two guest rooms, each with private bath, and a suite. The rooms are graciously appointed, and they share a common room with kitchenette, fireplace, and private deck. The suite, which holds up to four people and has a private entrance, has a private kitchen area as well as a deck. For a true wilderness experience, the proprietors also have a cabin for rent, as well as the **Tall Pines Yurt**, which is open year-round for summer or winter adventures. Bunk beds and a futon can accommodate up to four guests, and additional bedding can be provided. A fully equipped kitchen is included; an outhouse is steps away, as is a traditional Finnish sauna. **Pincushion Trails Inn** sits on 43 acres just 3 miles from Grand Marais and, perched on the Sawtooth Mountain ridgeline, affords impressive views and on-site access to hiking trails. This peaceful inn features four rooms, all with private bath, and a common living area with fireplace. **Cross River Lodge** is situated on Gunflint Lake. This property offers two lovely bed-and-breakfast rooms, each with private bath, and four cabins near or on the lake with fireplaces, complete kitchens, and decks with barbecues.

Lodges are common accommodations along the trail, usually offering both hotel rooms and cabin quarters. These lodges tend to be full service,

Ham Lake Burn

Toward the western end of the trail, you'll drive through the remnants of the 2007 Ham Lake Burn. The fire was set accidentally, but its devastation was thorough. The area was suffering from a drought, and the rapidly spreading fire burned through more than 36,000 acres on the US side (75,000 acres in total), the largest fire in nearly a century. A fire of this magnitude requires time for recovery, and you will see the stark outlines of burned tree shards, as well as the hopeful signs of green growth beginning to appear on the ground beneath them.

THE HAM LAKE BURN AREA ON THE GUNFLINT TRAIL

THE BEARSKIN LODGE ON THE GUNFLINT TRAIL

providing not only a place to sleep, but restaurants, outfitting and guide services, and equipment rental. **Big Bear Lodge and Cabins** has bed-and-breakfast rooms in its lodge and housekeeping cabins, as well as a full-service restaurant. **Bearskin Lodge** is a model of peace and retreat. The resort has 11 cabins and two lodges with town house accommodations. There's a hot tub and sauna on-site, and massage can be arranged. During the summer, boats, canoes, and pontoons are available, as well as bikes; and children's naturalist programs are offered on request. **Gunflint Lodge** has 23 cabins with varying amenities, from the more rustic Canoers Cabins (bunk beds, shared bath in a nearby building) to the Romantic Cottages (lake-view cabins with fireplace, hot tub, and full kitchen), to the Gunflint Lake Home (with two to four bedrooms, fireplace,

CABINS AT THE GUNFLINT LODGE

PATIO AT THE GUNFLINT LODGE

hot tub, and sauna). A restaurant on site offers an alternative to self-cooking in the cabin, and guests can partake in an extensive list of year-round activities, including winter and summer sports as well as massage. A beautiful stone patio adjacent to the bar is the perfect end-of-day stop.

IN THE AREA

Accommodations

ART HOUSE B&B, 8 7th Avenue West, Grand Marais. Call 218-370-1625. Website: www.arthousebb.com.

BALLY HOUSE B&B, 121 East 3rd Street, Grand Marais. Call 218-387-5099. www.ballyhousebnb.com.

BEARSKIN LODGE, 124 East Bearskin Road, Grand Marais. Call 218-388-2292; 800-338-4170. Website: www.bearskin.com.

BIG BEAR LODGE AND CABINS, 7969 Old Northwoods Loop, Gunflint Trail. Call 218-388-0172. Website: www.bigbearlodgemn.com.

CLEARWATER HISTORIC LODGE & CANOE OUTFITTERS, 774 Clearwater Road, Grand Marais. Call 218-388-2254. Website: clearwaterhistoric lodge.com.

COBBLESTONE COVE VILLAS, 17 South Broadway, Grand Marais. Call 218-387-2633; 800-247-6020. Website: www.gmhotel.net/properties/cobblestone-cove-villas.

CROSS RIVER LODGE, 196 North Gunflint Lake Road, Gunflint Trail. Call 866-203-8991. Website: www.crossriverlodge.com.

EAST BAY SUITES, 21 Wisconsin Street, Grand Marais. Call 800-414-2807. Website: www.eastbaysuites.com.

GRAND PORTAGE LODGE & CASINO, 70 Casino Drive, Grand Portage. Call 218-475-2401; 800-543-1384. Website: www.grandportage.com.

GUNFLINT LODGE, 143 South Gunflint Lake, Gunflint Trail. Call 800-328-3325. Website: www.gunflint.com.

HOLLOW ROCK RESORT, 7422 East MN 61, Grand Portage. Call 800-543-1384. Website: www.hollowrockresort.com.

MACARTHUR HOUSE B&B, 520 West 2nd Street, Grand Marais. Call 218-387-1840; 800-792-1840. Website: www.macarthurhouse.net.

NANIBOUJOU LODGE, 20 Naniboujou Trail, Grand Marais. Call 218-387-2688; www.naniboujou.com.

OPEL'S LAKESIDE CABINS, 1593 Croftville Road, Grand Marais. Call 218-663-7971. Website: www.opelslakesidecabins.com.

PINCUSHION TRAILS INN, 968 Gunflint Trail. Call 218-387-2009. Website: www.pincushiontrailsinn.com.

POPLAR CREEK GUEST HOUSE AND TALL PINES YURT, 11 Poplar Creek Drive, Gunflint Trail. Call 800-322-8327. Website: www.poplarcreekbnb.com.

WUNDERBAR EATERY & GLAMPGROUND, 1615 West MN 61, Grand Marais. Call 218-877-7655. Website: www.facebook.com/wunderbarmn.

Attractions and Recreation

BETSY BOWEN GALLERY, 301 1st Avenue West, Grand Marais. Call 218-387-1992. Website: www.woodcut.com.

THE BLUE MOOSE, 1301 West MN 61, Grand Marais. Call 218-387-9303. Website: www.thebluemoosemn.com.

CHIK-WAUK MUSEUM AND NATURE CENTER, 28 Moose Pond Drive, Grand Marais. Call 218-388-9915. Website: www.chikwauk.com.

DRURY LANE BOOKS, 12 East Wisconsin Street, Grand Marais. Call 218-387-3370. Website: www.drurylanebooks.com.

GRAND MARAIS ART COLONY, 120 West 3rd Avenue, Grand Marais. Call 218-387-2737. Website: www.grandmaraisartcolony.org.

GRAND MARAIS PLAYHOUSE, 51 West 5th Street, Grand Marais. Call 218-387-1284. Website: www.grandmaraisplayhouse.com.

GRAND PORTAGE CASINO, 70 Casino Drive, Grand Portage. Call 800-543-1384. Website: www.grandportage.com.

GRAND PORTAGE NATIONAL MONUMENT, 211 Mile Creek Road, Grand Portage. Call 218-475-0123. Website: www.nps.gov/grpo.

GRAND PORTAGE STATE PARK, 9393 East MN 61, Grand Portage. Call 218-475-2360. Website: www.dnr.state.mn.us/state_parks/grand_portage /index.html.

GUNFLINT MERCANTILE, 12 1st Avenue West, Grand Marais. Call 218-387-9228. Website: www.gunflintmercantile.com.

JOHNSON HERITAGE POST ART GALLERY, 115 West Wisconsin Street, Grand Marais. Call 218-387-2314. Website: www.johnsonheritagepost.org.

JOY AND COMPANY, 16 1st Avenue West, Grand Marais. Call 218-387-1004. Website: www.joy-and-company.com.

JUDGE C.R. MAGNEY STATE PARK, 4051 East MN 61, Grand Marais. Call 218-387-3039. Website: www.dnr.state.mn.us/state_parks/judge_cr _magney/index.html.

LAKE SUPERIOR TRADING POST, 10 South 1st Avenue West, Grand Marais. Call 218-387-2020. Website: www.lakesuperiortradingpost.com.

NORTH HOUSE FOLK SCHOOL, 500 West MN 61, Grand Marais. Call 218-387-9762; 888-387-9762. Website: www.northhouse.org.

SIVERTSON GALLERY, 14 West Wisconsin Street, Grand Marais. Call 218-387-2491; 888-880-4369. Website: sivertson.com.

Dining

ANGRY TROUT CAFÉ, 416 West MN 61, Grand Marais. Call 218-387-1265. Seasonal restaurant focused on local foods with a gourmet twist. Website: www.angrytroutcafe.com.

BLUE WATER CAFÉ, 20 Wisconsin Street, Grand Marais. Call 218-387-1597. Homestyle diner food, three meals a day. Website: www.bluewatercafe.com.

THE CROOKED SPOON, 17 West Wisconsin Street, Grand Marais. Call 218-387-2779. Contemporary, upscale American cuisine. Website: www.crookedspooncafe.com.

DOCKSIDE FISH MARKET & DELI, 418 West MN 61, Grand Marais. Call 218-387-2906. Retail market and deli focused on local fish. Website: www.docksidefishmarket.com.

GUNFLINT TAVERN, 111 West Wisconsin Street, Grand Marais. Call 218-387-1563. Fusion food, sandwiches, and pizza. Website: www.gunflinttavern.com.

HARBOR HOUSE GRILLE, 411 West MN 61, Grand Marais. Call 218-387-1889. Upscale American entrées and wood-fired-oven-baked pizzas. Website: www.harborhousegrille.com.

HUGHIE'S TACO HOUSE, 15 West MN 61, Grand Marais. Call 218-387-3382. Fresh Mexican food with flour tortillas made by hand. Website: www.facebook.com/pages/Hughies-Taco-House/329539440787781.

MY SISTER'S PLACE, 401 East MN 61, Grand Marais. Call 218-387-1915. Burgers, fresh fish, pizza, and salad. Website: www.mysistersplacerestaurant.com.

SVEN AND OLE'S, 9 West Wisconsin Street, Grand Marais. Call 218-387-1713. Local pizza institution. Website: www.svenandoles.com.

TRAIL'S END CAFÉ, 12582 Gunflint Trail. Call 218-388-2212; 800-346-6625. Basic but hearty meals, including burgers, sandwiches, and pizzas. Website: www.wayofthewilderness.com/cafe.htm.

WORLD'S BEST DONUTS, 10 East Wisconsin Street, Grand Marais. Call 218-387-1345. The name says it all. Website: www.worldsbestdonutsmn.com.

WUNDERBAR EATERY & GLAMPGROUND, 1615 West MN 61, Grand Marais. Call 218-877-7655. Hearty pub foods. Website: www.facebook.com /wunderbarmn.

Other Contacts

BOUNDARY COUNTRY TREKKING, 11 Poplar Creek Drive, Grand Marais. Call 218-388-4487; 800-322-8327. Website: www.boundarycountry.com.

BOUNDARY WATERS CANOE AREA. Website: www.canoecountry.com.

CLEARWATER HISTORIC LODGE & CANOE OUTFITTERS, 774 Clearwater Road, Grand Marais. Call 218-388-2254; 800-527-0554. Website: clearwaterhistoriclodge.com.

GRAND MARAIS AREA TOURISM ASSOCIATION. Call 218-387-2524; 888-922-5000. Website: www.visitcookcounty.com/community/grand-marais.

GUNFLINT TRAIL ASSOCIATION. Call 218-387-2524; 888-922-5000. Website: www.visitcookcounty.com/community/gunflint-trail.

SEAGULL OUTFITTERS, 12208 Gunflint Trail, Grand Marais. Call 218-388-2216. Website: www.seagulloutfitters.com.

WILDERNESS WATERS OUTFITTERS, 1712 East MN 61, Grand Marais. Call 218-387-2525.

3

WESTERN BOUNDARY WATERS
Highway 1 to Ely

ESTIMATED DISTANCE: 140 miles

ESTIMATED TIME: 3 hours

GETTING THERE: South of Grand Marais, near Illgen City, take MN 1 northwest to Ely. From Ely, take MN 169 south to MN 135, then to County Route 21 (CR 21) to Embarrass.

HIGHLIGHTS: The densely wooded area along MN 1; the Dorothy Molter Museum; the International Wolf Center; the North American Bear Center; the Soudan Underground Mine State Park; and the cold spot of the nation, the town of Embarrass.

South of Grand Marais, MN 61 connects with MN 1, a stretch of highway that veers inland from Lake Superior to Ely, a gateway city into the Boundary Waters. If you are planning to visit the Boundary Waters Canoe Area Wilderness, please see advice in Chapter 2 on obtaining the Superior National Forest Visitor Map, a critically important guide to the Wilderness.

When driving along MN 1 (also known as the Ely-Finland Trail), it's hard to imagine there was ever a time when this area was decimated by logging; today, the forests are thick along the road, with pine, spruce, birch, and aspen trees towering over the narrow highway. (An important aside, in some places, the trees are very close to the road and provide excellent camouflage for deer, so take your time.) The woods continue to thicken as you near Ely and the edge of the Boundary Waters.

The route to Ely takes you through **Superior National Forest**. This massive forest, more than 3 million acres, could just as easily have been named the Forest of Lakes—there are more than 2,000 lakes and countless

LEFT: LAKE VERMILION STATE PARK

connecting streams and rivers in this area, routes used for water travel thousands of years ago. Voyageurs used these waterways as their trade routes back and forth to Canada, and loggers used them to transport logs to mills. The forest itself is on the southern edge of the boreal forest biome, which also extends across northern Asia and Europe. The biome contains a complex mix of vegetation that veers from stands of mostly hardwood trees to stands of mostly conifers, varying according to soil composition.

Within the forest, wildlife thrives. More than 350 species of birds, reptiles, mammals, and amphibians have been identified, along with 50 species of fish. With luck, you can spot a gray wolf or moose, great gray owls or boreal chickadees. The lakes are full of walleye, trout, and even lake sturgeon.

After just a few miles on MN 1, you'll arrive at the little town of Finland. Not surprisingly, this town was founded by Finnish settlers. It's home to one of Minnesota's more tongue-in-cheek annual festivals, St. Urho's Day. The festival is a Finnish American response to Ireland's St. Patrick's Day and celebrates a fictional saint who reportedly drove the grasshoppers

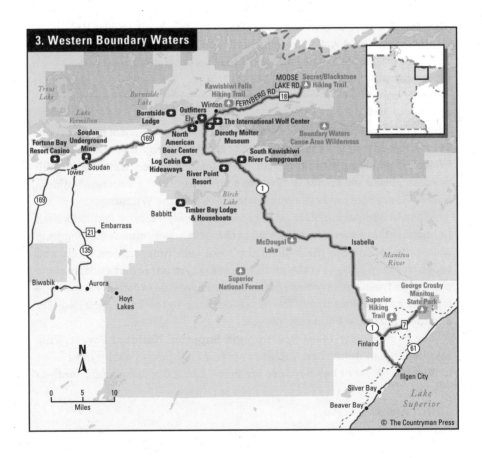

out of Finland (the country). Finland (the town) has a statue of this mythical saint, and every March celebrates his accomplishments.

From Finland, turn onto CR 7 and drive 7 miles to visit **George Crosby Manitou State Park**. The land was donated by mining executive George Crosby, and from the time of its designation as a state park, it was treated differently from others. A decision was made to design it specifically for backpackers and limit overall development within the park. Consequently, there is no central campground, but instead a collection of primitive campsites scattered throughout, accessible only by foot. There are 24 miles of hiking trails, including 5 miles of the **Superior Hiking Trail**, that run through rugged terrain, through old-growth forests, and along the Manitou River and Benson Lake.

HIGHWAY 1

Returning to MN 1 and continuing north, you'll cross the **Laurentian Divide**, which marks the dividing line between waters that flow north to Hudson Bay and those that flow south to Lake Superior. A few miles further, watch on your left for a sign directing you to Forest Road 106, a gravel road that takes you to the beautiful, undeveloped McDougal Lake, where a mile-long hiking trail explores the forest along the shoreline.

As you draw closer to Ely, you'll cross the South Kawishiwi River, a lovely sight unto itself. The South Kawishiwi River Campground has campsites that can be reserved and some that are held for drop-in visitors. The campground marks an entry point into the **Boundary Waters Canoe Area Wilderness** to the north. For more information about good reference materials and permits, please see the Boundary Waters information in Chapter 2.

At one time the city of Ely was primarily a logging and mining town. Today, tourism is a major force because of the town's proximity to the BWCAW. Still, even if your goal is to get to the wilderness, allowing yourself some time in Ely is a good idea. There's plenty to see and do.

If you're planning on heading into the BWCAW, there are several local outfitters that can help with equipment, permits, and guiding if needed. **Piragis Northwoods Company** is a large outfitting shop that sells and/ or rents a comprehensive selection of outdoor gear, including canoes and camping equipment. Piragis also offers guided canoeing and camping trips in the BWCAW. **Kawishiwi Lodge and Outfitters** is located on an entry point to a non-motorized lake and can handle complete or partial outfitting. **Canadian Waters** can get you to any of the Boundary Waters entry points and handles complete and partial outfitting as well as fly-in canoe trips. **Boundary Waters Guide Service** specializes in fully outfitted guided tours, and **Jordan's Canoe Outfitters** will work with any size group and any level of outfitting and guiding needed.

Canoeing, camping, and fishing are popular activities, but the area is also full of excellent hiking trails, everything from short, gentle hikes to overnight treks through rugged terrain. Cross-country skiing opportunities replace hiking in the winter. One particularly scenic hike is the **Kawishiwi Falls Hiking Trail**, east of Ely on CR 18 (also known as Fernberg Road). The trail is short, barely a mile, but travels to the edges of Fall Lake and Garden Lake, where steep cliffs overlook Kawishiwi Falls and the nearby power plant. Another interesting vantage point is found on the **Secret/Blackstone Hiking Trail**, further east on CR 18 and turning left onto Moose Lake Road. Here you can hike trails that will give you a glimpse of how the forest has been gradually changing since the 1999 Blowdown, when storms blew down millions of trees across nearly 40 percent of the BWCAW. In some areas,

KAYAK SALE AT PIRAGIS IN ELY

KAWISHIWI FALLS, ELY

every single mature tree was downed. However, where the blown trees are decaying, new life is growing.

In Ely, there's a unique piece of Boundary Waters history at the **Dorothy Molter Museum**. This is a loving tribute to the last person who lived in the Boundary Waters. Dorothy Molter lived a great deal of her adult life in a cabin in the BWCAW, and even though the US government evicted other tenants when the area was declared a wilderness, she was granted lifetime tenancy. During her many years in her rustic cabin, she brewed homemade root beer for boaters and fishers coming through her area, earning the nickname "the root beer lady." After her death, her log cabin was painstakingly disassembled and reassembled on the eastern edge of Ely and turned into a museum. The cabin is crammed full of Dorothy's things, and the adjacent gift shop sells books about her as well as cases of root beer (worth the purchase). The only downside is the noise of traffic from nearby MN 169, which can make visitors (this one, at least) wonder why they couldn't have sited the museum just a bit further down the road in an effort to recapture something more similar to the peace enjoyed by Molter in this natural setting.

Ely has two internationally acclaimed wildlife centers. **The International**

FERNBERG ROAD, ELY

Wolf Center is focused on education and information about wolves. The center tries to address public fears and concerns about wolf behaviors through media relations and public visits. There are hands-on exhibitions and "wolf cams" in the center's beautiful building, allowing visitors to watch wolves from a great distance; they also coordinate Learning Vacations, which bring visitors into the wilderness to meet "ambassador" wolves.

Similar in intent to the International Wolf Center is the **North American Bear Center**, 1 mile west of Ely. The Bear Center was founded by Dr. Lynn Rogers, a bear expert who has studied them in and around Ely for many years.

THE ELY BEAR CENTER

Although the building itself isn't as lavish as the Wolf Center, the Bear Center offers extensive and lively videos and exhibitions, including a look at the troubling case of Alaska's Grizzly Man. Staff and researchers are passionate and do an excellent job of making learning about bears fun. The "bear cams," streaming live on the center's website, have brought international attention to the Center in recent years, especially when black bear Lily gave birth live on the Internet. Be sure to watch the bears in their 2-acre habitat from the viewing deck.

From Ely, travel south on MN 169 to visit the **Soudan Underground Mine** at the **Lake Vermilion-Soudan Underground Mine State Park**. The Soudan Mine gives visitors insight into the daily life of miners who once worked this operation. Adventurous tourists can take a tour, which will carry them 27 stories beneath the ground (note: extensive walking is required, including through confined areas). Those who don't wish to go below can wander the grounds for free. The scenery from the hillside mine is breathtaking, particularly during fall foliage season. The park itself, one of the newest parks in Minnesota, is well worth the visit, with almost 10 shoreline miles on beautiful Lake Vermilion.

For a different kind of animal adventure, make winter plans at the **Wintergreen Dogsled Lodge**. With nearly 30 years of dogsled adventures under their belt, the proprietors of the Wintergreen Dogsled Lodge know a thing or two about taking visitors on a dogsled trip, whether they're first-timers or seasoned sledders. Trips can be arranged with stays at the lodge itself, just east of Ely, as lodge-to-lodge treks, or as camping excursions. Multiple-night or one-day-only trips are available, and themed trips (parent–daughter, photography) can be arranged as well.

Not surprisingly, the Boundary Waters area is surrounded by countless places to stay, everything from rustic mom-and-pop resorts to more elaborate deluxe accommodations.

Just outside the city of Ely is **Grand Ely Lodge**, the largest in Ely, with 61 rooms and suites. The resort is very family friendly, with kids under 10 staying and eating free with paid adults. There's an indoor pool and sauna, and lake activities are provided at the marina on Shagawa Lake. The **Evergreen Restaurant** is open all day and also sports a lounge. Mountain bikes are available to guests who want to use the **Trezona Trail** across the street, which connects to the International Wolf Center.

Right in the heart of downtown Ely, the **Adventure Inn** is a small but charming property spread across two buildings, one a log-cabin-style building with north woods themes, and the newer space a solar building in a Scandinavian style. Not far away is **A Stay Inn Ely**, a small establishment evocative of a European hostel but with private rooms and baths. Each has a color theme, and the Indigo Room would be appreciated by anyone who loves cozy attic spaces. The inn also boasts a large gathering room and full kitchen for common use, as well as a spacious deck.

A few miles outside Ely, you'll also find beautiful and diverse lodging choices. The **Timber Trail Lodge** offers 15 cabins, ranging from one to six bedrooms, as well as four motel units with kitchenettes. The resort can arrange boat rentals and guides, and massage is offered on-site. Guests can also take part in float plane rides, offered once per week. For scenic lake views and wooded privacy, **River Point Resort** may be a good option. The resort provides several waterfront cabins, villas, and chalets to choose

THE GATHERING ROOM AT ELY'S A STAY INN

from. Right at the edge of the BWCAW is the **Silver Rapids Lodge**, its cabins and suites located on a private peninsula within a chain of four lakes, and **Timber Bay Lodge and Houseboats** has both cabins and houseboats on Birch Lake.

For those hoping for a deep wilderness experience, **Log Cabin Hideaways** provides hand-hewn log cabins on the edge of the BWCAW. Each cabin comes with a canoe, but no electricity or indoor plumbing. Propane is provided for cooking, and most units have a Finnish sauna. Some of the cabins are accessible only by water, and none have neighbors as each cabin sits on its own secluded site.

Seemingly in the middle of nowhere, **Fortune Bay Resort and Casino** is on Lake Vermilion and offers attractive rooms and suites, an indoor pool, dining room, 24-hour casino, and golf course. An on-site marina provides fishing boats, pontoons, canoes, and paddleboats for rent, or you can bring your own boat and dock it at the marina.

You'll find several dining options in town. **Sir G's** serves Italian food,

BIRCH LAKE ON HIGHWAY 1

including pasta made in house. **Front Porch Coffee and Tea** is an inviting cafe with a limited but tasty menu of soups and pastries. If you're seeking steakhouse fare, the **Ely Steak House** fits the bill with fresh fish specials, prime rib on weekends, and steak whenever you like. Ely has its own brewery too: the **Boathouse Brewpub**, offering its own craft beers and serving up good pub staples. For lake fish, **Rockwood Restaurant & Lounge** specializes in walleye but offers steaks and burgers as well. **Gator's Grilled Cheese Emporium** serves up, as its name suggests, grilled-cheese sandwiches, but also a full menu of other sandwiches, including some unique options like the bacon-mac 'n' cheese sandwich. Breakfast dining is also available in Ely. **Insula Restaurant** is a relative newcomer focused on locally sourced fine dining with a fusion approach. At the Grand Ely Lodge, **Evergreen Restaurant** offers up three meals a day, and walleye and prime rib are served every night.

From ordinary souvenirs like shirts and mugs to specialty items like art and model train supplies, Ely's several blocks of shops offer a variety of merchandise. **The Brandenburg Gallery** showcases the award-winning nature photography of Jim Brandenburg, who has traveled the world for National Geographic and holds a special love for the Boundary Waters area (he makes it his home part of the year). **Wintergreen Northern Wear** produces its high-quality and attractive outdoor apparel in Ely and sells it at this local retail store. On the second floor of Piragis Outfitters is **Lisa's Second-Floor Bookstore,** accessible only by entering the outfitting store. A small but congenial gathering space for book lovers, the shop has a solid selection of fiction and local resource books. **Steger Mukluks & Moccasins** sells footwear inspired by Native American designs. Made in Ely from moose hide, the shop's shoes are highly regarded for their comfort and winter protection. **Legacy Toys** offers a wide variety of toys for all ages, as well as its own candy and a 400-gallon saltwater aquarium. **Mealey's Gift & Sauna Shop** is exactly that: a one-stop shop with saunas and sauna accessories but also high-quality gift and home décor items.

IN THE AREA

Accommodations

A STAY INN ELY, 112 West Sheridan Street, Ely. Call 218-365-6010. Website: www.jaspercompany.com/locations/jasper-inn.

ADVENTURE INN, 1145 East Sheridan Street, Ely. Call 218-365-3140. Website: www.adventureinn-ely.com.

Burntside Lodge

West of Ely, on Burntside Lake, **Burntside Lodge** has been offering gracious hospitality to guests since 1911, and is arguably one of Minnesota's most famous establishments. Family owned since 1941, the resort has always had a reputation for elegance, offering several cabins of varying size, all tucked within the woods or perched near the lake. The peaceful ambience found here is further ensured by the absence of TVs and telephones. On the National Register of Historic Places, the resort's log buildings were built exclusively by local builders using local materials and have been impeccably maintained. The dining room (open daily for dinner in-season, and on weekends only for breakfast) serves delicious dishes in a large, open room. The adjoining gift shop sells numerous items of local interest.

BURNTSIDE LODGE

BURNTSIDE LODGE, 2755 Burntside Lodge Road, Ely. Call 218-365-3894. Website: www.burntside.com.

FORTUNE BAY RESORT CASINO, 1430 Bois Forte Road, Tower. Call 800-992-7529. Website: fortunebay.com.

GRAND ELY LODGE, 400 North Pioneer Road, Ely. Call 218-365-6565; 800-365-5070. Website: www.grandelylodge.com.

LOG CABIN HIDEAWAYS, 1321 North CR 21, Ely. Call 218-365-4254. Website: www.logcabinhideaways.com.

RIVER POINT RESORT AND OUTFITTING COMPANY, 12007 River Point Road, Ely. Call 218-365-6604; 800-456-5580. Website: www.riverpointresort.com.

SILVER RAPIDS LODGE, 459 Kawishiwi Trail, Ely. Call 218-365-4877; 800-950-9425. Website: www.silverrapidslodge.com.

TIMBER BAY LODGE AND HOUSEBOATS, 8044 Timber Bay Road, Babbitt. Call 218-827-3682; 800-846-6821. Website: timberbay.com.

TIMBER TRAIL LODGE, 629 Kawishiwi Trail, Ely. Call 218-365-4879; 800-777-7348. Website: www.timbertrail.com.

Attractions and Recreation

BRANDENBURG GALLERY, 11 East Sheridan Street, Ely. Call 218-365-6563. Website: www.jimbrandenburg.com.

DOROTHY MOLTER MUSEUM, 2002 East Sheridan Street, Ely. Call 218-365-4451. Website: www.rootbeerlady.com.

GEORGE CROSBY MANITOU STATE PARK, 7616 CR 7, Finland. Call 218-353-8800. Website: www.dnr.state.mn.us/state_parks.

THE INTERNATIONAL WOLF CENTER, 1396 MN 169, Ely. Call 218-365-4695; 877-365-7879. Website: www.wolf.org.

LAKE VERMILION-SOUDAN UNDERGROUND MINE, MN 169, Soudan. Call 218-753-2245. Website: www.dnr.state.mn.us/state_parks/lake_vermilion_soudan/index.html.

LEGACY TOYS, 5 North Central Avenue, Ely. Call 218-249-0263; 855-328-8697. Website: www.legacytoys.com.

MEALEY'S GIFT & SAUNA SHOP, 124 North Central Avenue, Ely. Call 218-365-3639; 800-922-3639. Website: www.mealeysinely.com.

NORTH AMERICAN BEAR CENTER, 1926 MN 169, Ely. Call 218-365-7879. Website: www.bear.org.

STEGER MUKLUKS, 33 East Sheridan Street, Ely. Call 218-365-3322. Website: www.mukluks.com.

WINTERGREEN DOGSLED LODGE, 1101 Ring Rock Road, Ely. Call 218-365-6022; 877-753-3386. Website: www.dogsledding.com.

WINTERGREEN NORTHERN WEAR, 205 East Sheridan Street, Ely. Call 218-365-6602; 844-359-6233. Website: www.wintergreennorthernwear.com.

Dining

BOATHOUSE BREWPUB, 47 East Sheridan Street, Ely. Call 218-365-4301. Extensive menu of sandwiches, burgers, and bar food. Website: www.boathousebrewpub.com.

ELY STEAK HOUSE, 216 East Sheridan Street, Ely. Call 218-365-7412. Steakhouse and bar with fresh fish specials, prime rib on weekends, and steak whenever you like. Website: www.elysteakhouse.com.

EVERGREEN RESTAURANT, 400 North Pioneer Road, Ely. Call 218-365-6565. Three meals a day, with walleye and prime rib served every night. Website: www.grandelylodge.com/restaurant-bar/evergreen-restaurant.

FRONT PORCH COFFEE AND TEA, 343 East Sheridan Street, Ely. Call 218-365-2326. Full line of coffee and specialty drinks, as well as sandwiches, wraps, burritos, breakfast, and sweets. Website: www.elysfrontporch.com.

GATOR'S GRILLED CHEESE EMPORIUM, 955 East Sheridan Street, Ely. Call 218-365-7348. Not just grilled cheese, but a full line of inventive sandwiches. Website: www.gatorsinely.com.

INSULA RESTAURANT, 145 East Sheridan Street, Ely. Call 218-365-4855. Locally sourced fusion American dining. Website: www.insularestaurant.com.

ROCKWOOD, 302 East Sheridan Street, Ely. Call 218-365-7772. Walleye, steaks, and burgers. Website: www.rockwoodely.com.

SIR G'S, 520 East Sheridan Street, Ely. Call 218-365-3688. Italian food, including pasta made on-site. Website: www.sirgs.com.

Other Contacts

BOUNDARY WATERS CANOE AREA. Website: www.canoecountry.com.

BOUNDARY WATERS GUIDE SERVICE, Ely. Call 218-343-7951. Website: www.elyoutfittingcompany.com/boundarywatersguideservice.

CANADIAN WATERS, 111 East Sheridan Street, Ely. Call 218-365-3202; 800-255-2922. Website: www.canadianwaters.com.

ELY CHAMBER OF COMMERCE, 1600 East Sheridan Street, Ely. Call 218-365-9123. Website: www.ely.org.

JORDAN'S CANOE OUTFITTERS, 1701 MN 1, Ely. Call 800-644-9955. Website: www.jordanscanoeoutfitters.com.

KAWISHIWI LODGE AND OUTFITTERS, 3187 Fernberg Road, Ely. Call 218-365-5487. Website: www.lakeonecanoes.com.

PIRAGIS NORTHWOODS COMPANY, 105 North Central Avenue, Ely. Call 218-365-6745; 800-223-6565. Website: www.piragis.com.

SUPERIOR NATIONAL FOREST, 8901 Grand Avenue Place, Duluth. Call 218-626-4300. Website: www.fs.usda.gov/superior.

4

INTERNATIONAL FALLS AND VOYAGEURS NATIONAL PARK

ESTIMATED DISTANCE: 140 miles

ESTIMATED TIME: 3 hours

GETTING THERE: From the Twin Cities, take I-94 west to exit 178 and head northeast on MN 24 until you reach US 10. Follow US 10 to Little Falls, then follow MN 371 north to US 2 west. In Bemidji, turn onto US 71 north to International Falls. From International Falls, take MN 11 east until the road ends for the southwestern tip of Rainy Lake. Returning to International Falls, travel south on US 53 to County Route 122 (CR 122) north to reach Kabetogama.

HIGHLIGHTS: The border town of International Falls, with the Bronko Nagurski Museum and tours of the Boise Cascade Paper Mills; Rainy Lake; Voyageurs National Park; and Kabetogama Lake.

If you're coming from the Twin Cities, you have quite a drive to get to this part of the state, but it's well worth it. The land east of International Falls is stunning, with roller-coaster hills winding along the Rainy River and then reaching Rainy Lake itself. Historically, this route was valued by the voyageurs after whom the national park was named. It was also an important area for lumber mills, at the convergence of both miles of trees and the power of the Rainy River. The Boise Cascade Paper Mill has been a decades-long employer in the community and still benefits from its location. Centuries ago, missionaries looking to convert Native American tribes were in abundance in this region, as were immigrant farmers seeking out fertile land.

Does it get cold in the winter? Well, yes. International Falls has been referring to itself as the Icebox of the Nation for years, despite some competition in the coldest community contest with the town of Embarrass, to the

LEFT: KABETOGAMA LAKE

southeast. But even the cold can be advantageous for business; several auto manufacturers routinely test their vehicles here in the winter to make sure they can function in extreme weather.

The residents of this region have learned to adapt, and outdoor recreation is plentiful in the cold months. This is a part of the state where you can ski, snowmobile, and, most importantly, ice fish, which is made more comfortable by renting heated ice houses.

International Falls, named for a waterfall that used to be visible on the Rainy River but is now submerged in a reservoir, sits directly on the Canadian border and is a customs stop. Travel between the two countries is heavy; in fact, the International Falls international rail port is the second busiest in the entire country. The two countries have a good-natured relationship that in recent years has culminated in an annual International Tug of War contest: a 1,500-foot rope is strung across Rainy River with about 50 people on each side trying to pull the other side into the river.

The community's history is on display at two adjacent museums: the **Koochiching County Historical Museum** and the **Bronko Nagurski Museum**. The two museums share one building, each focused on history specific to the region. Bronko Nagurski is a local legend, a farm boy who became one of the best professional football players in the sport's history. His side of the museum details not only his life and sports career, but the impact of the times (the Depression, World War II) on his life and that of others. The County Historical Museum has a well-rounded collection of artifacts reflecting the area's history for Native Americans and French voyageurs, as well as its relationship to Canada. Museum volunteers and staff are well versed in the collections, and can answer questions and offer insightful tales.

Boise Cascade, one of the world's largest paper-making companies, offers both mill tours and woodland tours. Call ahead for reservations, as these tours are very popular.

Not surprisingly, this area is rife with outdoor activities, some more rustic than others. If golf is your game, stop by **Falls Country Club**. Designed by Joel Goldstrand, the Falls Country Club golf course is a challenging and beautiful course, and it is open to the public. The course is filled with pine trees, and streams wind their way throughout it.

You can stay in International Falls, but lodging alternatives are limited to chains like **AmericInn** and **Days Inn**. Most accommodations providing more of the "northern" experience are on the outskirts, or along Highway 11 East to Voyageurs National Park (details below).

Traveling out of International Falls on MN 11, enjoy the eastern portion of the **Waters of the Dancing Sky Scenic Byway.** This byway, which stretches most of the way across the Minnesota side of the border, narrows and curves its way along the Rainy River and Rainy Lake, with the road growing hillier as you approach the eastern end.

There are good options for meals. **The Coffee Landing** is a full-service

THE COFFEE LANDING IN INTERNATIONAL FALLS

RANIER

coffee, espresso, and tea shop, also offering a limited but tasty menu of breakfast items, pastries, and quiche. **The Rose Garden Restaurant** serves classic Chinese-American cuisine in large portions at reasonable prices while **The Chocolate Moose Restaurant Company** dishes up platter-sized portions of pancakes, burgers, pasta, and dinner entrées like steak and shrimp.

A few miles outside International Falls is the small town of Ranier, which sits near the spot where Rainy River flows out of Rainy Lake. Taking a quick visit to this quiet little town, it's hard to believe it was once a destination for Prohibition-era bootleggers smuggling whiskey from Canada. The bridge used by the bootleggers is now the oldest cantilevered bridge in the world. Befitting a bootlegging community, Ranier used to be quite the wild town, full of saloons and bordellos. Today it's more of an artist's haven, with amenities geared toward the outdoor enthusiast. **Tara's Wharf** is a small inn offering four suite accommodations in a charming "seaside" setting; their ice cream shop will keep everyone happy. **The Rainy Lake Grill** is open for most meals, but breakfast is its main attraction.

For a heartier dinner, stop by **Almost Lindy's**, a BBQ and pizza joint on Crystal Beach, east of Ranier.

The last stretch of MN 11 is dotted with small resorts, private cabins, and year-round homes. Several excellent lodging choices await you here, all with river and/or lake access and plenty of outdoor amenities. **Camp Idlewood** is composed of nine cabins with knotty pine interiors and full kitchens. Located on a beach, the resort provides its guests with access to a canoe, paddleboat, inner tubes, and tow ropes at no cost. Boats and motors can be rented, or you can bring your own; each cabin comes with one dock space included, and additional spaces can be rented. **Bear Ridge Guest House** offers just two accommodation options but is nevertheless an excellent choice for visitors to Rainy Lake. Located on a hill overlooking the lake, with a private deck to enjoy the view, Bear Ridge has a guesthouse suite with bedroom, full kitchen, and fireplace; a separate guest room has

A DOCK IN RANIER

SHA SHA RESORT

its own bath and living area. Located 12 miles east of International Falls, **Island View Lodge and Cabins** sits on the edge of Rainy Lake with gorgeous views and direct lake access. There are 15 cabins available, as well as several lodge rooms. An adjacent spa has a hot tub and sauna, and the lodge has a dining room and lounge. The **Thunderbird Lodge** has both lodge rooms and cabins, both of which include daily maid service. The resort is situated for good views of the lake and marina, and has a well-regarded dining room and lounge. Literally where MN 11 ends is **Sha Sha Resort**, which has the unique advantage of being surrounded by water on three sides. Log cabins are graciously appointed, and there is a very private cabin a mile north of the resort itself. Sha Sha also boasts an extensive multi-tiered deck overlooking Rainy Lake, complete with deck bar and boat-in docks, and a restaurant that knows exactly how to cook walleye.

Rainy Lake also provides access to Minnesota's only national park, **Voyageurs National Park**. Some of the oldest exposed rock formations in the world can be found here, carved out by the departures of at least four glaciers and leaving behind a series of four connected lakes. Centuries ago, French traders paddled these waters on their way to Canada, looking to trade animal pelts and goods with Native peoples. Today, Voyageurs National Park is a haven for those who love to be on the water, whether by

The Houseboat Lifestyle

To really relax and enjoy the waters of Rainy River and Rainy Lake, consider booking a houseboat. Rainy Lake is home to two companies that provide houseboat rentals. **Northernaire Houseboats** offers 10 houseboats of varying sizes and levels of amenities that can host two to 12 people, including some with screened-in decks. Rentals include a tow-behind boat, free delivery on the lake twice weekly (for groceries and so on), and a guide service for the first 4 miles to orient you to the maps and buoy systems. Order ahead, and your boat's kitchen will be stocked with foods and beverages of your choice.

NORTHERNAIRE HOUSEBOATS

Rainy Lake Houseboats rents several fully equipped, yacht-style houseboats that come with kitchens, a tow-behind boat, swim platforms and waterslides, and deck table and chairs. Houseboats are available for two to 12 guests. Some require a three-day minimum stay or weekly rental. Guide service is available with prearrangement, and groceries can be ordered in advance.

canoe, kayak, or houseboat. Hikers, snowshoers, and cross-country skiers travel the grounds year-round. A series of connected lakes and bays, as well as miles of untouched forest, provide an intimate north woods experience. Wildlife is abundant.

Ellsworth Rock Gardens

From the southern end of Kabetogama, you can take a boat to the lake's north shore and visit **Ellsworth Rock Gardens**, built over the course of 20 years by Jack Ellsworth, who designed and constructed more than 60 terraced flower beds on a stony outcrop, filling them with more than 13,000 flowers and surrounding them with 200 abstract rock sculptures. Following Ellsworth's death in 1974, the gardens languished. The national park service bought the property in 1978 and removed Ellsworth's buildings, leaving the gardens to deteriorate to the chagrin of many admirers. It wasn't until 1996 that public pressure finally led to reclamation efforts of Ellworth's gardens. Since 2000, the park service has hosted an annual "Garden Blitz" day, where contractors and volunteers converge on the Gardens to keep them from reverting back to forestland.

There are three visitor centers. Located 10 miles east of International Falls, the **Rainy Lake Visitor Center** serves as the park's main hub and is the only center open year-round. **The Kabetogama Lake Visitor Center**, on the southwest shores of Kabetogama Lake, and the **Ash River Visitor Center**, on the Ash River, are both open late May through September only.

From the Rainy Lake Visitor Center, you can take the **Oberholtzer Trail**, named after a northern Minnesota conservationist. The trail winds through the forest and alongside marshes, with views of the Black Bay Narrows. The following trails are reached exclusively by boat: **Black Bay Beaver Pond Trail** guides hikers to an active beaver pond; **Anderson Bay Trail** climbs a steep cliff and awards amazing views of Rainy Lake; while **Little American Island** Trail explores the historic site of the Little American Gold Mine.

Another option for seeing the natural beauty of the park is to reserve a spot on one of the three tour boats offered during the summer season. You can pick up last-minute tickets at either the Rainy Lake or Kabetogama Lake Visitor Centers, but departures from the Ash River Visitor Center must be booked ahead of time.

Campgrounds are available on a first-come, first-served basis (groups can reserve in advance with one of the visitor centers), but note that the campgrounds within the park are accessible only by boat. A free permit is required for camping, which can be obtained at the visitor centers or at self-permit stations within the park. If you're interested in camping but would rather be able to drive up to your campsite, look into reserving a site at the **Woodenfrog State Campground** on CR 122. Located in **Kabetogama State Forest**, part of Voyageurs National Park, Woodenfrog has campsites available from mid-May to mid-September that don't require boat access. If you stop by the Woodenfrog campgrounds, be sure to visit the Woodenfrog Refectory, a beautiful stone concession area built during the Depression by the Civilian Conservation Corps.

You can explore the northern part of the park via the Rainy Lake entrance, or you can return to International Falls and head south on US 53 to CR 122 to visit the southwest region of the park, around beautiful Kabetogama Lake. Birders should seek out the Echo Bay Trail near the Kabetogama Lake Visitor Center, which is an especially promising area for sighting birds, as there's a great blue heron rookery along the way. A longer (nearly 28 miles altogether) and more difficult hike, the Kab-Ash Trail connects the Kabetogama and Ash River areas and affords hikers generous access to the park. Many trails are open not only for hiking in the summer, but also for cross-country skiing and snowshoeing in the winter.

Lodging is abundant around Kabetogama Lake, with many mom-and-pop resorts and cabins available for rent. **Voyageur Park Lodge** offers 12 cottages for rent along Lake Kabetogama and plenty of peaceful privacy. Cabins come equipped with full kitchens, barbecue grills, and campfire sites (campfires are permitted only when conditions allow). Use of canoes, kayaks, and paddleboats is free; fishing boats, pontoons, and motors can

THE WOODENFROG REFECTORY AT KABETOGAMA LAKE

be rented on-site. **Herseth's Tomahawk Resort** consists of eight cabins and one mobile home. The resort has a large sand beach with free canoes and paddleboats, and motorized boats are available for rent. The proprietor is a certified scuba diver and is happy to arrange diving excursions into Lake Kabetogama.

Stretched along Lake Kabetogama on a sandy beach, **Moosehorn Resort** has nine cabins to choose from. An especially family-friendly resort, the cabins are located on a quiet bay offering calmer lake waters than in other spots. Canoes, kid-sized kayaks, and a playground area are free to guests, and boats are available for rental. **Kec's Kove Resort** offers eight cabins and a lodge with whirlpool and sauna. A massage therapist is available for guests, and motorized boats are available for rent. If you go fishing and need some help afterwards, Kec's can provide fish cleaning and freezing services. Paddleboats, canoes, and kayaks are complimentary. **Northern Lights Resort and Outfitting** rents out 10 cabins along Lake Kabetogama and provides a number of planned activities: guides can be arranged for fishing or other expeditions; a Ladies' Pontoon Cruise, with coffee and muffins, is offered weekly; and an adults' social cruise is also offered weekly in the evening.

IN THE AREA

Accommodations

AMERICINN, 1500 US 71, International Falls. Call 218-283-8000; 800-634-3444. Website: www.wyndhamhotels.com/americinn.

BEAR RIDGE GUEST HOUSE, 1841 MN 11, International Falls. Call 218-286-5710. Rates start at $110. Website: www.bearridgeguesthouse.net.

CAMP IDLEWOOD, 3033 CR 20, International Falls. Call 218-286-5551; 888-741-1228. Website: www.campidlewood.com.

DAYS INN, 2331 US 53, International Falls. Call 218-283-9441. Website: www.wyndhamhotels.com.

HERSETH'S TOMAHAWK RESORT, 10078 Gappa Road, Kabetogama. Call 218-875-2352; 888-834-7899. Website: hersethstomahawkresort.com.

ISLAND VIEW LODGE AND CABINS, 1817 MN 11 East, International Falls. Call 218-286-3511; 800-777-7856. Website: www.gotorainylake.com.

KEC'S KOVE RESORT, 10428 Gamma Road, Kabetogama. Call 218-875-2841; 800-777-8405. Website: www.kecscove.com.

KETTLE FALLS HOTEL, 10502 Gamma Road, Voyageurs National Park. Call 218-240-1724; 218-240-1726; off-season 218-875-2070. Website: www.kettlefallshotel.com.

MOOSEHORN RESORT, 10434 Waltz Road, Kabetogama. Call 218-875-3491; 800-777-7968. Website: www.moosehornresort.com.

NORTHERN LIGHTS RESORT AND OUTFITTING, 10179 Bay Club Drive, Kabetogama. Call 218-875-2591; 800 318-7023. Website: nlro.com.

NORTHERNAIRE HOUSEBOATS, 2690 CR 94, International Falls. Call 218-286-5221; 800-854-7958. Website: www.northernairehouseboats.com.

RAINY LAKE HOUSEBOATS, 2031 CR 102, International Falls. Call 800-554-9188. Website: www.rainylakehouseboats.com.

SHA SHA RESORT, 1664 MN 11 East, International Falls. Call 218-286-3241; 800-685-2776. Website: www.shashaonrainylake.com.

TARA'S WHARF, 2065 Spruce Street Landing, Ranier. Call 218-286-5699. Website: www.taraswharf.com.

Kettle Falls Hotel

For unique accommodations, try the **Kettle Falls Hotel**, located near the Kettle Falls and dams, which were built about the same time as the hotel. Accessible only by boat or plane and located on an odd geographical twist that allows you to stand on the Minnesota side while facing Canada to the south, this hotel is the only lodging available within Voyageurs National Park. Nearly a century old, Kettle Falls Hotel has a rich history. According to rumors, its construction in 1913 by timberman Ed Rose was financed by the infamous Nellie Bly. Rose in turn sold the hotel to Robert Williams for $1,000 and four barrels of whiskey, which set the stage for the years to come, with bootleggers selling whiskey from the hotel during Prohibition. Today the hotel is listed on the National Register of Historic Places. The hotel offers 12 rooms with shared baths, a full-service restaurant, and a saloon that still bears the marks of wilder early years.

THUNDERBIRD LODGE, 2170 CR 139, International Falls. Call 218-286-3151; 800-351-5133. Website: www.thunderbirdrainylake.com.

VOYAGEUR PARK LODGE, 10436 Waltz Road, Kabetogama. Call 218-875-2131; 800-331-5694. Website: www.voyageurparklodge.com.

Attractions and Recreation

BOISE CASCADE PAPER MILL, 2nd Street, International Falls. Call 218-285-5011.

KOOCHICHING COUNTY HISTORICAL MUSEUM/BRONKO NAGURSKI MUSEUM, 214 Sixth Avenue, International Falls. Call 218-283-4316. Website: www.koochichingmuseums.org.

VOYAGEURS NATIONAL PARK, 360 US 11 East, International Falls. Call 218-283-6600. Website: www.nps.gov/voya.

WATERS OF THE DANCING SKY, MN 11. Website: www.watersofdancing sky.org.

Dining

ALMOST LINDY'S, 3003 CR 20, International Falls. Call 218-286-3364. BBQ, pizza, and chicken. Website: www.almostlindys.com.

CHOCOLATE MOOSE RESTAURANT COMPANY, 2501 2nd Avenue West, International Falls. Call 218-283-8888. Three meals a day, with dinner offering supper club entrées. Website: www.chocolatemooserestaurant.com.

COFFEE LANDING, 444 3rd Street, International Falls. Call 218-373-2233. Coffee shop with breakfast and lunch. Website: www.facebook.com /coffeelandingcafe.

RAINY LAKE GRILL, 2079 Spruce Street, Ranier. Call 218-286-5584. Breakfast, appetizers, pizza. Website: rainy-lake-grill.business.site.

THUNDERBIRD LODGE, 2170 CR 139, International Falls. Call 218-286-3151; 800-351-5133. Steakhouse fare along with comfort foods and breakfast. Website: www.thunderbirdrainylake.com/dining-lounge.html.

Other Contacts

BOUNDARY WATERS CANOE AREA WILDERNESS PERMIT RESERVATION CENTER, 8901 Grand Avenue Place, Duluth. Call 218-626-4300; 877-444-6777. Website: www.recreation.gov.

ELY CHAMBER OF COMMERCE, 1600 East Sheridan Street, Ely. Call 218-365-6123; 800-777-7281. Website: www.ely.org.

INTERNATIONAL FALLS CONVENTION AND VISITOR BUREAU, 301 2nd Avenue, International Falls. Call 800-325-5766. Website: www.rainylake.org.

LAKE KABETOGAMA TOURISM BUREAU, 9707 Gamma Road, Lake Kabetogama. Call 218-875-2621; 800-525-3522. Website: www.kabetogama.com.

VOYAGEURS NATIONAL PARK ASSOCIATION, 126 North 3rd Street, Suite 400, Minneapolis. Call 612-333-5424. Website: www.voyageurs.org.

5

THE CANADIAN BORDER

West to Roseau

ESTIMATED DISTANCE: 160 miles

ESTIMATED TIME: 3 hours

GETTING THERE: From the Twin Cities, take I-94 west to exit 178 and head north-east on MN 24 until you reach US 10. Follow US 10 to Little Falls, then follow MN 371 North to US 2 West. In Bemidji, turn onto US 71 North. From there, drive to Blackduck and continue straight onto MN 72, following to MN 11 and Baudette.

HIGHLIGHTS: Fishing and boating on Lake of the Woods; the 3-mile beach at Zippel Bay State Park; historic Fort St. Charles; Roseau's Pioneer Village; and bird-watching in Lost River State Forest.

The border lakes region was shaped by former glacial lakes and settled by Chippewa Indians, followed by French traders and eventually Scandinavians, looking for fertile farmland. People farm here still, but outdoor recreation is a favorite pastime of both residents and visitors. Part of the border boundary is the Rainy River, which flows from its source, Rainy Lake, on the eastern end of the border. Rainy River divides the United States and Canada right up to the point where it meets Lake of the Woods, an enormous lake stretching far north into Canada. This is one of the most remote spots in the state, and what it lacks in amenities, it makes up for in peaceful beauty.

The northwestern stretch of the state is especially beloved by visitors who want to enjoy outdoor activities, such as fishing (both summer and winter), boating, hiking, hunting, snowmobiling, snowshoeing, and cross-country skiing. Consequently, many resorts in this area are open year-round to cater to clients who favor activities in the different seasons. Since winter can be

LEFT: ROSEAU'S PIONEER VILLAGE

unpredictable, it's extremely unwise to head out to this part of the state in the middle of January without a snow emergency kit and a charged-up cell phone in your vehicle. Pay close attention to the weather, as snowstorms with dangerous winds and wind chills can arise quickly.

The lakes that punctuate the region are known for excellent fishing and boating. Winter fishing has grown in popularity through better technology; today many northern lakes are dotted by buildings ranging from little more than shacks to larger, heated buildings with attached Porta-Potties, known as sleepers, but all considered ice houses, to be used for winter fishing. Ice fishing and other winter sports like cross-country skiing, snowmobiling, and snowshoeing have made the northern region a year-round destination rather than a summer-only spot.

Lake of the Woods is one of the nation's largest lakes (after the Great Lakes and Salt Lake), and it's become a favored place of fishermen from all over the country and Canada. The region is proud of its walleye population, but there are many kinds of fish for the catching: lake sturgeon, northern pike, smallmouth and largemouth bass, perch, and muskie are just some of the plentiful fish. You can bring your own boat and manage your fishing yourself, or you can hire a guide to assist you through one of the many guide services (and through many of the dozens of resorts throughout the area).

There is a separate summer and winter fishing season. Winter's ice fishing has gained considerable ground as more resorts offer ice houses for rent, many of which are outfitted with propane heaters and cooktops. The popularity of sleeper fish houses, outfitted like rustic cabins, also continues to

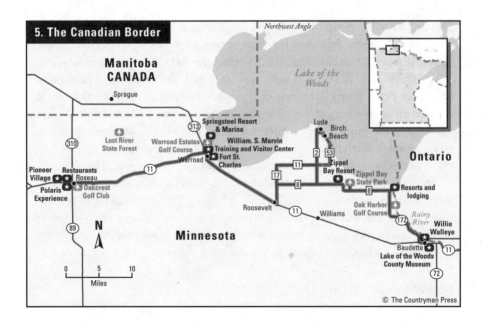

Golfing in the Far North

Golf's charm continues to be felt in the northernmost region of the state. There are several courses available to the public in this area:

Oak Harbor Golf Course in Baudette is a nine-hole course open May 1 to October 15, weather permitting.

Oakcrest Golf Club in Roseau is an 18-hole championship course that winds along the river and twists through the woods. Open mid-May to mid-October, weather permitting.

Warroad Estates Golf Course is an 18-hole course that straddles the US–Canadian border. Open April 15 to October 15, weather permitting.

Northwest Angle Country Club, located at the farthest northern part of the continental United States: the Northwest Angle. When a golf course's location is described as "north of Northern Minnesota," you know you're truly going "up north." A nine-hole course that may not be the most pristinely groomed one you've ever played, but you may never be able to experience quite so much wildlife while golfing, either. Open May through September, weather permitting.

grow. Fish spearing is another activity drawing increasing interest. Official seasons and regulations can be found through the Minnesota Department of Natural Resources (information at the end of this chapter).

Deer hunting in Minnesota begins in late October for bow hunters and early November for firearms. Besides deer hunting, duck, grouse, and goose hunting are all popular activities. Because there is so much open land near Lake of the Woods, it's easy to mistake private property for public hunting grounds. Check with the local tourist offices or with your resort owners, who can provide necessary information to help you avoid trespassing. The Minnesota DNR has specific licensing and regulation information. Many of the resorts in this area can recommend, or are available for hire, as hunting guides to help you maximize your time.

There are over 400 miles of snowmobile trails in the Lake of the Woods area, most groomed and maintained locally.

While there are indeed attractions and historical sites in this part of the state, the emphasis here is outside, not inside.

You'll get your first taste of the favored local sport when you arrive in Baudette on MN 11, and **Willie Walleye** is there to greet you. No visit to the northern lakes would be complete without a photo op at the walleye equivalent of Paul Bunyan. Forty feet long and weighing two tons, Willie represents Baudette's claim of being the "Walleye Capital of the World," a claim, it should be noted, disputed by other popular walleye destinations in the state.

WILLIE WALLEYE IN BAUDETTE

The **Lake of the Woods County Museum** in Baudette is a small but well-curated museum with exhibitions on various aspects of northern Minnesota's history and development, including a re-created homestead kitchen, school, country store, and tavern, as well as information on the geology of the area.

The nicest hotel in Baudette itself is the **AmericInn**, which offers rooms and suites, an indoor pool, cold-weather hook-ups, a fish-cleaning area, and free high-speed Internet access. Upgraded rooms include fireplaces. Just outside of Baudette is the **Wildwood Inn Bed & Breakfast**, a secluded home in a pristine setting with five suites, all with private bath.

North of Baudette on MN 172, where the Rainy River meets Lake of the Woods, you can find the **Border View Lodge**. This resort has several cabins, all of which are fully equipped and include the option of daily maid service (bed making, dish washing). Border View also offers ice houses, both for daily use and for accommodation for that all-night ice fishing getaway, and there's a bar and restaurant in the lodge. Not far away is the **Wigwam Resort**. The Wigwam offers both hotel rooms in the lodge and cabins for rental. Guests can book accommodations only, or they can reserve packages that include meals at the resort's restaurant and charter fishing with a guide. Also nearby is the **Sportsman's Lodge**, with numerous cabins, sleeper fish houses, and a lodge with 30 rooms.

If you're looking for a quick bite to eat, check out the **Northlake Café** for burgers or **Alice's Family Restaurant** for breakfast. There's also **Rosalie's Restaurant & Lounge**, open daily for lunch and dinner, and the bar stays open late.

Continue north on MN 172, which closely follows the shoreline of Rainy River up to Lake of the Woods. Turn west onto County Route 8 (CR 8), which will bring you to **Zippel Bay State Park**. Fishing, swimming, camping, bird-watching—Zippel Bay State Park offers these and more in its 3,000-plus acres along Lake of the Woods. Six miles of hiking trails during the summer are expanded to 11 miles in winter for cross-country skiers. During the summer, get your fill of the vast Lake of the Woods by hiking along Zippel Bay State Park's 3-mile beach. A word to the wise: before heading to the park, stop at one of the local bait-shop gas stations and ask what the best repellent is for deerflies, which can be a nuisance in summer.

West of the park, near the town of Williams, is **Zippel Bay Resort**.

THE BEACH AT ZIPPEL BAY STATE PARK

Situated right on the bay, the resort offers both budget and deluxe (with fireplace and hot tub) log cabin accommodations. The cabins are attractive and spacious, located on the water's edge, and the resort has a restaurant and provides an outdoor pool for the summer months. During winter, make sure to spend some time at the Zippel Igloo, an on-ice "igloo" with several holes for fishing, catered food and drinks, and a satellite TV. Packages are available with or without meals. During the winter, sleeper ice houses are also available for rent.

At this point, you can choose to continue west on CR 8 until you reach CR 17, then head south to return to MN 11 heading west to Warroad. Or, if you'd like to spend more time enjoying the view of the vast Lake of the Woods, you can take CR 53 (note: this is a gravel road) until you make a right turn on CR 51. Make an almost immediate left on CR 52 (also known as Sandy Shores Drive), and follow it north along the lakeshore to Birch Beach. Continue inland on CR 52 to MN 2, which will take you north to Lude, one of the northernmost spots in Minnesota

ZIPPEL BAY RESORT CABINS

that doesn't involve crossing international waters. From Lude, you will return down MN 2, making a right turn onto MN 11 and following that to MN 17. Take a left turn there and return to CR 11, traveling to Warroad.

In Warroad, **Fort St. Charles** is a worthy stop. In the early 1700s, a French explorer and trader by the name of Pierre Gaultier de Varennes, sieur de la Vérendrye, established this fort as a base for trading and launching expeditions. However, lack of food and hostility from local Sioux made the fort difficult to maintain, and it was abandoned after 1760. The buildings were discovered and reconstructed as a historical site in the mid-1900s.

Another worthwhile point of interest is the **William S. Marvin Training and Visitor Center** at CR 11 and MN 313. The Marvin Visitor Center is a historic, industrial exhibition, featuring the growth and technology behind Marvin Windows and Doors. Highlights include a theatrical account of the fire that destroyed the Marvin plant in 1961 and how the Marvin company rebuilt and expanded. Tours of the Marvin plant itself are available by appointment at 218-386-4333, Monday through Friday only.

From all this sightseeing you're likely to work up an appetite. At **Izzy's Lounge and Grill,** you'll find the bar fully stocked, and the grill dishing up enormous burger and chicken platters. Service is friendly, and Izzy's casual environment, with its large stone fireplace, is downright cozy. **The Nomad Tavern** is a seasonal pizza joint with a bar as well, and **Phoenix Restaurant & Lounge** offers similar options. For a great breakfast or brunch, try **Joe's Place**, and for something a little more upscale, the **Willows Restaurant** is a good bet, located just off CR 74 (also known as Lake Street NE). Willows

RIVER VIEW PARK, ROSEAU

THE POLARIS EXPERIENCE, ROSEAU

serves up steak, shrimp, and burgers while diners enjoy a stellar view of the lake. Here, your after-dinner entertainment is taken care of too—the restaurant is located in the Seven Clans Casino.

Just outside the city of Warroad is the **Springsteel Resort & Marina**, where you can reserve a cabin either on the lakeshore or tucked back into the woods. You'll find a restaurant and bar on site, and year-round fishing as well. If you're looking for accommodations a little out of the ordinary, check out the **St. Mary's Lofts,** right in Warroad itself. Housed in the world's largest all-weather log church, the motel room is built into the former balcony and offers 22-foot-high ceilings and a hot tub.

From Warroad, travel west on MN 11 through the **Lost River State Forest** to reach Roseau. Lost River State Forest is an excellent stop for birders, with typical sightings including great gray owls, northern hawks, boreal chickadees, and magnolia warblers. Roseau marks a transition in the landscape, as the large forests to the east begin to give way to the prairies of the Red River Valley in the west. The changing scenery also provides unique opportunities for spending time outdoors, as you can easily find yourself deep within the forest and then very quickly travel to prairie grasslands, experiencing striking differences in flora and fauna along the way.

Roseau is also known as the birthplace of snowmobiles, and the town's role in the world of snowmobiling are on display at the **Polaris Experience**. One of the leading manufacturers of snowmobiles, Polaris built this visitor center adjacent to its plant to showcase the company's history. Exhibitions range from examples of the earliest snowmobile prototypes to today's sleeker machines. Tours of the Polaris plant itself are scheduled daily at

EARL'S DRIVE IN, ROSEAU

2 p.m.; call ahead or stop by the office to sign up. Admission is free.

Just west of Roseau is the **Pioneer Village**, a lovingly preserved testament to the pioneer days of northwestern Minnesota's agricultural history. Of the 16 buildings, most are restored artifacts, maintained primarily by volunteer labor (volunteer opportunities are available on Tuesdays—call the village for more information). Visitors are welcome to explore on their own or take a guided tour through the post office, parish hall, church, barn, blacksmith shop, and log cabin. Bathroom facilities are, fittingly, of the outhouse variety—a vintage Porta-Potty.

Accommodations within Roseau itself are somewhat limited. The **AmericInn** is one of the nicest hotels in Roseau, offering rooms and suites, an indoor pool, and cold-weather hook-ups. Nearby is the **North Country Inn and Suites**, a motel with 49 rooms and suites, all with refrigerators and microwaves, and daily continental breakfast. There is an indoor pool and hot tub as well.

For a good meal, check out the **Brickhouse Restaurant and Bar**, located near the Polaris Experience. Casual bar food is found at **Gene's Bar and Grill**, and breakfast and lunch at **Nelson's Cafe**. Or if you'd like to enjoy an old-fashioned dining experience, try **Earl's Drive In** for burgers and malts.

IN THE AREA

Accommodations

AMERICINN BAUDETTE, 1179 Main Street, Baudette. Call 218-634-3200. Website: www.wyndhamhotels.com/americinn.

AMERICINN ROSEAU, 1110 3rd Street NW, Roseau. Call 218-463-1045. Website: www.wyndhamhotels.com/americinn.

BORDER VIEW LODGE, 3409 MN 172 NW, Baudette. Call 800-776-3474. Website: www.borderviewlodge.com.

NORTH COUNTRY INN AND SUITES, 902 3rd Street NW, Roseau. Call 888-300-2196. Website: www.northcountryinnandsuites.com.

SPORTSMAN'S LODGES, 3244 Bur Oak Road NW, Baudette. Call 218-634-1342; 800-862-8602. Website: www.sportsmanlodges.com.

SPRINGSTEEL RESORT & MARINA, 38004 Beach Street, Warroad. Call 218-386-1000; 800-605-1001. Website: www.springsteelresort.net.

ST. MARY'S LOFTS, 202 Roberts Avenue NE, Warroad. Call 218-386-2474. Website: www.scottjohnsoncompanies.com.

WIGWAM RESORT, 3502 Four Mile Bay Drive NW, Baudette. Call 218-634-2168; 800-448-9260. Website: www.wigwamresortlow.com.

WILDWOOD INN BED & BREAKFAST, 3361 Cottonwood Road NW, Baudette. Call 218-634-1356. Website: www.wildwoodinnbb.com.

ZIPPEL BAY RESORT, 6080 39th Street NW, Williams. Call 800-222-2537. Website: www.zippelbay.com.

Attractions and Recreation

FORT ST. CHARLES, The Point, Lake Street NE, Warroad. Call 218-223-4611.

LAKE OF THE WOODS COUNTY MUSEUM, 119 8th Avenue SE, Baudette. Call 218-634-1200. Website: www.lakeofthewoodshistoricalsociety.com.

NORTHWEST ANGLE COUNTRY CLUB, Angle Inlet. Call 218-223-8001. Website: www.pasturegolf.com/courses/nwangle.htm.

OAK HARBOR GOLF COURSE, 2805 24th Street NW, Baudette. Call 218-634-9939. Website: www.oakharborgolfcourse.com.

OAKCREST GOLF CLUB, 5th Street South, Roseau. Call 218-463-3016. Website: www.oakcrestgolfcourse.com.

PIONEER VILLAGE, MN 11, Roseau. Call 218-463-1045; 218-463-1118. Website: www.roseaupioneerfarm.com.

THE POLARIS EXPERIENCE, 205 5th Avenue SW, Suite 2, Roseau. Call 218-463-4999. Website: www.polarisindustries.com.

WARROAD ESTATES GOLF COURSE, 37293 Elm Drive, Warroad. Call 218-386-2025. Website: www.warroadestates.com.

WILLIAM S. MARVIN TRAINING AND VISITOR CENTER, 704 MN 313 North, Warroad. Call 218-386-4334. Website: www.marvin.com/our-story /visitor-center.

WILLIE WALLEYE, Main Street and 1st Avenue East, Baudette.

ZIPPEL BAY STATE PARK, 3684 54th Avenue NW, Williams. Call 218-783-6252. Website: www.dnr.state.mn.us/state_parks/zippel_bay/index.html.

Dining

ALICE'S FAMILY RESTAURANT, 203 West Main Street, Baudette. Call 218-634-1165. Diner breakfast and lunch.

BRICKHOUSE RESTAURANT AND BAR, The Creamery, MN 89 South, Roseau. Call 218-463-0993. Website: www.mnbrickhouse.com.

EARL'S DRIVE IN, 1001 3rd Street NE, Roseau. Call 218-463-1912.

GENE'S BAR AND GRILL, 1095 3rd Street NW, Roseau. Call 218-463-1957. Burgers and sandwiches. Website: www.facebook.com/Genes-Bar-and-Grill-103689823006461.

IZZY'S LOUNGE AND GRILL, 801 State Avenue North, Warroad. Call 218-386-2723. Website: www.patchmotel.com/lounge-grill.

JOE'S PLACE, 318 Lake Street, Warroad. Call 218-386-2900. Breakfast and brunch. Website: www.facebook.com/Joes-Place-214079825282316.

NELSON'S CAFÉ, 104 Main Avenue North, Roseau. Call 218-463-2277. Diner comfort food. Website: www.facebook.com/pages/Nelsons-Cafe/115438815 145925.

NOMAD TAVERN, 1109 MacKenzie Street NE, Warroad. Call 218-386-4808. Pizza and bar. Website: www.facebook.com/nomadtavernwarroad.

NORTHLAKE CAFÉ, 913 2nd Street NW, Baudette. Call 218-634-9807. Burgers and sandwiches. Website: www.facebook.com/Northlake-Cafe-123091301081019.

THE PHOENIX RESTAURANT & LOUNGE, 603 Cedar Avenue NW, Warroad. Call 218-386-1618. Pizza place with bar. Website: www.facebook.com /thephoenixwarroad.

ROSALIE'S RESTAURANT & LOUNGE, 1229 Main Street West, Baudette. Call 218-634-9422. Lunch spot and supper club with a bar open late. Website: www.facebook.com/pages/Rosalies-Restaurant-Lounge/689218364512912.

THE WILLOWS, 34966 605th Avenue, Warroad. Call 218-386-2969; 800-815-8923. Website: www.sevenclanscasino.com.

Other Contacts

CONVENTION AND VISITOR BUREAU OF ROSEAU, 121 Center Street East, Roseau. Call 218-463-0009. Website: goroseau.com.

LAKE OF THE WOODS TOURISM, Baudette. Call 218-634-1174; 800-382-3474. Website: www.lakeofthewoodsmn.com.

MINNESOTA DEPARTMENT OF NATURAL RESOURCES. Call 651-296-6157; 888-646-6367. Website for fishing information: www.dnr.state.mn.us /regulations/fishing/index.html. For hunting information: www.dnr.state .mn.us/regulations/hunting/index.html.

WARROAD CONVENTION AND VISITOR BUREAU, 201 Lake Street NE, Warroad. Call 218-386-3543; 800-328-4455. Website: www.visitwarroad .com.

6

NORTHERN LAKES AND FORESTS, PART 1

South from Bemidji

ESTIMATED DISTANCE: 120 miles

ESTIMATED TIME: 3 hours

GETTING THERE: From the Twin Cities, take I-94 west to exit 178 and head northeast on MN 24 until you reach US 10. Follow US 10 to Little Falls, then follow MN 371 north to US 2 west to Bemidji.

HIGHLIGHTS: The Art Walk in Bemidji; Itasca State Park; Dorset, the "Restaurant Capital of the World"; the Heartland Trail; Chippewa National Forest.

This is the area of Minnesota well-known for something simultaneously enormous and tiny: the headwaters of the Mississippi, found in Itasca State Park. When you consider how mighty the Mississippi grows even before leaving Minnesota, let alone the immensity it reaches during its course to the Gulf of Mexico, it's amazing to experience the river as a gentle trickle that's easy enough to wade across. These headwaters are found in a densely forested part of the state, where large old-growth tracts of pine trees abound alongside wetlands, and hundreds of little lakes appear around every corner. The abundance of water is reflected in the name of one of the region's largest towns, Bemidji, which is Ojibwe for "lake with water flowing through." Many of the settlements here grew out of the logging industry, but today tourism is a major source of revenue for towns like Bemidji, Park Rapids, and Walker.

Bemidji is the county seat and home to Bemidji State University, located on the shores of Lake Bemidji. The city's downtown area is compact and includes several points of interest to visitors. The area's logging, pioneer, and Native American histories are on display at the **Beltrami County History Center**. The center resides within the restored 1912 Great Northern

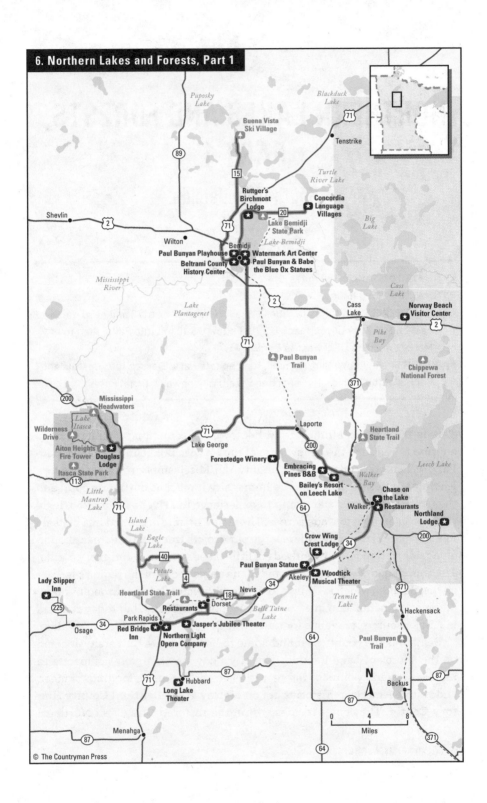

6. Northern Lakes and Forests, Part 1

Puposky Lake

Blackduck Lake

71

Buena Vista Ski Village

Tenstrike

89

15

Turtle River Lake

Ruttger's Birchmont Lodge ★

Concordia Language Villages ★

Shevlin

2

71

20

Lake Bemidji State Park

Big Lake

Wilton

Bemidji

Lake Bemidji

Paul Bunyan Playhouse ★ ★ Watermark Art Center
Beltrami County ★ ★ Paul Bunyan & Babe
History Center   the Blue Ox Statues

Mississippi River

Lake Plantagenet

2

Cass Lake

Cass Lake

Norway Beach ★ Visitor Center

2

71

Paul Bunyan ⚑ Trail

Pike Bay

Chippewa ⚑ National Forest

200

Mississippi Headwaters

Lake Itasca

371

Wilderness Drive

Aiton Heights ⚑ Fire Tower
Douglas ★ Lodge
⚑ Itasca State Park

113

Little Mantrap Lake

71

Lake George

Forestedge Winery ★

Laporte

200

Heartland ⚑ State Trail

Leech Lake

Embracing ★ Pines B&B

Bailey's Resort ★ on Leech Lake

Walker Bay

Chase on ★ the Lake
★ Restaurants
Northland ★ Lodge

Island Lake

Eagle Lake

40

4

Potato Lake

64

Walker

200

Crow Wing ★ Crest Lodge

34

Lady Slipper Inn ★

225

Heartland State Trail

Paul Bunyan Statue ★

Akeley ★ Woodtick
         Musical Theater

Nevis

34

Tenmile Lake

371

Hackensack

Osage

34

Park Rapids

18

Dorset

Restaurants ★

Belle Taine Lake

64

Red Bridge ★ Inn
Northern Light ★ Opera Company

★ Jasper's Jubilee Theater

Paul Bunyan ⚑ Trail

87

Backus

71

87

Hubbard ★
Long Lake Theater

Menahga

87

64

371

N

0   4   8
Miles

© The Countryman Press

Railway Depot, the last depot built by railroad baron James J. Hill. The building's architecture itself is worth a visit, but the collection it houses is also entertaining and enlightening, with items varying from Native American artifacts to a restored telegraph office. A separate research area offers historians access to archival materials.

Families are welcome at the **Headwaters Science Center**. Essentially a children's science museum, the HSC offers a variety of hands-on activities, as well as a collection of live animals (snakes, turtles, salamanders) for kids to learn about and handle.

The Watermark Art Center is located in the historic Carnegie Library building on the lakeshore, which is listed on the National Register of Historic Places. Inside are three galleries that display the work of national and regional artists, which also serve as venues for hosting live music and poetry readings. New exhibitions appear monthly from February through December. The Art Center also sponsors a series of First Fridays, which showcase art and live performances both in the center and around Bemidji.

Close to the lakefront is the **Paul Bunyan Playhouse**. With over 55 years of productions, this is one of the country's longest continuously operating summer stock theaters. The Paul Bunyan Playhouse employs both professional actors from around the country as well as local talent for its summer season. Veterans of the Playhouse have gone on to professional theater careers in the Twin Cities.

THE PAUL BUNYAN PLAYHOUSE, BEMIDJI

The lakefront itself also has several attractions. The **Bemidji Sculpture Walk** is an outdoor sculpture garden curving along the shores of Lake Bemidji. Stop by the visitor information center on the lakefront and pick up a self-guided tour brochure to begin exploring the sculptures and murals that appear along the lakeside and downtown.

A visit to Bemidji isn't quite complete without taking a photo with the statues of the legendary **Paul Bunyan and Babe the Blue Ox**. Besides, a trip to the statues makes for a good starting point for visiting the Art Walk. The statues are situated right next to the **Paul Bunyan Amusement Park**, which is open every day in summer, offering rides for small children and old-fashioned miniature golf.

The Paul Bunyan Trail winds around the east side of Lake Bemidji on its way to **Lake Bemidji State Park**. The park may not have the Mississippi headwaters, but it is a worthy stop, with acres of forest, access to Lake Bemidji for boating and fishing, a paved bike trail, and scores of birds for watching. The 110-mile Paul Bunyan Trail runs from Lake Bemidji State Park to Brainerd, and is a popular choice for cyclists. You'll find several bike-in campsites along the way, as well as bicycle rentals in many of the towns along the route.

Continue north on US 71 until you reach CR 15. Follow CR 15 north to find **Buena Vista Ski Village**. The mountains are not extraordinarily tall, but Buena Vista offers beautiful scenery to enjoy alongside its 16 runs. Cross-country skiing, tubing, snowboarding, and horse-drawn sleigh rides are all offered while there's snow. In summer, the winter ski resort becomes

Concordia Language Villages

North of Bemidji are the **Concordia Language Villages**. Take US 71 north to MN 197 (also known as Bemidji Avenue North), turning right, then turn left at Thorsonveien NE to reach the campus. This renowned language school, headquartered in Moorhead, holds the majority of its classes and camps at an expansive site just outside Bemidji. The languages (including French, German, Spanish, Korean, Russian, Norwegian, and Swedish) are taught in villages, small towns created to resemble a town in the country of origin. Around one corner, you'll find a beautiful German town; around the next, a colorful Spanish center. Most of the villages in Bemidji are centered near Turtle Lake, but a few are about 10 miles north. Each village is separate from the other, and programs are offered for both children and adults. Even if you're not planning on learning a foreign language, visiting the villages for the sightseeing and loving re-creations of international villages makes this site worth a stop.

Buena Vista Ranch, a logging village and visitor center. Activities include covered wagon tours, horsemanship training clinics, and fall foliage rides. Reservations are recommended; call for information.

Bemidji has several options for lodging, mostly chains, but with a couple of exceptions. The **DoubleTree by Hilton** and the **Hampton Inn** are located right on Lake Bemidji, and only a short walk from the tourist information center and the beginning of the Sculpture Walk. Full breakfast is included in the rates, and all rooms have high-speed Internet access. The Hampton Inn also houses the **Green Mill** pizza restaurant, open for lunch and dinner. Near the Paul Bunyan Mall is the **AmericInn Motel & Suites**. The AmericInn offers 59 units, 26 of which are suites. The property has an indoor pool, whirlpool, and sauna, and the rates include continental breakfast. Also near the mall is the **Holiday Inn Express**. Most quarters have two queen beds, while a few upgraded rooms feature king beds and hot tubs.

Located near Lake Bemidji on the Paul Bunyan Trail, **Lake Bemidji Bed & Breakfast** offers three rooms, all with private bath, upgraded bed coverings, and full breakfast. A common great room serves as the breakfast spot, where you'll enjoy lovely views of the lake, and the backyard boasts a fire pit and double hammock for guest relaxation.

Just outside town is a family resort that's something of a summer vacation tradition for visitors on Lake Bemidji. Take US 71 to MN 197, then to CR 21 to find **Ruttger's Birchmont Lodge**, which offers both lodge and cabin accommodations. The Cedar Lodge offers the most luxurious suites, with fireplaces and lakefront vistas, while the Main Lodge offers more affordable options. Cedar Lodge is open year-round, while the Main Lodge is open only in the summer. In addition to the two lodges, there are 22 cottages, most of which are available from mid-May to Labor Day, and seven villas (larger than the cottages), which are open year-round. The resort has a restaurant and bar, which are open during the summer months. There is an indoor pool and hot tub, available for use all year, and boat and bike rental during the summer. A large sandy beach makes for a great summer resting spot, and during the summer Ruttger's offers a supervised kids' program for children ages 4 through 12.

Bemidji has a number of good restaurant options. The quintessential small-town **Raphael's Bakery Café** serves delicious breakfasts and lunches, and sells baked goods to go. The menu is limited (salads, sandwiches, soups), but the baked goods are pleasingly fresh, and the soups are homemade. Another fine spot for home cooking and baked goods is the **Minnesota Nice Café**. **Brigid's Cross** is a cheerful Irish pub with the usual suspects (fish and chips, ploughman's platter, shepherd's pie) and several not-so-Irish dishes (macaroni and cheese bites, mini burger basket). The food is hearty, and the restaurant offers a full bar and a variety of entertainment, from open mics to trivia contests and live music. **Keg & Cork** is a friendly neighborhood bar and grill, beloved by the locals. The same can be said for **Dave's Pizza**, a community institution serving up delicious pizzas and pastas. **Lucky Dogs** sells hot dogs and brats, some produced locally at **Stittsworth's**, and the **Wild Hare Bistro and Coffeehouse** features a full slate of coffee drinks as well as thoughtful breakfast and lunch entrées.

For upscale dining, **Tutto Bene** is wonderful choice. Housed in a beautiful historic building in downtown Bemidji, the restaurant specializes in high-end Italian entrées and drinks. Another option is **Sparkling Waters**, a supper club located on a narrow strip of land between Lake Irving and Lake Bemidji. **North Shore Grille**, part of the **Bemidji Town and Country Club**, also serves supper club food heavy on meats and large plates on a seasonal basis.

From Bemidji, take US 71 south to MN 200 west to reach **Itasca State Park/Mississippi headwaters**. Itasca is Minnesota's oldest state park and famous for being home to the origins of the Mississippi River. The quest to find the headwaters of the Mississippi led explorers to various sites around the Bemidji area, but in 1832 Henry Schoolcraft, led by Anishinaabe guide Ozawindib, found the true source. The name Itasca derives from Schoolcraft's combining parts of the Latin words for truth and head, veritas and caput, into one word. Later in the nineteenth century, the region where the park is now located faced deforestation due to excessive logging. Surveyor Jacob Brower, alarmed at the loss of natural habitat, then began an

BRIGID'S CROSS IRISH PUB, BEMIDJI

THE MISSISSIPPI HEADWATERS, ITASCA STATE PARK

intense campaign to persuade the state government to preserve the area. He succeeded—by one vote.

Today the headwaters are a major attraction, but they make up just a small section of this 32,000-acre park. Within it are 49 miles of hiking trails and 16 miles of paved biking trails, including the 10-mile Wilderness Drive (shared by bikes and cars), a winding, hilly stretch of road that meanders through the forests. To get a full view of the park, hike up to the top of the Aiton Heights Fire Tower, which you can reach from the Wilderness Drive. In the winter, trails are open for cross-country skiing, snowshoeing, and snowmobiling. You can rent bikes within the park, as well as boats, canoes, and fishing equipment.

Other sites to visit include Wegmann's Cabin, a pioneer artifact, and a 500-year-old Indian cemetery. Conifers inhabit the Wilderness Sanctuary, a 2,000-acre stand of white and red pines, some of which are upwards of 300 years old. The Bohall Wilderness Trail guides you through the pines and onto an overlook at Bohall Lake. There are campsites throughout the park, but consider staying at Douglas Lodge, located near Lake Itasca. The lodge was built in 1905 with native timber and houses five guest rooms, a dining room, and a lounge. There is also a clubhouse with rooms available, as well as several cabins.

If staying at the park isn't an option, there are other good choices for lodging nearby, including a pair of bed-and-breakfasts. The **Lady Slipper Inn in**

FIRETOWER AT ITASCA STATE PARK

Osage, near Park Rapids, is situated on 160 acres of woodland with canoe-ing, kayaking, and paddle-boarding among the many recreational opportu-nities available. The home has five guest rooms, all with private bath, double whirlpool tubs, fireplaces, and private sitting areas. In Park Rapids proper, you'll find the **Red Bridge Inn**, a Victorian-style hotel along the Fish Hook River, adjacent to the **Heartland State Trail**. Guests have access to fishing boats, pontoons, and paddle boats, as well as a fire pit along the river. The property has four rooms and two suites, all with private bath; one of the suites includes a full kitchen and private deck.

LANDING AT ITASCA STATE PARK

Itasca State Park is by no means the only alternative for experiencing scenic lakes and trees in this part of the state. When you leave the park, take MN 200 back to US 71 and turn south. You'll follow the edge of the park for a few miles, then go by Little Mantrap Lake. Shortly after that, US 71 veers to the southeast, and you'll pass Island Lake and Eagle Lake. When you reach CR 40, turn left to enter an area teeming with lakes surrounded by forests and rolling farmland. Follow CR 40 as it wanders east between Eagle Lake and Potato Lake, then turns south between Potato Lake and the aptly named Blue Lake. Take a right turn onto CR 4 and travel south of Ingram Lake, then turn left onto CR 18. When CR 18 intersects with CR 7, turn left, and soon you'll be in Dorset.

THE HISTORIC DOUGLAS LODGE AT ITASCA STATE PARK

Dorset may be small, but it makes for a great stop if you're driving the back roads or want to enjoy the **Heartland State Trail**, which has a trailhead with parking in the village. The Heartland

COMPAÑEROS MEXICAN RESTAURANT

Trail is a 49-mile trail connecting Park Rapids to Cass Lake. Given the many lakes, wetlands, and woodlands along its path, not only is the trail scenic, but an excellent opportunity to explore the local wildlife. Deer, porcupines, beaver, muskrats, and occasional bobcats and coyotes all live in proximity to the trail.

Dorset is also home to the **Heartland Trail Bed & Breakfast**, a renovated 1920s community school building located on the Heartland Trail. The inn offers five spacious guest rooms, all with private baths and fireplaces, and a full breakfast is served daily. Stay here, eat in the village, explore the Heartland Trail, and catch live performances nearby, either at the **Long Lake Theater** in Hubbard—a summer stock theater offering four to five productions each year along with holiday productions of A Christmas Carol, or at the **Northern Light Opera Company** in Park Rapids. The name of this company is a play on words, with "light" referring to "light opera" more so than "northern lights." This grassroots organization has been diligently putting on productions, primarily of Gilbert and Sullivan, since 2001. Their success can be seen in their growth and in the branching out of their repertoire to include shows like *Into the Woods*. Also in Park Rapids is **Jaspers Jubilee Theater,** a lively, family-friendly live variety show incorporating music, magic, juggling, yodeling, dancing, and comedy skits.

If you're looking for dining beyond what Dorset has to offer, Park Rapids provides some unique alternatives. With more than 80 years of service in the heart of this small town, the **MinneSoda Fountain,** a 17-stool confectionery, falls in the category of "don't miss." Leave the calorie counter at home. **The Good Life Cafe** has contemporary takes on diner classics, including an updated wild rice hotdish and a Thai peanut butter burger. **The Great Northern Cafe** follows a more traditional diner path, with basic sandwiches and burgers, along with a full slate of hot sandwiches (meat and gravy on bread with potatoes) and dinner plates that include chicken-fried steak and liver and onions. For a more formal dining option, **Necce's Italian Ristorante** has pasta, steak, and seafood.

From Dorset, travel back to CR 18 on CR 7 and head east. The road slips

Dorset: Restaurant Capital of the World

This tiny town has, tongue firmly in cheek, billed itself as the **Restaurant Capital of the World**, and certainly it's hard to believe any other town has as many restaurants per capita as this one does. With just 26 residents, Dorset has four restaurants, one for every 6.5 villagers. What's more surprising is that while the restaurants may not be profiled in *Food & Wine* anytime soon, they are all worthy of a visit if you're passing through. Just follow the boardwalk down the main street (or take a detour from the Heartland Trail if you're out hiking or biking), and you'll find a good meal somewhere.

Compañeros. Americanized Mexican food served in cheerful abundance.

Dorset Chick'n Coop. This dinner café serves steaks and seafood and has a full bar, and also offers brunch on weekends.

Dorset House. Choose from the buffet or from a pizza and burger menu; homemade pies and ice cream for dessert.

LaPasta Italian Eatery. Breakfast features include the standard pancakes and omelets, along with stuffed French toast and potato pancakes; lunch offers several pasta dishes along with burgers and sandwiches; dinner is an ever-changing roster of Italian cuisine.

between Belle Taine Lake and Shallow Lake before merging with MN 34 in Nevis. It's then just a short jaunt to Akeley, home of the state's largest Paul Bunyan statue, as well as the **Woodtick Musical Theater**. Billing its show as similar to those in Branson, Missouri, the Woodtick Theater offers a musical variety show each summer that's appropriate for all ages. The music encompasses country, folk, bluegrass, and gospel, and is accompanied by a comedy show.

A good choice for accommodations is the **Crow Wing Crest Lodge**, offering 19 cabins on the 11th Crow Wing Lake. Cabins vary from rustic to deluxe. The lodge itself was built by the Red River Logging Company in 1898 as part of its logging operations. When the logging industry declined, the lodge changed hands and served a variety of purposes, functioning as a chicken farm at one time and a girls' etiquette camp at another. The resort prides itself on its environmentally conscious practices. The proprietors recycle lake water, avoid all pesticides or herbicides, and use only all-natural

PICNIC SHELTER AT NORWAY BEACH

CHARLIE'S BOATHOUSE, WALKER

cleaning products. Kids' activities are offered daily during the summer, that is, if they aren't already sufficiently entertained by the sandy beach, with its beach toys, paddleboats, and kayaks, or the resort's playground.

Continuing north on MN 34, you'll arrive in the town of Walker, on the shores of Leech Lake. Leech Lake is a major fishing destination, and is teeming with walleye, perch, crappies, pike, and largemouth and small-mouth bass. Of course, you don't have to fish to appreciate the lake; boating is another favored activity. The Heartland and Paul Bunyan Trails both run through the area and are popular with bikers and snowmobilers.

Walker and Leech Lake are part of the **Chippewa National Forest**. With over 666,000 acres, Chippewa National Forest provides ample opportunities for outdoor adventures. The forest has 160 miles of hiking trails and cross-country ski trails, 330 miles of snowmobiling trails, 23 developed campgrounds, 380 camping sites, and a sandy swimming beach. Three visitor centers offer programs and information: **Norway Beach, Cut Foot Sioux**, and **Edge of the Wilderness Discovery Center**. For water lovers, the forest holds two of Minnesota's five biggest lakes, and there are nine canoe routes across various rivers and Leech Lake. Please note that some of these routes are more treacherous than others; when planning a canoe trip, check with the Chippewa National Forest for recommendations based on your skill level. The forest also boasts the largest breeding population of bald eagles in the lower 48 states.

Walker offers numerous options for lodging, from the standard hotel or motel to more unique options. Located on the lakeshore, **Chase on the**

Lake is an upscale resort and spa complex with a well-regarded restaurant on site. **Embracing Pines Bed & Breakfast**, outside Walker on CR 38, has three warmly appointed rooms. Guests also have use of the sauna, bikes, and canoes. Also on CR 38 is **Bailey's Resort on Leech Lake**, with nine cabins on the lake and boats and bikes available to rent. On the southern shore of Leech Lake is **Northland Lodge**, with 17 custom-built log homes that can accommodate two to 25 people and have whirlpool tubs and fireplaces.

There are also several good restaurants in the area. **The Boulders** mixes fine dining with a casual atmosphere and is perfect for a special occasion. Specialties include steak, salmon, lamb chops, and a beautifully prepared and served paella. A more low-key option is the **Lucky Moose Bar and Grill**, housed in a log building. The old-fashioned but newly renovated **Ranch House Supper Club** prepares delicious steaks and prime rib, plus all-you-can-eat specials each night. **Charlie's Up North** is another good bet for steaks, and serves excellent fish and roasted chicken as well. In the summer, **Charlie's Boathouse**, right next door, offers an open-air version of Charlie's wrapped around a bar built out of an old boat. For another casual option and family-style meals, check out **Benson's Eating and Drinking Emporium**.

When you leave Walker, follow MN 200 north to Laporte, then turn south on MN 64 to visit **Forestedge Winery**. Forestedge produces wines from rhubarb, chokecherries, raspberries, and plums grown on site and has won several awards for its innovative beverages. A wine-tasting room and shop is open May through December, and a separate gift shop sells arts and crafts items, particularly culinary accessories that the winery's owners have collected around the country or even made themselves.

From Forestedge, return to MN 200 on MN 64. Follow MN 200 to US 71 to return to Bemidji.

IN THE AREA

Accommodations

AMERICINN MOTEL & SUITES, 1200 Paul Bunyan Drive NW, Bemidji. Call 218-751-3000. Website: www.wyndhamhotels.com/americinn.

BAILEY'S RESORT ON LEECH LAKE, 33216 CR 38, Walker. Call 218-547-1464; 800-458-7540. Website: www.baileysresort.com.

CHASE ON THE LAKE, 502 Cleveland Boulevard, Walker. Call 218-547-7777; 888-242-7306. Website: www.chaseonthelake.com.

CROW WING CREST LODGE, 31159 CR 23, Akeley. Call 218-652-3111; 800-279-2754. Website: www.crowwing.com.

DOUBLETREE BY HILTON, 115 Lake Shore Drive NE, Bemidji. Call 218-441-4400. Website: www.doubletree3hilton.com.

DOUGLAS LODGE, Itasca State Park. Call 866-857-2757. Website: www.dnr .state.mn.us/state_parks/itasca/lodging/units_rooms.html.

EMBRACING PINES BED & BREAKFAST, 32287 Mississippi Road, Walker. Call 218-224-3519; 218-731-5026. Website: www.embracingpines.com.

HAMPTON INN, 1019 Paul Bunyan Drive South, Bemidji. Call 218-751-3600; 800-426-7866. Website: www.hamptoninn.com.

HEARTLAND TRAIL BED & BREAKFAST, 20220 Friar Road, Park Rapids. Call 218-732-3252. Website: www.heartlandbb.com.

LADYSLIPPER INN BED & BREAKFAST, 51722 270th Street, Osage. Call 218-583-3353. Website: www.ladyslipperinn.com.

LAKE BEMIDJI BED & BREAKFAST, 915 Lake Boulevard NE, Bemidji. Call 218-556-8815. Website: www.lakebemidjibandb.com.

NORTHLAND LODGE, 2802 Northland Lane NW, Walker. Call 800-247-1719. Website: www.andersonsleech-lake.com/northland.

RED BRIDGE INN, 118 North Washington, Park Rapids. Call 218-237-7337; 855-237-7337. Website: www.redbridgeinn.com.

RUTTGER'S BIRCHMONT LODGE, 7598 Bemidji Road NE, Bemidji. Call 218-444-3463; 888-788-8437. Website: www.ruttger.com.

Attractions and Recreation

BELTRAMI COUNTY HISTORY CENTER, 130 Minnesota Avenue SW, Bemidji. Call 218-444-3376. Website: www.beltramihistory.org.

BEMIDJI SCULPTURE WALK, lakefront, Bemidji. Website: www.bemidji sculpture.org.

BUENA VISTA SKI VILLAGE AND RANCH, 19276 Lake Julia Drive NW, Bemidji. Call 218-243-2231; 800-777-7958. Website: www.bvskiarea.com.

CHIPPEWA NATIONAL FOREST, 200 Ash Avenue NW, Cass Lake. Call 218-335-8600. Website: www.fs.usda.gov/chippewa.

CONCORDIA LANGUAGE VILLAGES, 8607 Thorsonveien NE, Bemidji. Call 218-586-8600; 800-222-4750. Website: www.concordialanguagevillages .org.

FORESTEDGE WINERY, 35295 MN 64, Laporte. Call 218-224-3535. Website: www.forestedgewinery.com.

HEADWATERS SCIENCE CENTER, 413 Beltrami Avenue NW, Bemidji. Call 218-444-4472. Website: www.hscbemidji.org.

HEARTLAND TRAIL, Park Rapids. Website: www.dnr.state.mn.us/state_ trails/heartland/index.html.

ITASCA STATE PARK, 36750 Main Park Drive, Park Rapids. Call 218-699-7251. Website: www.dnr.state.mn.us/state_parks/park.html.

JASPERS JUBILEE THEATER, 17339 MN 34, Park Rapids. Call 218-255-2300. Website: www.jasperstheater.com.

LAKE BEMIDJI STATE PARK, 3401 State Park Road NE, Bemidji. Call 218-755-3843. Website: www.dnr.state.mn.us/state_parks/lake_bemidji/index .html.

LONG LAKE THEATER, 12183 Beacon Road, Hubbard. Call 218-732-0099. Website: www.longlaketheater.net.

NORTHERN LIGHT OPERA COMPANY, 11700 Island Lake Drive, Park Rapids. Call 218-237-0400. Website: www.northernlightopera.org.

NORTHERN LIGHTS CASINO AND HOTEL, 6800 Y Frontage Road NW, Walker. Call 800-252-7529. Website: www.northernlightscasino.com.

PAUL BUNYAN AMUSEMENT PARK, lakefront, Paul Bunyan Drive N and 2nd Street, Bemidji.

PAUL BUNYAN AND BABE THE BLUE OX, lakefront, Bemidji. Daily. Website: www.visitbemidji.com.

PAUL BUNYAN PLAYHOUSE, 314 Beltrami Avenue, Bemidji. Call 218-751-7270. Website: www.thechieftheater.com.

WATERMARK ART CENTER, 505 Bemidji Avenue North, Bemidji. Call 218-444-7570. Website: watermarkartcenter.org.

WOODTICK MUSICAL THEATER, MN 34, Akeley. Call 218-652-4200; 800-644-6892. Website: www.woodtick-theater.com.

Dining

BENSON'S EATING AND DRINKING EMPORIUM, 400 Minnesota Avenue, Walker. Call 218-547-1896. Family-style pizzas, burgers, and sandwiches. Website: www.bensonsemporium.com.

THE BOULDERS, 8363 Lake Land Trail NW, Walker. Call 218-547-1006. Upscale steak and seafood. Website: www.thebouldersrestaurant.net.

BRIGID'S CROSS, 317 Beltrami Avenue, Bemidji. Call 218-444-0567. A cheerful Irish pub. Website: www.facebook.com/brigidscrossirishpub.

CHARLIE'S UP NORTH/CHARLIE'S BOATHOUSE, 6841 MN 371 NW, Walker. Call 218-547-0222. Steaks, seafood, and broasted chicken. Website: www.charliesupnorth.com.

COMPAÑEROS, 20427 MN 226, Dorset. Call 218-732-7624. Homemade Mexican-American. Website: www.facebook.com/Companeros-245085807861.

DAVE'S PIZZA, 15th Street and Irvine Avenue, Bemidji. Call 218-751-3225. Long-time community stalwart serving pizza and pasta. Website: www.davespizza.biz.

DORSET CHICK'N COOP, 20456 MN 226, Dorset. Call 218-732-4072. Seafood, steaks, and broasted chicken. Website: www.facebook.com/dorsetchicken.

DORSET HOUSE, 20427 MN 226, Dorset. Call 218-732-5556. American foods and ice cream. Website: www.facebook.com/dorset-House-Family-Restaurant-120057944701033.

GOOD LIFE CAFÉ, 220 Main Avenue South, Park Rapids. Call 218-237-4212. Contemporary takes on classic bar foods. Website: www.thegoodlifecafepr .com.

GREAT NORTHERN CAFÉ, 218 1st Street E, Park Rapids. Call 218-732-9565. Hearty diner food. Website: www.greatnortherncafe.com.

KEG & CORK, 310 Beltrami Avenue NW, Bemidji. Call 218-444-7600. A friendly neighborhood bar and grill. Website: www.kegncorkbemidjimn .com.

LAPASTA ITALIAN EATERY, Dorset. Call 218-732-0275. Italian-American. Website: www.facebook.com/Dorset-General-Store-La-Pasta-Italian-Eatery -291731654068.

LUCKY DOGS, 201 Beltrami Avenue NW, Bemidji. Call 218-444-0288. Gourmet hot dogs and brats. Website: www.luckydogsbemidji.com.

LUCKY MOOSE BAR AND GRILL, 441 Walker Bay Boulevard, Walker. Call 218-547-0801. Comfort foods, pizzas, sandwiches, and steaks. Website: www .luckymoosebargrill.com.

MINNESODA FOUNTAIN, 205 South Main, Park Rapids. Call 218-732-3240. Diner food and ice cream. Website: www.facebook.com/TheMinneSoda Fountain.

MINNESOTA NICE CAFÉ, 315 Irvine Avenue NW, Bemidji. Call 218-444-6656. Enormous homecooked breakfast and lunches and baked goods. Website: www.minnesotanicecafe.com.

NECCE'S ITALIAN RISTORANTE, 311 Main Avenue, Park Rapids. Call 218-237-4625. Pasta, pizza, and Italian entrees. Website: www.necces.net.

NORTH SHORE GRILLE, 2425 Birchmont Beach Road, Bemidji. Call 218-751-4535. Seasonal supper club. Website: www.bemidjigolf.com/north shoregrille.php.

RANCH HOUSE SUPPER CLUB, 9420 MN 371 Northwest, Walker. Call 218-547-1540. Old-fashioned supper club, with steaks and prime rib, plus all-you-can-eat specials each night. Website: www.facebook.com/Ranch -House-Supper-Club-111589395547205.

RAPHAEL'S BAKERY CAFÉ, 319 Minnesota Avenue, Bemidji. Call 218-759-2015. The quintessential small-town bakery and café. Website: www .gr8buns.com.

SPARKLING WATERS, 824 Paul Bunyan Drive South, Bemidji. Call 218-444-3214. Prime rib, steak, seafood. Website: www.sparklingwatersbemidji .com.

TUTTO BENE, 300 Beltrami Avenue NW, Bemidji. Call 218-751-1100. Upscale Italian food in a historic building. Website: www.tuttobene.us.

WILD HARE BISTRO AND COFFEEHOUSE, 523 Minnesota Avenue, Bemidji. Call 218-444-5282. Coffee, breakfast, and lunch. Website: www .wildharebistro.com.

Other Contacts

LEECH LAKE TOURISM BUREAU, Walker. Call 800-735-3297. Website: www.leechlake.org.

PARK RAPIDS CHAMBER, 1204 Park Avenue South, Park Rapids. Call 218-732-4111. Website: www.parkrapids.com.

VISIT BEMIDJI, Bemidji. Call 218-759-0164; 877-250-5959. Website: www .visitbemidji.com.

7

NORTHERN LAKES AND FORESTS, PART 2

North and East of Bemidji

ESTIMATED DISTANCE: 250 miles

ESTIMATED TIME: 5 hours

GETTING THERE: From the Twin Cities, take I-94 west to exit 178 and head northeast on MN 24 until you reach US 10. Follow US 10 to Little Falls, then follow MN 371 north to US 2 west to Bemidji.

HIGHLIGHTS: The Forest History Center; Scenic State Park; the Joyce Estate; the Lost 40; the rolling, curving highways that take you through miles of forests and wetlands and around the countless lakes in the region.

The land north and east of Bemidji is a wilderness often underestimated and underexplored. Most of this area is contained in the Chippewa National Forest (see Chapter 6 for more information about the forest), but there are adjacent and overlapping state forests here too, including **Welsh Lake State Forest, Koochiching State Forest**, and **Blackduck State Forest**. This part of the state doesn't have as much to offer in terms of amenities like restaurants, mini-golf, or movie theaters, but what it does have is breathtaking stretches of old-growth forests; wildflowers in bloom in all seasons but winter; abundant wildlife and bird-watching; myriad opportunities for fishing, hiking, biking, snowshoeing, cross-country skiing, snowmobiling, or even just a wonderful day's drive to enjoy sunlight flashing through pine trees; and of course the quiet you can find only in a remote part of the state.

From Bemidji, take US 2 east into **Chippewa National Forest**. Weather permitting, take a break at Norway Beach, a swimming area with a mile-long sandy beach and pristine waters on Cass Lake. The beach has tall pine trees for a backdrop, making it seem even more remote than it really is.

LEFT: FIRETOWER AT THE FOREST HISTORY CENTER, GRAND RAPIDS

As US 2 heads away from Lake Winnie, you'll approach the city of Grand Rapids. From here, you'll explore the **Edge of the Wilderness Scenic Byway**, but before heading into that wilderness, consider taking time to visit the **Forest History Center**, south of the city at the junction of US 2 and US 169. One of the center's main attractions is a re-created turn-of-the-century logging camp with costumed characters for guides. Visitors can board a floating cook shack, climb a 100-foot fire tower, and crawl through a decayed log while learning about Minnesota's logging history. A trail system takes visitors through the forest and along the Mississippi River to see where, during the heyday of logging, the logs were sent down the river.

Along US 169 is the **Judy Garland Museum**. Judy Garland was born in Minnesota in 1922 and spent her first four years here. The house she lived

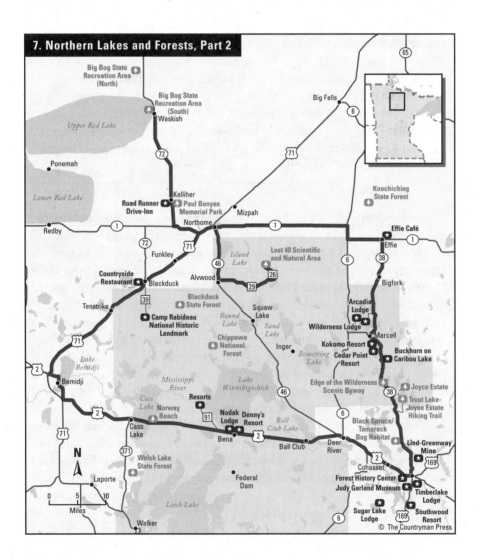

A Lake Full of Fish

A bit further down US 2, you'll start to see signs for **Lake Winnibigoshish**, or, as it's known locally, Lake Winnie. Lake Winnie is the fifth-largest lake in the state, and 95 percent of its shoreline is undeveloped, meaning you'll find long stretches of untouched forest and shoreline here. Even better, the lack of development means the lake isn't fished out, but teeming with walleye, perch, and pike. The Minnesota DNR uses Lake Winnie in its walleye restocking program, trapping and collecting walleye to repopulate other lakes around the state. Just off US 2 are **Nodak Lodge** and **Denny's Resort**; north of US 2 on County Route 91 (CR 91), you can find **McArdle's Resort, Four Seasons Resort**, and **Becker's Resort** on the southwestern shore. The resorts are open year round and offer plenty of help with fishing and hunting, and additional amenities like pools and playgrounds.

THE BEACH AT MCARDLE'S RESORT

in has been moved from its original street to a location on US 169, a busy highway across from Home Depot, which detracts slightly from the house's charm. Garland's home has been lovingly restored with considerable attention to detail, and the curators have procured a wide variety of artifacts, including the carriage Dorothy rode in upon her arrival at Oz. The museum did have a pair of ruby slippers, but those were stolen in 2005. The FBI were able to locate the slippers in 2018, but when—or if—they'll be returned to the museum is unclear.

Grand Rapids can be a great spot to set up camp, so to speak, and explore the surrounding area. Some good options for your stay include the **Green Heron Bed & Breakfast**, the **Southwood Resort, Sugar Lake Lodge, Buckhorn on Caribou Lake**, and **Timberlake Lodge**. There are also plenty of places to go for good dining: **Florio's Grill & Tavern** specializes in classic Minnesota steakhouse fare (think BBQ ribs, steak, and fish dinner); **Otis's Bar and Grill** at Sugar Lake Lodge, offers casual pubfare; **Forest Lake Restaurant** is another steakhouse, but one that also serves breakfast and lunch; the **17th Street Grill** at Timberlake Lodge offers upscale American dining; and **Brewed Awakenings Coffeehouse** has an extensive line of coffee drinks as well as gourmet breakfast and lunch items.

Just north of Grand Rapids is MN 38, which is the road for the Edge of the Wilderness Byway. You can choose to simply drive the 47 miles to Effie, which is enjoyable in and of itself, with the heavy forests and wetlands and, in the warm months, profusions of wildflowers. Although the byway is beautiful at any time of year, if you have the flexibility, make the journey in the fall, when the colors are spectacular.

But there are some deviations from MN 38 worth pursuing. Just north of Grand Rapids, at milepost 3.4, is the **Lind-Greenway Mine** on the southern shore of Prairie Lake. This former mine, on the edge of the Iron Range, left behind a 200-foot-tall mountain of rock and low-grade iron ore (taconite) fragments, an intense red-black in color. Visitors are welcome to select a fragment as a souvenir.

EDGE OF THE WILDERNESS BYWAY

Resuming in a northerly direction, you'll drive through the **Black Spruce/ Tamarack Bog Habitat**. Lining both sides of the road, this habitat was formed 16,000 years ago at the tail end of the glacial period. Spruce and tamarack tower over the road, and if you were to wander into the bog, you'd find the ground wet and spongy.

Another facet of the area's history is on display at the **Camp Rabideau National Historic Landmark**, one of the best-preserved Civilian Conservation Corps projects in the country. You can take a guided tour, or you can go on your own; interpretive displays with detailed information are present throughout.

Joyce Estate Hike

For a more adventurous detour—and a glimpse into a way of life long gone—turn right on CR 60 and drive several miles to Blue Water Lake Road, where you'll find a parking lot for the **Trout Lake-Joyce Estate Hiking Trail**. From the trailhead, the hike to Joyce Estate is about 6 miles round-trip. The estate was built on the shores of Trout Lake between 1917 and 1935 by David Joyce, who made his fortune in the logging industry. He built a massive complex out of native stone and lumber: 40 buildings, a seaplane hangar, a nine-hole golf course, and a clubhouse. The caretaker's complex itself was composed of 17 buildings. The estate is a fascinating place to explore how the wealthy lived, decades ago, in the woods.

There are few towns along the southern end of the Edge of the Wilderness Byway, but as you continue north you'll drive through Marcell, built a century ago as a logging town and, unusual for most older logging towns, still operating as such. The town Bigfork's roots are also in logging but it has since developed into a place that caters to tourists.

The Byway ends in Effie, named in 1903 after the community postmaster's daughter. After 47 miles of rolling, densely forested terrain, the landscape

EDGE OF THE WILDERNESS

Big Bog State Recreation Area

Big Bog State Recreation Area is divided into two parts, southern and northern. The southern portion is a campground and cabin area, with sandy swimming beaches and fishing access. The northern section contains the Big Bog itself, a 500-square-mile peat bog, the largest in the lower 48 states. Carefully constructed to do as little damage as possible, a mile-long environmentally sensitive boardwalk now permits visitors to wander a mile into the bog. Interpretive signs explain the sights on either side. Parts of the bog are overgrown with

trees, while other areas are wide-open wetlands. Depending on the season, you may spot rare orchids, or possibly some carnivorous plants.

BOARDWALK AT BIG BOG STATE RECREATION AREA

morphs into gentle, open farmland. Effie is a logical stopping point for lunch, and the **Effie Café** has good diner food. If you want to do more exploring, there are several worthwhile resorts where you can set up camp along the Byway. Recommendations include the **Arcadia Lodge** on Big Turtle Lake, **Cedar Point Resort** on North Star Lake, **Kokomo Resort** on North Star Lake, and **Wilderness Lodge** on Big Turtle Lake.

THE EFFIE CAFÉ, EFFIE

The next stage of the journey turns westward, following MN 1. This is a sparsely populated road that twists and turns, sometimes through thick forests, sometimes along wetlands and bogs, other times past farmland. The majority of this route takes you through Kooch-iching State Forest.

Once you reach US 71, you have some options. The first is to turn south on US 71 and return to Bemidji (with a few suggested stops along the way). The second is to continue west on MN 1 to Northome, then travel north on MN 72

THE SUNSET ON HIGHWAY 1

PAUL BUNYAN'S GRAVE, KELLIHER

to Waskish, where you can visit the Big Bog State Recreation Area (see sidebar).

On your way to the Big Bog, you can take in a bit of local humor by stopping at the **Paul Bunyan Memorial Park** in Kelliher to pay respects to Paul himself—his enormous "grave" is right alongside the road, with a headstone that reads, "Here lies Paul and that's all." In summer, you can take a break at the **Road Runner Drive-Inn** for a burger and shake.

The other option at the junction of MN 1 and US 71 is to turn south on MN 46 to Alvwood, then drive east on CR 29. Once you reach CR 26, turn north and drive to Forest Road 2240. Shortly after starting on the Forest Road, you'll come to the parking lot for the **Lost 40 Scientific and Natural Area (SNA)**. The Lost 40, which is actually 144 acres, is a tract of land that was accidentally misidentified as a lake by a surveyor during the logging boom times. Consequently, it remained untouched while forests around it were decimated. There are pine trees that are more than 300 years old in the Lost 40, and wildflowers are prolific in the late spring. A 1-mile hiking trail guides you through this special and beautiful landscape.

ONE OF THE BIG BLACK DUCKS IN BLACKDUCK

The remaining stretch of this journey continues south on US 71, through towns as tiny as Funkley (population 15) to larger towns like Blackduck (which has not just one, but two large black duck statues, one on the highway and the other in the town's center). You can stop for a bite to eat at **Restaurant 71**, where you can get a solid sandwich or burger.

IN THE AREA

Accommodations

ARCADIA LODGE, 52001 CR 294, Bigfork. Call 218-832-3852. Website: www.arcadialodge.com.

BECKER'S RESORT, 17048 Wild Rice Drive, Bena. Call 218-665-2268. Website: www.beckersresort.com.

BUCKHORN ON CARIBOU LAKE, 45101 Buckhorn Resort Road, Marcell. Call 218-256-0089. Website: www.buckhornoncaribou.com.

CEDAR POINT RESORT, 38268 Cedar Point Road, Marcell. Call 218-832-3808; 800-450-6613. Website: www.cedarptresort.com.

DENNY'S RESORT, 15017 16th Avenue NE, Bena. Call 218-665-2222. Website: www.dennysresort.com.

FOUR SEASONS RESORT, 925 River Drive NW, Bena. Call 218-665-2231. Website: www.fishingwinnie.com.

GREEN HERON BED & BREAKFAST, 2810 Meyers Bay Road, Grand Rapids. Call 218-999-5795. Website: www.greenheronbandb.com.

KOKOMO RESORT, 48301 MN 38, Marcell. Call 218-832-3774; 888-848-7407. Website: www.kokomoresort.com.

McARDLE'S RESORT, 1014 West Winnie Road NW, Bena. Call 218-665-2212; 800-535-2398. Website: www.mcardlesresort.com.

NODAK LODGE, 15080 Nodak Drive, Bena. Call 218-665-2226; 800-752-2758. Website: www.nodaklodge.com.

SOUTHWOOD RESORT, 32460 Southwood Road, Grand Rapids. Call 218-259-8886; 888-815-6645. Website: www.southwoodresort.com.

SUGAR LAKE LODGE, 37584 Otis Lane, Cohasset. Call 218-327-1462. Website: www.sugarlakelodge.com.

TIMBERLAKE LODGE, 144 SE 17th Street, Grand Rapids. Call 218-326-2600; 866-800-2200. Website: www.timberlakelodgehotel.com.

WILDERNESS LODGE, 51760 Becker Road, Bigfork. Call 218-743-3458. Website: www.thewildernesslodge.com.

Attractions and Recreation

BIG BOG STATE RECREATION AREA, MN 72, Waskish. Call 218-647-8592. Website: www.dnr.state.mn.us/state_parks/big_bog/index.html.

CAMP RABIDEAU NATIONAL HISTORIC LANDMARK, Scenic Highway NE, Blackduck. Call 218-335-8600. Website: www.fs.usda.gov/recarea/chippewa/recarea/?recid=26640.

EDGE OF THE WILDERNESS SCENIC BYWAY. Call 888-754-0011. Website: www.edgeofthewilderness.com.

FOREST HISTORY CENTER, 2609 CR 76, Grand Rapids. Call 218-327-4482; 888-727-8386. Website: www.sites.mnhs.org/historic-sites/forest-history-center.

THE JUDY GARLAND MUSEUM, 2727 Pokegama Avenue South, Grand Rapids. Call 218-327-9276; 800-664-5839. Website: www.judygarlandmuseum.com.

LOST 40 SCIENTIFIC AND NATURAL AREA (SNA), Forest Road 2240, Chippewa National Forest. Website: www.dnr.state.mn.us/snas/list.html.

PAUL BUNYAN MEMORIAL PARK, MN 72, Kelliher. Call 218-647-8470. Website: www.kelliher.govoffice.com.

Dining

17TH STREET GRILL, 144 SE 17th Street, Grand Rapids. Call 218-326-2600. Upscale American fine dining. Website: www.timberlakelodgehotel.com/17th-street-grill.

BREWED AWAKENINGS COFFEEHOUSE, 24 NE 4th Street, Grand Rapids. Call 218-327-1088. Extensive coffee drink menu and meals as well. Website: www.brewedawakenings.biz.

EFFIE CAFÉ, 100 NW CR 5, Effie. Call 218-743-3607. Breakfast, lunch, and dinner. Website: www.facebook.com/EffieCafe.

FLORIO'S GRILL AND TAVERN, 105 Old Main Street, Cohasset. Call 218-999-7077. Burgers, breakfast, sandwiches, and walleye. Website: www .floriosgrillandtavern.com.

FOREST LAKE RESTAURANT, 1201 NW 4th Street, Grand Rapids. Call 218-326-3423. Steakhouse open for three meals a day. Website: www .forestlakerestaurant.com.

OTIS'S BAR AND GRILL, 37584 Otis Lane, Cohasset. Call 218-327-1462. Casual pub open for lunch and dinner with burgers, sandwiches, and other entrées. Website: www.sugarlakelodge.com/the-resort/dining.

RESTAURANT 71, 240 Summit Avenue West, Blackduck. Diner fare in generous portions. Call 218-835-3333. Website: www.facebook.com/Restaurant 71MN.

ROAD RUNNER DRIVE-INN, 321 Clark Avenue South, Kelliher. Call 218-647-8717. Classic drive-in fare. Website: www.facebook.com/roadrunner drivein.

Other Contacts

CHIPPEWA NATIONAL FOREST. Website: www.fs.usda.gov.

GRAND RAPIDS CHAMBER OF COMMERCE, 1 NW 3rd Street, Grand Rapids. Call 218-326-6619; 800-472-6366. Website: www.grandmn.com.

8

BRAINERD LAKES
Gull Lake and Environs

ESTIMATED DISTANCE: 95 miles
ESTIMATED TIME: 2 hours
GETTING THERE: From the Twin Cities, take US 169 north to Onamia.
HIGHLIGHTS: Lake Mille Lacs; the Pequot Lakes Fire Tower; the little town of
    Nisswa; the grand lodges of Brainerd.

If lakes are what people think of when they think about Minnesota, it's likely that they're thinking about the Central Lake District, particularly the Brainerd area. Slightly over two hours north of the Twin Cities, these popular lakes have long attracted those looking for a summer weekend getaway. In response to the demand, mom-and-pop resorts and upscale enclaves have sprung up to cater to all types of interests. Brainerd and its twin city Baxter are the most prominent communities, but the small towns surrounding Brainerd, such as Nisswa, Pequot Lakes, and Crosslake, are also good bets.

Beyond the many lakes in the Brainerd region lies another option for water enthusiasts. Located east of Brainerd, Minnesota's second-largest lake, Lake Mille Lacs is an idyllic area for visitors. Both areas are blessed with natural beauty in abundance, plenty of outdoor recreational opportunities, and historic sites to visit.

Because these desirable lake regions are close enough to the Twin Cities to enable weekend trips, traffic can be congested. The addition of traffic lanes on MN 371 has improved the route to Brainerd, but neither Brainerd nor Baxter are towns designed for managing heavy traffic flow; be prepared for occasional delays.

Located on the Mille Lacs Reservation, **Lake Mille Lacs** is just about as

LEFT: PIRATE'S COVE MINI GOLF, BRAINERD

popular in winter as it is in summer, thanks to a continually growing interest in ice fishing. The region has responded by adding more options for icehouse rental, including deluxe accommodations with electricity and heat. Year-round, the outdoor options seem almost endless: fishing, hunting, boating, biking, hiking, cross-country skiing, snowshoeing, snowmobiling—it's all here, along with spectacular sunrises and sunsets.

Note: US 169 is the main route along the lake, but periodically a frontage road will scoot closer to Mille Lacs for a stretch before merging back with

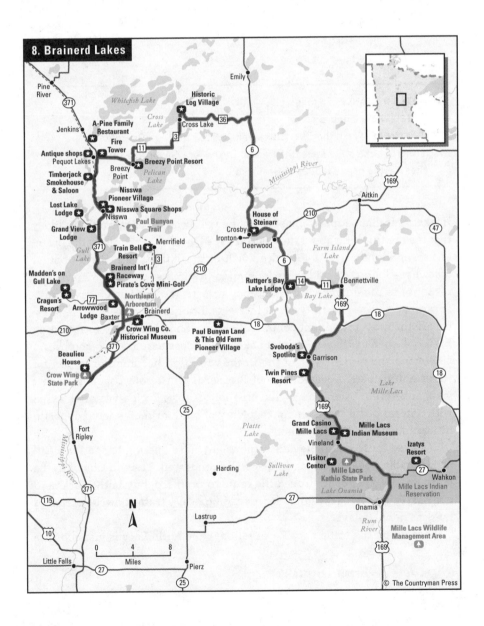

© The Countryman Press

LAKE MILLE LACS

US 169. Though the two roads are nearly identical in path, the frontage road takes you that much closer to the lake and is worth slowing down for.

Mille Lacs Wildlife Management Area is a small, carefully preserved 61-acre tract of forests and wetlands. Camping is allowed during hunting season, and those with permits can hunt deer, bear, and small game.

There are still other activities in the area in which to partake. A full-scale gambling complex with slots, blackjack, and bingo, **Grand Casino Mille Lacs** also holds several restaurants, a hotel, a theater with frequent live performances, a Kids Quest child-care area, and an extensive video arcade. Near Mille Lacs Kathio State Park, **the Mille Lacs Indian Museum** is a joint venture between the Mille Lacs Band and the Minnesota Historical Society. The museum's thoughtful, detailed collection of exhibitions show how Native Americans of the region lived and worked centuries ago. The crafts room has an especially lovely collection of beadwork and birch-bark basketry. An adjacent trading post serves as a re-creation of a 1930s-era trading post and is open year-round on weekends to sell Native American gift items.

The Mille Lacs area is heavily geared toward the outdoorsman, with many resorts offering camping and cabins, along with boat rentals and fishing

Thousands of Years of History

A National Historic Landmark, **Mille Lacs Kathio State Park** has been home to a number of significant archaeological discoveries. Hundreds of years before Europeans arrived, the Dakota people settled this land. Among the Dakota artifacts uncovered here have been copper tools dating back 9,000 years. By the eighteenth century, the Ojibwe were moving into the area too, and they continue to live around Mille Lacs. For more information on the region's history and heritage, check out the park's visitor center.

As with any state park, the outdoors here is the big draw. The Rum River flows through the park from its source in Lake Mille Lacs, and visitors can use canoes or rowboats to explore. A swimming beach is open during the summer, as are a 100-foot observation tower and a wide variety of campsites and cabins (some of which are available year round). There are 35 miles of hiking trails and 27 miles of horseback trails, both winding through second-growth stands of birch, maple, and oak trees. Winter enthusiasts can cross-country ski, snowshoe, or snowmobile on groomed trails. Among the types of wildlife frequently seen here are hawks, owls, deer, beavers, and eagles.

assistance. However, there are upscale options as well. **Izatys Resort** is a luxury complex of townhouses and villas (ranging from two to four bedrooms), as well as a lodge offering hotel rooms on the shores of Lake Mille Lacs. Boat rental, two 18-hole golf courses, fishing and hunting guides, tennis courts, and indoor and outdoor pools are all available on-site, as is a well-regarded fine-dining restaurant. **Grand Casino Mille Lacs** also offers excellent accommodations of different types, including a number of luxurious suites with four-person hot tubs and separate living areas. The large indoor swimming pool and commonly shared whirlpool are in a nicely decorated wing. The casino's four restaurants include **Plums**, a quick-service burger-and-pizza café, open 24 hours a day, Wednesday through Sunday. There's also a buffet restaurant, a casual grill restaurant, and a steakhouse available for dinner only. **Twin Pines Resort** is a quintessential family-friendly resort with cabins and motel rooms on Lake Mille Lacs, and a restaurant and bar open all day. The property is a good value, with summer

TWIN PINES MOTEL, GARRISON

and winter fishing guides available (as well as icehouse rental in winter) and a restaurant and bar on-site.

For dining options beyond those found within the area's many hotels, check out **Svoboda's Spotlite**. Breakfast is served all day at this friendly café and local institution. The home-cooked foods are simple but delicious, and the prices are reasonable.

Just past Garrison on the northwestern edge of Lake Mille Lacs, US 169 veers north. Stay on US 169 until you reach County Route 11 (CR 11) heading west. At this point, you're moving toward the Brainerd Lakes area, and you'll wind your way past several smaller lakes and through wooded areas. Sure, there are faster ways to get from point A to point B, but they're not nearly as scenic as CR 11, as it meanders along the south shore of Farm Island Lake before reaching Bay Lake. (Please note that you'll cross county lines en route, so CR 11 becomes CR 14.) Take CR 6 north to Deerwood, where you'll connect with MN 210, driving in an appropriately sinuous manner around Serpent Lake to Crosby. Besides its lakeside location and opportunities for outdoor adventures, another reason to stop here is to book a room at the **House of Steinarr**. Housed in a former Methodist church, the House of Steinarr offers five rooms with disparate themes, including Odin's Loft, decorated with armor and weapons, and the Locker Room, decorated for Minnesota Vikings football fans. Breakfast is included in the room rates.

THE MILLE LACS INDIAN MUSEUM AND TRADING POST

On nights of full occupancy, guests can participate in an interactive Viking dinner theater performance, complete with Viking feast.

Driving into the Brainerd Lakes area, you'll come upon one of the earliest major resort areas outstate. Nineteenth-century logging took a toll on this region, so by the end of that century when loggers were leaving, entrepreneurial residents made good use of the area's myriad lakes, sandy beaches, and excellent hunting and fishing to establish the communities around Brainerd as a vacation idyll. The little towns of Nisswa, Breezy Point, Pequot Lakes, Merrifield, Crosslake, and Lake Shore have each established themselves as hospitable bases from which to enjoy all that the region has to offer.

Take MN 6 north to CR 36 west, driving through **Crow Wing State Forest** and **Cross Lake Game Refuge** and around Square Lake and Velvet Lake. CR 36 ends at Tiff Lake. From that point, travel north on CR 66 to Crosslake on the shores of Cross Lake (no, that's not a typo—the town is one word, the lake two). Crosslake boasts an interesting historic exhibition at the **Historic Log Village** on CR 66. The Log Village is a collection of original log buildings transplanted to this corner of the state and available for tours in the summer.

From Crosslake, travel south on CR 3 to CR 11 west, which runs along the northern border of Pelican Lake before turning south to Breezy Point. This small lakeside town is home to **Breezy Point Resort**. Located on Pelican Lake, the resort presents a huge variety of accommodations to choose from—lodge rooms, one- and two-bedroom apartments, and a series of

HISTORIC LOG VILLAGE, CROSSLAKE

Antiquing

If you enjoy antiquing, the Pequot Lakes area has some browse-worthy shops.

Annie's Attic, 34010 2nd Avenue, Jenkins
Antique Emporium of Nisswa, 5518 CR 18, Nisswa
Castoffs, 4242 Jokela Drive, Pequot Lakes
The Flour Sack Antiques Shop, 29119 MN 371, Pequot Lakes
Treasures N Tiques, 34016 MN 371, Pequot Lakes

Also keep your eye out for highway signs that lead the way to antique shops or private sales off the main road.

lodgings referred to as "unique retreats": log cabins, A-frame cabins, and full houses. For recreation, there are two 18-hole golf courses, an indoor pool, and an extensive sandy beach with boat rentals available. The summer months bring live musical performances, while winter delivers yet another round of activity, including a nine-hole golf course on the lake, skating rinks, cross-country skiing (equipment available for rental), and a snow tubing hill adjacent to the resort. The resort has two full-service restaurants, the most attractive of which is the Antlers Dining Room, built with post-and-beam construction and featuring two large antler chandeliers.

Continue westward on CR 11 to Pequot Lakes. As you approach the town, you'll see signs directing you to the **Pequot Lakes Fire Tower**. A short but steep hike takes you through dense woods to a hill that leads to this 100-foot tower. Definitely not for the faint of heart or weak of knees, but if you'd like a spectacular view of the surrounding forestland, you can also climb the tower itself.

The Paul Bunyan Trail (see Chapter 6 for more information about the trail) runs right through town in a north–south direction. Pequot Lakes also offers a good selection of shopping and restaurants. **The A-Pine Family Restaurant** has been around for years, catching attention with its distinctive A-frame building. For something more substantial, check out the **Timber-jack Smokehouse & Saloon**.

Traveling south on MN 371, you'll arrive in Nisswa, tucked along the southern edge of Nisswa Lake near Roy Lake, and not far from the northern edge of Gull Lake. Even though it's close to the Brainerd/Baxter area, Nisswa is more serene and still has the feel of a small village. The Heartland Trail and Paul Bunyan Trail are nearby.

You can get another taste of history at the **Nisswa Pioneer Village**. The Pioneer Village comprises nine buildings, including log homes and a schoolhouse, while the old caboose and train depot holds railroad relics. An annual Scandinavian festival attracts large crowds.

Less historic but just as fun (if not more so) are the annual **Nisswa Turtle Races**. No worries about breakneck speeds in these races, held every Wednesday, rain or shine, in the summer months. The races are immensely popular with kids, and participation can easily reach into the hundreds. If you don't have your own turtle, it's possible to rent one. Races start at 2 p.m.

Just south of Nisswa's Main Street is **Grand View Lodge**. Grand View hearkens back to the grand old days of lake resorts. Built in 1919, this venerable institution has maintained its historic elegance while modernizing its amenities to accommodate today's resort travelers. The resort offers lodge rooms, cabins, and suites and villas on the property's golf course. An indoor pool and water slide shares a building with a fitness center, but in good weather, swimming takes place at the sandy beach. Boats can be rented, as can bikes and horses for riding. There are three 18-hole golf courses and a nine-hole course. The full-service spa is open year-round, as are the resort's six restaurants. Two separate kids' clubs, one for ages 3 to 6 and the other for ages 7 to 12, give parents a break from full-time child care.

In the neighboring community of Lake Shore, you can find **Lost Lake Lodge**. This small but lovely seasonal resort has beautifully outfitted cabins in a quiet, tucked-away location on Lost Lake. Rates are all-inclusive, meaning guests receive full breakfast and four-course dinners daily, included in their rates, and the food is well worth it. Canoes, fishing boats, and bikes are

GRAND VIEW LODGE, NISSWA

Nisswa Square Shops

One of the most fun things to do in Nisswa is to while away a few hours visiting the shops along Main Street in a little shopping district called **Nisswa Square**.

Turtle Town Books & Gifts. A bookseller for book lovers, with a wide range of reading material for grown-ups and kids.

Totem Pole. All Minnetonka moccasins, all the time.

BluPaisley Boutique. Casual and elegant clothing and jewelry.

Simpler Thymes of Nisswa. A gift shop focused on personal luxuries, including lotions, soaps, candles, gourmet foods (many locally produced), robes, and women's accessories.

NISSWA SQUARE

The Chocolate Ox. A shop full of sugary temptations, from higher-end truffles to vintage candies and kiddie favorites.

Adirondack Coffee. A warm and cozy coffee shop that also retails its roasted-on-site coffee products.

The Fun Sisters Boutique. Fun indeed—a shop full of inexpensive accessories and makeup for girls of all ages.

Lundrigans Clothing. Casual but high-quality men's and women's clothing for the north woods lifestyle.

also included in the rates, and fishing guides as well as massage therapists can be hired at an additional fee.

Just a few miles south of Nisswa on MN 371 is the Brainerd Lakes area. Brainerd is a town that experienced a rapid-fire start to its history. In 1870, when the railroad arrived, the town consisted of a lone trading post. Along with rail came the loggers, for whom the railway was a necessity, and the town's growth was explosive. By the time the loggers left, tourism had already created an economic base that has continued to flourish, unsurprisingly given the hundreds of lakes in close proximity to the town and its twin, the city of Baxter.

Arguably one of the most popular lake areas in the state, the Brainerd Lakes region has undergone a shift over the last several years. The small-town community with dozens of small mom-and-pop resorts is evolving into a larger-scale resort destination, with more lodging, restaurants, and off-the-lake entertainment activities. The small resorts remain and are thriving, as are the grander old-style hotel resorts, but they're being supplemented with newer chain hotels, including some that have amenities like indoor water parks. The increased efforts to bring in more traffic year-round have succeeded, and that means the area is perhaps not as peaceful as some of the others nearby. That said, for visitors wanting a wider variety of options for their vacation, the Brainerd area is hard to beat.

As you start driving into Brainerd, you'll see **Pirate's Cove Mini-Golf and the Billy Bones Raceway** on the left side of MN 371 north. Pirate's Cove is a fun and well-maintained pirate-themed mini-golf course. You can play one of the two 18-hole courses, or play both at a discount. Next door is the Billy Bones Raceway, which has three go-cart tracks. Another form of entertainment can be found at **Paul Bunyan Land and This Old Farm Pioneer Village** on MN 18. The destination is part historic village and part amusement park, with attractions like a 26-foot-tall talking Paul Bunyan, amusement rides, and the Pioneer Village, which includes an original log cabin, dentist's office, schoolhouse, and post office. For more intense thrills, check out one of Brainerd's most famous attractions, **Brainerd International Raceway**, presenting drag racing and road racing at its finest. Paul Newman has been among its many racing participants.

For a more serious take on the area, visit the **Crow Wing County Historical Museum**. A lively museum that used to be the sheriff's office and county jail, the site houses a wide-ranging collection of Native American artifacts and historical items that detail the region's lumber, railroad, and mining history as well.

In the midst of the strip-mall highway landscape, the **Northland Arboretum** provides a taste of the nature that can be found outside the town. Rather incongruously located behind the **Westgate Mall** in Brainerd, this nature preserve covers 500 acres of forest and prairie that have prevailed on the site of a former landfill. Open year-round, the arboretum has several miles of hiking and cross-country ski trails.

A final stop for this route is just south of Brainerd on MN 371: **Crow Wing State Park**, not only a pristine state forest, but a landmark of the area's

CROW WING STATE PARK

fur-trading past. During the area's heyday, the town of Crow Wing flourished, but when the railroad decided to pass through Brainerd rather than Crow Wing, the town's fate was sealed. Today the nearly 2,100-acre park has several miles of hiking trails (some of which are groomed for cross-country skiing in the winter) and excellent canoeing opportunities, including a canoe-in campsite. Within the park is the Beaulieu House, the last remaining building from the fur trading days.

Lodging runs the gamut from small mom-and-pop cabin resorts to big elaborate full-service complexes. **Cragun's Resort** falls into the latter category. Besides the beautifully appointed rooms, cabins, and reunion houses, Cragun's offers a 22,000-square-foot indoor sports complex with tennis and basketball courts, a running track, and a fitness center. The hotel itself features an indoor pool, and a full-service spa is on site. There are three restaurants open year round, plus two others open in the summer. Fifty-four holes of golf will keep golfers happy, while boaters and fishing aficionados have direct access to Gull Lake (note: Cragun's does not allow personal watercraft, or jet-skis, to be stored or launched from their property). Bike rentals are available, and snowmobiles can be hired during the winter.

Next door to Cragun's is **Madden's on Gull Lake**, another of the state's largest and nicest resorts, offerings rooms, cabins, and reunion houses. Three 18-hole golf courses adorn the property, along with a nine-hole social course. Fishing, boating, hiking, swimming, and tennis are all offered, as is trapshooting (with one week's notice) and seaplane certification. There is a full-service spa on site, and children's programs run from July through mid-August for kids ages 4 to 12. The resort also includes seven restaurants, three fine dining and four casual.

Ruttger's Bay Lake Lodge has been welcoming guests since 1898, and it is now a massive complex with condos, villas, cottages, lodge rooms, and a vacation house. There's an abundance of activities, from golf and fishing to spa services, a kid's camp, and even a high ropes course. Three on-site restaurants provide every culinary desire.

A newer resort, the **Arrowwood Lodge** opened in 2005. The lodge features sizable rooms and suites (including a Cinema Suite, featuring a 64-inch surround-sound, flat-screen TV), and reflects the newer generation of resorts with its 30,000-square-foot indoor water park, complete with tube and body slides, zero-entry pool, and indoor/outdoor hot tub.

For something completely different—but very family-friendly and wonderfully tranquil—travel north of Brainerd on CR 4 to **Train Bell Resort**. Here you'll find several well-maintained lakeside cabins as well as a condo complex, but the resort keeps its cozy feeling with the assistance of weekly activities such as a pancake breakfast, minnow races, and Friday night dances. Fishing boat rentals are available, and kayaks and paddleboats at the sandy beach are included with lodging.

371 DINER, BRAINERD

There are plenty of dining options too in Brainerd. A popular family choice is the **371 Diner**, right on US 371. The restaurant is a replica of a '50s diner and offers a respectable (if high-calorie) menu of burgers, sandwiches, and ice cream treats. Kids' meals are served in a cardboard racecar. Close to the diner is the **Black Bear Lodge and Saloon**, which serves standard bar and grill fare, including sandwiches and burgers, steaks, and seafood. **Prairie Bay Grill** offers pizza, pasta, sandwiches, and "meat and potato" dishes in a casual but upscale environment. Kids are welcome, as are vegetarians, who have several options on the menu. **Boomer Pizza** is a great choice for those looking for a gourmet pizza experience.

In the older downtown of Brainerd is the **Sawmill Inn**. It doesn't look like much on the outside, but the Sawmill is the classic small-town café, complete with huge breakfasts and hearty sandwiches. Nearby is the **Barn**, a bar and grill offering the classic Midwest loose-meat sandwiches (they're better than they sound). Bring cash; the Barn doesn't accept plastic. The **Front Street Café** is another home-cooking spot with hot turkey sandwiches and walleye. Down the road is **The Local 218**, which offers robust meat and potato entrées with sandwiches and seafood in more of a supper club venue. Just down the street from The Local 218 is **Triangle Drive-Inn Treats**, a vintage ice cream shop that's open seasonally.

IN THE AREA

Accommodations

ARROWWOOD LODGE, 6967 Lake Forest Road, Baxter. Call 218-822-5634; 877-687-5634. Website: arrowwoodbrainerdlodge.com.

BREEZY POINT RESORT, 9252 Breezy Point Drive, Breezy Point. Call 800-432-3777. Website: www.breezypointresort.com.

CRAGUN'S RESORT, 11000 Craguns Drive, Brainerd. Call 218-825-2700; 800-272-4867. Website: www.craguns.com.

GRAND CASINO MILLE LACS, 777 Grand Avenue, Onamia. Call 800-626-5825. Website: www.grandcasinomn.com.

GRAND VIEW LODGE, 23521 Nokomis Avenue, Nisswa. Call 218-963-8756; 866-801-2951. Website: www.grandviewlodge.com.

HOUSE OF STEINARR, 210 1st Avenue NW, Crosby. Call 218-839-2900. Website: www.steinarr.com.

IZATYS RESORT, 40005 85th Avenue, Onamia. Call 320-532-4574. Website: www.izatys.com.

LOST LAKE LODGE, 7965 Lost Lake Road, Lake Shore. Call 218-963-2681; 800-450-2681. Website: www.lostlake.com.

MADDEN'S ON GULL LAKE, 11266 Pine Beach Peninsula, Brainerd. Call 218-829-2811; 800-233-2934. Website: www.maddens.com.

RUTTGER'S BAY LAKE LODGE, 25039 Tame Fish Lake Road, Deerwood. Call 218-678-2885; 800-450-4545. Website: www.ruttgers.com.

TRAIN BELL RESORT, 21489 Train Bell Road, Merrifield. Call 218-829-4941; 800-252-2102. Website: www.trainbellresort.com.

TWIN PINES RESORT, 7827 US 169, Garrison. Call 320-692-4413. Website: www.twinpinesmillelacs.com.

Activities and Recreation

ANNIE'S ATTIC, 34010 2nd Avenue, Jenkins. Call 218-568-5225. Website: www.facebook.com/anniesattic371.

ANTIQUE EMPORIUM OF NISSWA, 5518 CR 18, Nisswa. Call 218-963-3911.

BILLY BONES RACEWAY, 17944 State Highway 371, Brainerd. Call 218-828-4245. Website: www.billybonesraceway.com.

BLUPAISLEY BOUTIQUE, 25527 Main Street, Nisswa. Call 218-961-0105. Website: blupaisley.com.

BRAINERD INTERNATIONAL RACEWAY, 5523 Birchdale Road, Brainerd. Call 218-824-7223; 866-444-4455. Website: www.brainerdraceway.com.

CASTOFFS SECONDHAND, 4242 Jokela Drive, Pequot Lakes. Call 218-568-6155. Website: www.facebook.com/vintagefunstore/?rf=1720092031558151.

THE CHOCOLATE OX, 25452 Main Street, Nisswa. Call 218-963-4443. Website: www.thechocolateox.com.

CROW WING COUNTY HISTORICAL MUSEUM, 320 Laurel Street, Brainerd. Call 218-829-3268. Website: www.crowwinghistory.org.

CROW WING STATE PARK, 3124 State Park Road, Brainerd. Call 218-825-3075. Website: www.dnr.state.mn.us/state_parks/crow_wing/index.html.

FLOUR SACK ANTIQUES, 29119 MN 371, Pequot Lakes. Call 218-568-5658. Website: www.facebook.com/Flour-Sack-Antiques-110227245706646.

THE FUN SISTERS BOUTIQUE, 5380 Merill Avenue, Nisswa. Call 218-961-0071. Website: www.thefunsisters.com.

HISTORIC LOG VILLAGE, CR 66, Crosslake. Call 218-692-5400. Website: www.crosslakehistoricalsociety.org.

LUNDRIGANS CLOTHING, 25521 Main Street, Nisswa. Call 218-963-2647; 866-310-1041. Website: lundrigansclothing.com.

MILLE LACS INDIAN MUSEUM, 43411 Oodena Drive, Onamia. Call 320-532-3632. Website: www.sites.mnhs.org/historic-sites/mille-lacs-indian-museum.

MILLE LACS KATHIO STATE PARK, 15066 Kathio State Park Road, Onamia. Call 320-532-3523. Website: www.dnr.state.mn.us/state_parks/mille_lacs_kathio/index.html.

MILLE LACS WILDLIFE MANAGEMENT AREA, 29172 100th Avenue, Onamia. Call 320-532-3537. Website: www.dnr.state.mn.us/wmas/index.html.

NISSWA PIONEER VILLAGE, 25611 Main Street, Nisswa. Call 218-963-3570.

NISSWA TURTLE RACES, Nisswa Trailside Information Center, Nisswa. Call 218-963-2620. Website: www.nisswa.com/pages/NisswaTurtleRaces.

NORTHLAND ARBORETUM, 14250 Conservation Drive, Brainerd. Call 218-829-8770. Website: www.northlandarb.org.

PAUL BUNYAN LAND AND THIS OLD FARM PIONEER VILLAGE, 17553 MN 18, Brainerd. Call 218-764-2524. Website: www.paulbunyanland.com.

PEQUOT LAKES FIRE TOWER, CR 11, Pequot Lakes. Call 218-568-5860.

PIRATE'S COVE MINI-GOLF, 17992 MN 371 North, Brainerd. Call 218-828-9002. Website: www.piratescove.net.

SIMPLER THYMES OF NISSWA, 25410 Main Street, Nisswa. Call 218-963-9463. Website: www.faceboook.com/pages/Simple-Thymes-of-Nisswa/1468083270172106.

TOTEM POLE, 25485 Main Street, Nisswa. Call 218-963-3450. Website: www.facebook.com/totempolemn.

TREASURES N TIQUES, 34016 MN 371, Pequot Lakes. Call 218-820-7931. Website: www.facebook.com/AntiquesUniquesnCoolOldStuff.

TURTLE TOWN BOOKS & GIFTS, 25491 Main Street, Nisswa. Call 218-963-4891; 800-635-7809. Website: www.turtletownnisswa.com.

Dining

371 DINER, 14901 Edgewood Drive, Baxter. Call 218-829-3356. Fun diner space serving burgers, sandwiches, salads, and soups. Website: www.facebook.com/371diner.

A-PINE FAMILY RESTAURANT, 33039 Old MN 371, Pequot Lakes. Home-cooked, hearty meals. Call 218-568-8353. Website: www.apinerestaurant.com.

ADIRONDACK COFFEE, 25469 Main Street, Nisswa. Call 218-967-0111. Coffee drinks, sandwiches, and treats. Website: www.lovemymug.com.

THE BARN, 711 Washington Street, Brainerd. Call 218-829-9297. Classic American diner food. Website: www.facebook.com/TheBarnBrainerd.

BLACK BEAR LODGE AND SALOON, 14819 Edgewood Drive, Brainerd. Call 218-828-8400. Casual eatery offering walleye, steaks, pasta, and prime rib. Website: www.blackbearlodgemn.com.

BOOMER PIZZA, 14039 Edgewood Drive North, Baxter. Call 218-454-4900. Gourmet, creative pizza. Website: boomerpizza.com.

FRONT STREET CAFÉ, 616 Front Street, Brainerd. Call 218-828-1102. Hearty American food.

GRAND CASINO MILLE LACS, 777 Grand Avenue, Onamia. Call 800-626-5825. Multiple dining spots, casual to upscale. Website: www.grandcasinomn.com.

IZATYS, 40005 85th Avenue, Onamia. Call 320-532-4574. Both casual and more formal dining with frequently changing menus. Website: www.izatys .com.

THE LOCAL 218, 723 Mill Avenue, Brainerd. Call 218-270-3195. Upscale American food and cocktails. Website: www.local-218.com.

LOST LAKE LODGE, 7965 Lost Lake Road, Lake Shore. Call 218-963-2681. Gourmet foods, with many items locally sourced. Website: www.lostlake .com.

PRAIRIE BAY GRILL, 15115 Edgewood Drive, Baxter. Call 218-824-6444. Family-friendly eatery with sandwiches, pizzas, pot roast, and dinner bowls. Website: www.prairiebay.com.

SAWMILL INN, 601 Washington Street, Brainerd. Call 218-829-5444. Great diner food. Website: www.sawmillinnbrainerd.com.

SVOBODA'S SPOTLITE, 9563 Madison Street, Garrison. Call 320-692-4692. Home cooking in generous portions. Website: www.facebook.com /Svobodas-Spotlite-Family-Restaurant-471416619597532.

TIMBERJACK SMOKEHOUSE & SALOON, 4443 CR 168, Pequot Lakes. Call 218-568-6070. Hearty plated dinners and cocktails. Website: www .facebook.com/Timberjack-Smokehouse-Saloon-164674166895315.

TRIANGLE DRIVE-INN TREATS, 714 Mill Avenue, Brainerd. Call 218-838-3512. Seasonal ice cream shop. Website: www.facebook.com/TriangleDrive InnTreatsllc/?rf=211239122312594.

ZORBAZ ON THE LAKE, 36215 CR 66, Crosslake. Call 218-692-4567. Local favorite with substantial entrées, sandwiches, and burritos. Website: www .zorbaz.com.

Other Contacts

BRAINERD LAKES CHAMBER, 7393 MN 371, Brainerd. Call 218-829-2838; 800-450-2838. Website: www.explorebrainerdlakes.com.

MILLE LACS LAKE AREA TOURISM, 630 West Main Street, Isle. Call 320-676-9972; 888-350-2692. Website: www.millelacs.com.

9

ST. CROIX RIVER VALLEY AND AMERICA'S LITTLE SWEDEN

ESTIMATED DISTANCE: 120 miles

ESTIMATED TIME: 4 hours

GETTING THERE: From the Twin Cities, take I-35W north to US 8 east to Chisago City. Follow US 8 east through Lindstrom, Center City, and Taylors Falls. Take US 8 south to MN 95 (St. Croix Trail) to reach Franconia. Continue on MN 95 to MN 97, turning right to arrive in Scandia. Return to MN 95 and travel south to County Route (CR 4) (Maple Street) to stop in Marine on St. Croix. Follow MN 95 south to Stillwater. From Stillwater, you can take MN 96 or MN 36 back to the Twin Cities.

HIGHLIGHTS: The Scandinavian bakeries in the "America's Little Sweden" towns; the steep bluffs and cliffs of Interstate State Park; the Taylors Falls Angel Hill District; the Gammelgården Museum; the Franconia Sculpture Garden; antiquing and dining in Stillwater.

There are lakes in this area, but the primary source of outdoor recreation in the St. Croix Valley rests along the riverbanks. This small but highly scenic region derives its beauty from the St. Croix River and the surrounding landscapes. The wealthy New England families that settled here more than a century ago re-created their New England villages along the riverside, small towns that remain intact, and as charming as they were when they were first built. Along with the New Englanders came the Scandinavians, building tight agricultural and cultural enclaves. Logging and the fur trade drove the growth of the area during the nineteenth century, and today's visitors can still find remnants of those trades, primarily in place names, but the small towns are quaint and wonderful to wander around, and going up the river can

LEFT: COFFEE POT WATER TOWER, LINDSTROM

9. St. Croix River Valley and America's Little Sweden

Women's Environmental Institute

Wild River State Park

95

North Branch

12

Wild Mountain

95

16

87

St. Croix River

35

Balsam Lake

46

8

Stacy

Chisago County Historical Society
Lindstrom

Historic District Center City

Eichten's Bistro & Market

Taylors Falls
Folsom House

St. Croix Visitor Center
St. Croix Falls

8

St. Croix Dalles
Interstate State Park

Chisago City

25

WineHaven Winery and Vineyard

Nya Duvemåla

8

Franconia Sculpture Park

Dresser

Wyoming

35

Osceola

10

Forest Lake

Columbus

35

Forest Lake

Scandia

Gammelgården

3

Hay Lake School Museum & Erickson Log Home

97

95

Wisconsin

65

35W

William O'Brien State Park

Stone House Museum
Marine General Store

Marine on Saint Croix
Marine Mill

St. Croix Chocolate Company

35

35E

Lino Lakes

Hugo

Minnesota

Somerset

95

64

New Richmond

White Bear Lake

Vadnais Heights

White Bear Lake

Mahtomedi

244

96

Warden's House Lodging & shops
Aamodt's Hot Air Balloon Rides

Stillwater

Stillwater Lift Bridge
Stillwater River Boats

35

65

36

694

North St. Paul

5

Lake Elmo

Bayport

36

Maplewood

120

Oakdale

94

St. Paul

35E

10

West St. Paul

52

South St. Paul

494

10

Inver Grove Heights

55

Cottage Grove

Woodbury

Wiederkehr Balloon Rides

Lakeland

Stillwater Balloons

Lake St. Croix

Afton

Lake St. Croix Beach
Afton House Inn

ST CROIX TRAIL

95

Afton Alps

Afton State Park

Hudson

95

35

Roberts

12

Hammond

94

River Falls

65

29

N

0   3   6

Miles

Mississippi River

St. Croix R.

29

65

© The Countryman Press

provide insight into some of Minnesota's Scandinavian heritage. The St. Croix Valley is still full of natural beauty, from rivers to woodlands to prairie to glacial trails, and is a park lover's dream region. Some of Minnesota's most beautiful state parks are in this area, running along the river and offering nearly every kind of recreational opportunity, including swimming, canoeing, hiking, camping, horseback riding, cross-country skiing, and snowshoeing. Artists have not been immune to the area's beauty, and the arts community is strong and growing throughout the Valley.

LINDSTROM SIGN IN SWEDISH AND ENGLISH

Inland from the river, in an area heavily populated with lakes and farmland, is a part of the state known as **America's Little Sweden**. A series of small towns settled by Swedish (and other Scandinavian) immigrants, America's Little Sweden is a place where you can still hear faint traces of Swedish accents and may see store and street signs in both English and Swedish. Most of these communities have active relationships with sister cities in Sweden, and the food and culture still strongly reflect that ancestry.

Chisago City was host to novelist **Vilhelm Moberg**, author of a four-part cycle of novels known as the Emigrants series, which he researched here. Today, he is remembered by a park statue bearing his name. The town's name itself comes from the Native American phrase *ki chi saga*, which means "fair and lovely waters." It's an aptly named community, surrounded by lakes that have made it an enduring tourist destination. For a good meal in Chisago City, you can wander over to **George's Smokin' BBQ**. Just east of town is **WineHaven Winery and Vineyard**, an award-winning vineyard that's been family owned and operated for four generations. Take US 8 to CR 80, then the first left onto 292nd Street to find the winery and its tasting room.

Nearby is the town of Lindstrom,

VILHELM MOBERG STATUE, CHISAGO CITY

home to the **Chisago County Historical Society**, which houses exhibitions tracing the area's history and also provides maps for self-guided walking tours through the Swedish Circle. Moberg's novels feature a fictional couple named Karl Oskar and Kristina. In Lindstrom, you'll find a statue of the literary couple—along with a water tower shaped like a Swedish coffeepot. From Lindstrom, travel south on CR 25, then east on Glader Boulevard to reach **Kichi-Saga Park**, home to **Nya Duvemåla**. This old house was an inspiration to Moberg, who modeled Karl Oskar and Kristina's fictional home after it. A boulder in front of the house was donated by Volvo from Åseda, Sweden, to honor Moberg's fictional work.

While in Lindstrom, stop for a bite to eat at the **Swedish Inn**; the Swedish pancakes are especially delicious. You can also visit the **Lindstrom Bakery** for both Swedish and non-Swedish baked goods, many of which are organic. The **Northwoods Roasterie & Coffee Shop** offers additional options—a full slate of coffee drinks, as well as a small but thoughtful lunch menu (be sure to check out the lunch waffle).

Founded in 1851, Center City has the distinction of being the oldest continuously settled Swedish community in Minnesota. (On a non-Swedish-related note, the town is also home to the internationally renowned Hazelden Center for addiction treatment.) Center City is on the shores of Kichi-Saga, or "the Big Lake." It's also known as Swede Lake, and used to be a single enormous body of water until expansion of the railroads led to it being broken up into five smaller lakes. Center City is home to **Chisago Lake Evangelical Lutheran Church**, which has existed in its current building since 1889 and held services since 1854. Original homes of the Swedish pioneers can be viewed throughout the **Center City Historic District on Summit Avenue**, a neighborhood with numerous houses of first- and second-generation families, built in period style.

THE KARL OSKAR HOUSE, LINDSTROM

Just outside Center City on US 8 is **Eichten's Bistro & Market**, a restaurant and food shop filled with bison and artisan cheeses produced locally by Eichten's Hidden Acres farm. Try a bison burger—the Blue Mox with Minnesota cave-aged blue cheese warrants special attention. You can also pick up some cheese and sausage for the road while you're here.

Continuing on US 8 will lead you to Taylors Falls. It's hard to imagine a more dramatic entrance to a community: the road suddenly curves and opens up to soaring views of the **St. Croix Dalles**, a deep canyon gouged out during the last ice age. The St. Croix River has steep bluffs on both sides, with forests of pine, oak, and maple trees lining them.

Incorporated in 1858, Taylors Falls has retained its small-town sensibilities as well as its sense of tradition. **Folsom House,** along with several of its neighbors, looks as though it was plucked out

EICHTEN'S BISTRO & MARKET, CENTER CITY

of a New England landscape and replanted in Taylors Falls. Home of a lumber baron and state senator, the Folsom House is a study in life 150 years ago. The home was owned by five generations of Folsoms, and family members tended to store furnishings and belongings rather than divest them, so the museum exists as a treasure trove of authentic pieces, including kitchenware, clothing (even a Civil War uniform), and furniture. After visiting the Folsom House, take some time to explore (by foot or by car) the homes on the hills above the museum, known collectively as the **Angel Hill District**.

There are historic lodging options in Taylors Falls. The **Old Jail** offers three suites and a cottage in two buildings, one a former jail, the other having housed a wide variety of businesses: saloon, chicken-plucking factory, and mortuary. Despite the premises' strange history, the suites are lovely, each including a private bath, and some outfitted with old-fashioned record players. One of the suites features a bathroom in a cave, and another is not recommended for people over six feet tall. Another lodging option, the **Cottage Bed & Breakfast** consists of only one unit, but it's a suite with a private dining area overlooking the St. Croix River in an eighteenth-century house.

When it's time for dinner, check out **Tangled Up in Blue**, a French fusion restaurant, with high-end fare and a good wine list. **The Chisago House Restaurant** is located in a charming old building and serves three meals a day, plus robust weekend dinner buffets (think prime rib, BBQ ribs, and baked and fried fish). If you're looking for something more casual (and you're visiting in the summer), stop by **The Drive In**. The atmosphere is retro, with a giant rotating root beer cup, and burgers and malts are served to your vehicle by carhops. The Drive In is located right next door to a minigolf course. Another good choice is **Schoony's Malt Shop & Pizzeria**, specializing in (what else?) malts and pizzas. **Juneberry Café** is a seasonal café

FOLSOM HOUSE, TAYLORS FALLS

serving gourmet sandwiches and salads, along with ice cream, and the **Goat Saloon** is a cheery bar with hearty pub options.

The biggest draw of the Taylors Falls area is outdoor recreation. The headquarters for information is the **St. Croix Visitor Center**, in St. Croix Falls, Wisconsin, which is just across the river from Taylors Falls. As the St. Croix ambles south along the Minnesota border, canoeing and camping are popular activities, but check with the visitor center before making plans—there are restrictions regarding use of campsites and boats to protect the river and the land on either side of it. In times of low rainfall, fire restrictions are strictly enforced.

Take US 8 to the only stoplight and turn left, then follow CR 16 to **Wild Mountain**. Wild Mountain takes advantage of the rolling terrain in the river area to run 25 ski and boarding runs during the winter, along with a snow-tubing course. During the summer, there's a water park with alpine slide and go-cart tracks, as well as public and private charter river cruises, canoe and kayak rental, and an RV park and campground.

The dramatic terrain plays a role in several state parks in the area. North of Taylors Falls on MN 95, turn onto CR 12 to find **Wild River State Park**. This sizable park spans 18 miles of the St. Croix River and offers hiking and cross-country ski trails. You'll find a guesthouse and camping within the park, including campsites for visitors with horses. Spring provides some of the most beautiful wildflower displays in the state. For those with GPS units

WILD RIVER STATE PARK

and an itch to explore, the Minnesota DNR website provides coordinates for historical searches within the park. If you'd like to find lodging nearby, check out the Women's Environmental Institute at Amador Hill. Located in an organic apple orchard on the edge of Wild River State Park, the WEI offers four rooms for guests or groups. Two of the rooms share a bath, and the largest room has a fireplace. The quarters are simple but attractive, and its location can't be beat.

At the junction of US 8 and MN 95 is the **Franconia Sculpture Park**. The park is, intentionally, a work in progress. There are more than 75 installations

FRANCONIA SCULPTURE PARK

in this outdoor "gallery," and each year somewhere between 15 and 25 artists are invited to work and contribute art on a rotating basis. The sculptures are spread across a field with flat mowed paths; self-guided tours and guided tours are offered. Not only are many of the pieces in process, but several are hands-on for visitors—very attractive for kids.

Traveling south on MN 95 to MN 97 will bring you to Scandia, the first Swedish settlement in Minnesota. Scandia's heritage is on display at **Gammelgården**, a living history museum paying tribute to the Scandinavian roots of the region. Several original immigrant homes and other buildings, including a church, have been restored on 11 acres of farmland. The site is open for public tours during the summer, but year-round the museum offers a vast array of special events and classes, including music festivals, sausage-making classes, and annual Midsommar Dag (Midsummer Day) and Lucia Day celebrations.

GAMMELGARDEN CHURCH, SCANDIA

Glacial Potholes?

nterstate State Park is located on US 8, just as you arrive in Taylors Falls. The park's name reflects its cross-river location, with the park stretching from Minnesota to Wisconsin. River access makes kayaking and canoeing popular sports, and intriguing geological formations, including exposed lava flows and glacial deposits, provide motive for exploration. Of particular interest are the glacial potholes, immense holes (the deepest one is 60 feet) in the bedrock where the Glacial St. Croix River forced its way through. Interstate State Park features more of these glacial potholes in one area than does any other place in the world. Rock climbing here is popular, and during the fall, the autumn colors provide a major draw.

INTERSTATE STATE PARK

If Gammelgården doesn't offer enough history for you, check out the nearby **Hay Lake School Museum and Erickson Log Home**, a mile south of Scandia on CR 3. Listed on the National Register of Historic Places, this museum consists of a former schoolhouse and a log home built in the late 1800s.

Just down the street from Gammelgården, you can find breakfast or lunch at the **Scandia Café**. It's a classic small-town café, often busy with locals who come in for the daily soup specials and turkey luncheon.

From Scandia, return to US 95 and drive south to **William O'Brien State Park**. This small but lovely park was named after a lumber baron who had originally cleared the land of trees. The park is now, more than a century later, reforested and full of wildlife and river access. Open year round, the park offers trails for cross-country skiing and snowshoeing, as well as campsites with electricity for winter camping. There's a swimming beach with a large picnic area adjacent, and summer canoeing on the river is made easy by the park's canoe rental and shuttle service. Birdwatchers can spot hundreds of different birds. The visitor center has a seasonal checklist of species that might be seen, from the common Canadian goose and northern flicker to the uncommon (but still possible!) great blue heron, ruffed grouse, and scarlet tanager.

Just 2 miles south of William O'Brien State Park on MN 95 is Marine on St. Croix, a tiny riverside village. The town was originally founded as a sawmill, the Marine Mill, the first commercial sawmill on the St. Croix River. Today the Marine Mill is gone, but its site is maintained by the Minnesota Historical Society. You can wander down trails with interpretive signs explaining the site's significance and photographs of what once existed. Eventually, the trail leads you to an overlook above the river.

HAY LAKE SCHOOL, SCANDIA

You can see more of the village's history at the **Stone House Museum**. Aptly named for its Scandinavian stone architecture, the Stone House Museum was originally the town meetinghouse. Today it's a repository for artifacts and photographs documenting the Scandinavian settlers of the early nineteenth century.

For a brief respite, you can pick up snacks to go (among many other things) at the **Marine General Store**. Nearby is the **St. Croix Chocolate Company**, purveyor of amazing (and amazingly beautiful) chocolates, as well as local wines and pizza on weekend nights.

Stillwater, south of Marine on St. Croix, calls itself the "Birthplace of Minnesota." Built by lumber barons and transplanted New Englanders, it's one of the oldest cities in the state. Like other towns in the region, Stillwater suffered the loss of its primary industry and experienced a slump in the early twentieth century. However, the natural beauty surrounding the area combined with the charm of the downtown streets and buildings drove a renaissance that has since created thriving shops and galleries and a busy tourist trade, particularly on summer weekends, when driving down Main Street often requires patience and time. Travelers with both are awarded with the opportunity to stop, shop, and wander along the river where they can watch the **Stillwater Lift**

THE MARINE GENERAL STORE, MARINE ON ST. CROIX

Bridge in operation and see sailboats and yachts dotting the water. Visitors to Stillwater may find the abundance of excellent dining options here nearly unreasonable. Whether you are wandering on your own, with family, or seeking a romantic couple's getaway, Stillwater is a lovely place to spend a day or two. Factor in the recreation and dining options south of the city, and you may want to extend your stay.

Of course there's plenty of history to be discovered in this area. **The Warden's House** was built in 1853 and was used as a residence for prison wardens and superintendents until 1941, when the building was sold to the Washington County Historical Society. Several of the rooms are furnished as they would have been in the late nineteenth century, while a few rooms are reserved for displays relevant to the region's overall history, including that of the lumber industry. The Joseph Wolf Caves were once used for breweries, and today tours illuminate both the caves and the history behind the brewing.

Options for exploring the river town abound, both by land and by sea. **Stillwater River Boats** offers cruises on the St. Croix River with your choice of a lunch, dinner, brunch, or live music. Boats are also available for private charter, and reservations are recommended. For something more

STILLWATER

personal, try **Gondola Romantica**. Who needs Venice? This company brings romantic gondola rides right onto the St. Croix River. Options include everything from 20-minute sightseeing cruises to a five-course dinner cruise. The company offers customized cruises as well. Gondolas hold six people, but if you'd like a private excursion, reserve ahead. For land excursions, the **Stillwater Trolley** operates enclosed, climate-controlled trains that take visitors on a 45-minute guided tour of the Stillwater area.

One of the many joys of Stillwater is its abundance of historic (and romantic) inns and bed-and-breakfasts. Spending a weekend in this river town is a treat—and a popular one. Book ahead.

The Lowell Inn is the granddaddy of historic hotels in Stillwater. Built in 1927 on the site of a former lumberjack hotel, this stately building boasts 23 impeccably decorated rooms, some with stained-glass windows, antique furnishings, and fireplaces, but all with modern conveniences. Several rooms

Hot-Air Balloon Rides

Given the beautiful scenery and charming small towns in this region, it's only logical that hot-air balloon rides would be a popular pastime. The following companies all offer hot-air balloon service daily from May through October, weather permitting. Contact the individual companies for off-season possibilities (contact information is at the end of this chapter).

Stillwater Balloons: Morning or late afternoon departures are available during summer, but balloon rides (dependent on weather) can be procured all year long. Each flight concludes with a champagne celebration. **Wiederkehr Balloons**: Morning and afternoon departures are available for up to eight passengers booked on a 12-passenger balloon. Champagne is served at the conclusion of the ride. **Aamodt's Hot Air Balloon Rides**: Hot-air balloon rides are offered with departures from the owner's apple orchard in Stillwater. Rides are reserved for two people only and include a champagne toast. Most rides are scheduled late in the day to take advantage of the views over the St. Croix, but sunrise departures can also be accommodated.

have hot tubs, and the romance here runs high. The hotel is also home to a highly regarded restaurant.

The Water Street Inn is a small luxury inn with rooms and suites, most with gas fireplaces. The rooms are decorated as would have befitted the upscale visitors of the lumber boom days, and several packages are offered involving meals, flowers, and massages. A well-regarded restaurant and pub round out the amenities.

Lora is a new hotel right downtown Stillwater. A smaller property with just 40 rooms and suites, the hotel makes excellent use of the building's historic character while offering a modern, upscale set of amenities.

The lower St. Croix Valley enjoys an affluent residential population and close proximity to the Twin Cities, providing it with an abundance of notable dining options, even off-season. A unique way to explore the city's many culinary offerings is to take a **Foodies on Foot** tour, a guided food adventure through Stillwater. There are regularly scheduled tours, but also the option to bring your own group and create a private specialty tour.

While it's open year-round, the **Dock Café** is the place to be during the warm-weather months. Situated right on the banks of the St. Croix, the restaurant has outdoor seating that provides diners with a full view of river life. Not surprisingly, the outdoor patio is popular—plan to arrive early, or wait. However, the indoor ambience is attractive as well, with a fireplace and wide windows. Menu items leans heavily toward steaks and seafood. Another great outdoor option is **Portside**, which offers a rooftop patio overlooking the river.

THE LIFT BRIDGE, STILLWATER

Bed & Breakfasts

The Elephant Walk is an elaborate Victorian house, the residence of globe-trotting owners who have filled the interior with finds from their travels in Europe and Asia. Each of the four sumptuously decorated rooms has a theme: the Rangoon, Chiang Mai, Cadiz, and Raffles rooms are all decorated according to their geographic designation. All rooms have fireplaces and refrigerators with complimentary nonalcoholic beverages; a bottle of wine and appetizers, as well as a four-course breakfast, are included in the rates.

The whimsical **Ann Bean Mansion** has a colorful history, complete with tales of lumber-baron riches and marital scandal. Today, the inn features five lovely rooms, all with fireplaces and private baths. The Tower Room is a particularly cozy choice. Rooms come with plush robes, and rates include an afternoon glass of wine and full breakfast daily.

The Aurora Staples Inn offers five rooms and suites, all with whirlpools, fireplaces, and private baths. The home's library, parlor, dining room, and porch are all available to guests as well, who are also encouraged to visit the property's beautiful gardens during the summer.

Sitting on a hillside above Stillwater, the **Rivertown Inn** provides beautiful views along with four rooms and five suites, each of which is elaborately decorated and named after a literary heavyweight (Lord Byron, Longfellow, etc.). The inn is open year round, but summer visitors will enjoy the use of the private gardens and screened-in gazebo. All accommodations include luxurious bedding, plush robes, turn-down service with handmade chocolates, full breakfast, and an evening social hour.

The James Mulvey Inn Carriage House has two luxury suites with double whirlpools, balconies, and fireplaces, set on 1½ acres. Breakfast is included at a nearby restaurant.

The lovingly restored 1895 Queen Anne home **Lady Goodwood** offers several original details, include a parlor fireplace. The three guest rooms are all lavishly decorated in Victorian style and have private baths; the St. Croix Suite comes with a round king-sized bed.

The William Sauntry Mansion has five rooms, all with private bath and three with Tylo Swedish steam showers. The rooms are decorated in Victorian style, and guests receive a four-course breakfast each day.

Within the historic Lowell Inn are two noteworthy restaurants. The formal restaurant, in the elegant **George Washington Room**, serves classic dinner entrées such as duck à l'orange and beef Wellington, while the **Matterhorn Room** serves a four-course Swiss dinner fondue each evening. Other upscale dining options include the **Domacin Winebar** and **Revé Bistro and Bar.**

Other eateries worth a visit include the **Main Café**, open through lunch but also serving breakfast through closing time; **Marx Fusion Bistro**, offering an eclectic menu with Caribbean, Asian, and Italian-American foods; and **Brick & Bourbon** with its upscale take on café favorites. Focusing on locally sourced ingredients, **Lolo American Kitchen** serves up gourmet takes on burgers and tacos, while **Velveteen Speakeasy** will please those in search of an old-fashioned hideaway. For excellent coffee drinks and homemade baked goods, **Tin Bins** is a popular spot.

Stillwater's main city center, along the riverfront, has developed into a visitor shopping haven, full of small, charming shops, with hardly a chain store to be seen. Antique enthusiasts flock to this community for its large concentration of antique stores and dealers, but there are plenty of other kinds of retail as well.

North Main Studio is open only by appointment, but the planning is worth the trouble to visit this atelier where local resident and artist Carl Erickson displays, sells, and creates his pottery. Another spot for art lovers, **Tamarack Gallery** showcases local and national artists of various media, including painting, etching, sculpture, and photography.

Open daily for tastings and tours, **Northern Vineyards** is an award-winning winery right on the main street of Stillwater, vinting Minnesota and Wisconsin grapes. In summer, enjoy a glass of wine on the back patio overlooking the lift bridge across the river. Nearby is the **Wedge & Wheel**, a retail cheese shop that also offers dining and classes in different subjects.

With hundreds of thousands of titles available, **Loome Theological Book-sellers** is a bookshop for serious collectors. You'll also find framed engravings for purchase, as well as medieval manuscript leaves.

Located in a historic mill, **Staples Mill Antiques** comprises nearly 80 antique dealers spread over three floors—a great spot for both serious antiquing and window-shopping. Another must for antique enthusiasts is the **Midtown Antique Mall**, with more than 100 dealers, including several that sell furniture.

To reach the final stop on this route, take MN 95 south to Afton, the home of two notable outdoor areas:

Afton Alps is one of Minnesota's biggest ski resorts, with 40 trails and 18 lifts, a snowboard park, and a tubing hill. During the summer, the resort is open for mountain bikers, and golfers can enjoy an 18-hole course.

Afton State Park is a beautiful nature preserve that also provides a strenuous workout for visitors. The park offers 20 miles of hiking trails, most of which include sharply steep inclines, but the views of the St. Croix River are worth the effort. Horseback riding is permitted in one area of the park, and several miles of trails are open for cross-country skiers in winter. Year-round camping is available.

If you'd like to linger at this end of the trail, reserve a room at the **Afton**

House Inn. Afton House has 46 rooms, most with a canopy or four-poster bed, and deluxe accommodations feature balconies overlooking the St. Croix River. The location near Afton Alps makes this hotel a good choice for a ski weekend, providing you with a warm, romantic hideaway to return to at the end of the day. The inn has a restaurant and bar on site.

IN THE AREA

Accommodations

AFTON HOUSE INN, 3291 South St. Croix Trail, Afton. Call 651-436-8883. Website: www.aftonhouseinn.com.

THE ANN BEAN MANSION, 319 West Pine Street, Stillwater. Call 651-430-0355; 877-837-4400. Website: www.annbeanmansion.com.

AURORA STAPLES INN, 303 North 4th Street, Stillwater. Call 651-351-1187. Website: www.aurorastaplesinn.com.

COTTAGE BED & BREAKFAST, 950 Fox Glen Drive, Taylors Falls. Call 651-465-3595.

THE ELEPHANT WALK, 801 West Pine Street, Stillwater. Call 651-430-0359; 888-430-0359. Website: www.elephantwalkbb.com.

JAMES MULVEY INN CARRIAGE HOUSE, 807 Harriet Street South, Stillwater. Call 651-430-8008. Website: www. jamesmulveyinn.com.

LADY GOODWOOD, 704 1st Street South, Stillwater. Call 651-439-3771; 866-688-5239. Website: www.ladygoodwood.com.

LORA, 402 South Main Street, Stillwater. Call 651-400-7922. Website: www .lorahotel.com.

LOWELL INN, 102 North 2nd Street, Stillwater. Call 651-439-1100. Website: www.lowellinn.com.

THE OLD JAIL, 349 Government Street, Taylors Falls. Call 651-465-3112. Website: www.oldjail.com.

RIVERTOWN INN, 306 Olive Street West, Stillwater. Call 651-430-2955. Website: www.rivertowninn.com.

WATER STREET INN, 101 Water Street South. Call 651-439-6000. Website: www.waterstreetinn.us.

WILLIAM SAUNTRY MANSION, 626 4th Street North, Stillwater. Call 651-430-2653. Website: www.sauntrymansion.com.

WOMEN'S ENVIRONMENTAL INSTITUTE AT AMADOR HILL, 15715 River Road, North Branch. Call 651-583-0705. Website: www.w-e-i.org.

Attractions and Recreation

AAMODT'S HOT AIR BALLOON RIDES, Stillwater. Call 651-351-0101. Website: www.aamodtsballoons.com.

AFTON ALPS, 6600 Peller Avenue South, Hastings. Call 651-436-5245; 800-328-1328. Website: www.aftonalps.com.

AFTON STATE PARK, 6959 Peller Avenue South, Hastings. Call 651-436-5391. Website: www.dnr.state.mn.us/state_parks/afton/index.html.

CHISAGO COUNTY HISTORICAL SOCIETY, 12795 Lake Boulevard, Lindstrom. Call: 651-257-5310. Website: www.chisagocountyhistory.org.

CHISAGO LAKE EVANGELICAL LUTHERAN CHURCH, Center City. Call 651-257-6300. Website: www.chisagolakelutheranchurch.org.

FOLSOM HOUSE, 272 West Government Street, Taylors Falls. Call 651-465-3125. Website: www.sites.mnhs.org/places/historic-sites/folsom-house.

FOODIES ON FOOT, Stillwater. Call 855-236-6343. Website: www .foodiesonfootmn.com.

FRANCONIA SCULPTURE PARK, 29836 St. Croix Trail, Shafer. Call 651-257-6668. Website: www.franconia.org.

GAMMELGÅRDEN, 20880 Olinda Trail, Scandia. Call 651-433-5053. Website: www.gammelgardenmuseum.org.

GONDOLA ROMANTICA, 425 East Nelson Street, Stillwater. Call 651-439-1783. Website: www.gondolaromantica.com.

HAY LAKE SCHOOL MUSEUM AND ERICKSON LOG HOME, 14020 195th Street North, Marine on St. Croix. Call 651-433-4014. Website: wchsmn.org/museums/hay-lake.

INTERSTATE STATE PARK, 307 Milltown Road, Taylors Falls. Call 651-465-5711. Website: www.dnr.state.mn.us/state_parks/interstate/index.html.

LOOME THEOLOGICAL BOOKSELLERS, 229 Main Street South, Stillwater. Call 651-430-1092. Website: www.loomebooks.com.

MARINE GENERAL STORE, 101 Judd Street, Marine on St. Croix. Call 651-433-2445. Website: www.marinegeneralstore.com.

MIDTOWN ANTIQUE MALL, 301 Main Street South, Stillwater. Call 651-430-0808. Website: www.midtownantiques.com.

NORTH MAIN STUDIO, 402 North Main Street, Stillwater. Call 651-351-1379.

NORTHERN VINEYARDS, 223 Main Street North, Stillwater. Call 651-430-1032. Website: www.northernvineyards.com.

NYA DUVEMÅLA, 29061 Glader Boulevard, Lindstrom.

ST. CROIX CHOCOLATE COMPANY, 11 Judd Street, Marine on St. Croix. Call 651-433-1400. Website: www.stcroixchocolateco.com.

STAPLES MILL ANTIQUES, 410 North Main Street, Stillwater. Call 651-430-1816. Website: www.staplesmillantiques.com.

STILLWATER BALLOONS, 135 St. Croix Trail North, Lakeland Shores. Call 651-439-1800. Website: www.stillwaterballoons.com.

STILLWATER RIVER BOATS, 525 South Main Street, Stillwater. Call 651-430-1234. Website: www.stillwaterriverboats.com.

STILLWATER TROLLEY, 400 East Nelson Street, Stillwater. Call 651-430-0352. Website: www.stillwatertrolley.com.

STONE HOUSE MUSEUM, 241 5th Street, Marine on St. Croix. Call 651-433-3636.

TAMARACK GALLERY, 112 South Main Street, Stillwater. Call 651-439-9393. Website: www.tamarackgallery.com.

WARDEN'S HOUSE MUSEUM, 602 North Main Street, Stillwater. Call 651-439-5956. Website: wchsmn.org/museums/wardens-house-museum.

WEDGE & WHEEL, 308 Chestnut Street East, Stillwater. Call 651-342-1687. Retail cheese shop with dining and classes. Website: www.wedgeandwheel.com.

WIEDERKEHR BALLOONS, Lakeland. Call 651-436-8172.

WILD MOUNTAIN & TAYLORS FALLS RECREATION, 37200 Wild Mountain Road, Taylors Falls. Call 651-465-6315. Website: www.wildmountain.com.

WILD RIVER STATE PARK, 39797 Park Trail, Center City. Call 651-583-2125. Website: www.dnr.state.mn.us/state_parks/wild_river/index.html.

WILLIAM O'BRIEN STATE PARK, 16821 O'Brien Trail North, Marine on St. Croix. Call 651-433-0500. Website: www.dnr.state.mn.us/state_parks/william_obrien/index.html.

WINEHAVEN WINERY AND VINEYARD, 9757 292nd Street, Chisago City. Call 651-257-1017. Website: www.winehaven.com.

Dining

BRICK AND BOURBON, 215 Main Street, South, Stillwater. Call 651-342-0777. Extensive cocktail list and playful, upscale menu. Website: www.brickandbourbon.com.

CHISAGO HOUSE RESTAURANT, 361 Bench Street, Taylors Falls. Call 651-465-5245. Three meals a day and special weekend buffets. Website: www.chisagohouse.com.

DOCK CAFÉ, 425 East Nelson Street, Stillwater. Call 651-430-3770. Supper club fare on the banks of the St. Croix River. Website: www.dockcafe.com.

DOMACIN RESTAURANT & WINEBAR, 102 South 2nd Street, Stillwater. Call 651-439-1352. American/Mediterranean with a thoughtful wine list. Website: www.domacinwinebar.com.

THE DRIVE IN, 572 Bench Street, Taylors Falls. Call 651-465-7831. Classic drive-in food with generous portions. Website: www.taylorsfallsdrivein.com.

EICHTEN'S BISTRO & MARKET, 16440 Lake Boulevard, Center City. Call 651-257-1566. Sandwiches, salads, and daily breakfast. Website: www .eichtenscheese.com.

GEORGE'S SMOKIN' BBQ, 29346 Old Towne Road, Chisago City. Call 651-257-1566. Pulled pork and chicken, brisket, and comfort-food sides. Website: smokingeorgesbbq.com.

THE GOAT SALOON, 367 Bench Street, Taylors Falls. Call 651-240-0120. Hearty bar food. Website: www.facebook.com/The-Goat-359109264485177.

JUNEBERRY CAFÉ, 360 Bench Street, Taylors Falls. Seasonal café with pastries, gourmet salads and sandwiches, and ice cream. Website: www .juneberrycafe.com.

LINDSTROM BAKERY, 12830 Lake Boulevard, Lindstrom. Call 651-257-1374. Pastries, including traditional favorites like rosettes. Website: www .facebook.com/Lindstrom-Bakery-Inc-120703007945281.

LOLO AMERICAN KITCHEN, 233 Main Street, South, Stillwater. Call 651-342-2461. Gourmet street foods and small plates. Website: www .loloamericankitchen.com.

LOWELL INN, 102 North 2nd Street, Stillwater. Call 651-439-1100. Both upscale and casual dining on site. Website: www.lowellinn.com.

THE MAIN CAFÉ, 108 Main Street South, Stillwater. Call 651-430-2319. Extensive breakfast and lunch menus. Website: www.themaincafe.wixsite .com.

MARX FUSION BISTRO, 241 Main Street South, Stillwater. Call 651-439-8333. Fusion restaurant with Caribbean, Asian, and Italian-American cuisine. Website: www.marxwbg.com.

NORTHWOODS ROASTERIE & COFFEE SHOP, 12710 North 1st Avenue, Lindstrom. Call 651-257-5240. Coffee shop with limited but thoughtful lunch menu (check out the lunch waffle). Website: www.northwoodsroasterie.com.

PORTSIDE, 317 South Main Street, Stillwater. Call 651-342-1502. Sandwiches, flatbreads, and salads. Website: www.portsidestillwater.com.

REVÉ BISTRO & BAR, 200 East Chestnut Street, Stillwater. Call 651-342-1594. Upscale American food. Website: www.revebistroandbar.com.

SCANDIA CAFÉ, 21079 Olinda Trail North, Scandia. Call 651-433-4054. Omelets, burgers, and old-style hot plates. Website: www.thescandiacafe .com/menu.

SCHOONY'S MALT SHOP & PIZZERIA, 384 Bench Street, Taylors Falls. Call 651-465-3222. Pizza and ice cream. Website: www.schoonys.com.

SWEDISH INN, 12678 Lake Boulevard, Lindstrom. Call 651-257-2571. Traditional American foods, breakfast, and burgers. Website: www.facebook .com/Swedish-Inn-115562678570817.

TANGLED UP IN BLUE, 425 Bench Street, Taylors Falls. Call 651-465-1000. Classic fine dining featuring standards like beef carpaccio and duck breast à l'orange (menu changes frequently). Website: www .tangledupinbluerestaurant.net.

TIN BINS, 413 East Nelson Street, Stillwater. Call 651-342-0799. Bakery and coffee drinks. Website: www.tinbinscafe.com.

VELVETEEN SPEAKEASY, 132 2nd Street North, Stillwater. Call 651-342-2571. Hidden bar with upscale bar fare and an extensive drink menu. Website: thevelveteenspeakeasy.com.

Other Contacts

FALLS CHAMBER OF COMMERCE, St. Croix Falls. Call 715-483-3580. Website: www.fallschamber.org.

GREATER STILLWATER CHAMBER OF COMMERCE, 200 Chestnut Street East, Stillwater. Call 651-439-4001. Website: www.greaterstillwaterchamber .com.

SWEDISH CIRCLE TOURS. Website: www.swedishcircletours.com.

10

NORTHERN MISSISSIPPI RIVER BLUFF COUNTRY

Hastings to Lake City

ESTIMATED DISTANCE: 70 miles

ESTIMATED TIME: 2 hours

GETTING THERE: From the Twin Cities, take I-494 to MN 55, then take MN 56 to MN 61. Follow MN 61 to Frontenac.

HIGHLIGHTS: New England-style architecture and historic sites of Hastings and Red Wing; antique shopping and dining in those towns and in Lake City; the stopped-in-time village of Old Frontenac; views of the Mississippi and Lake Pepin. (Note: you could combine this journey with the La Crescent to Wabasha trip in Chapter 11.)

According to geologists, volcanoes and ancient seas first sculpted this part of the state, followed by glaciers that carved out several of its many rivers, including the Mississippi. The starting point for this trip is Hastings, where the St. Croix, Mississippi, and Vermillion rivers all converge, and the Cannon River meets the Mississippi in Red Wing, all due to the work of glaciers 10,000 years ago. As with so many other river towns in Minnesota, this area's proximity to early modes of transportation boded well for the creation and expansion of industry here. Milling and lumber operations were critical to the growth and stability of these towns, but the natural beauty of the region has led to a rise in revenue from tourism as well. Today the rivers are a major source of recreation and sightseeing.

The first stop on this itinerary is the town of Hastings, whose city center contains 63 buildings on the National Register of Historic Places. Here you'll find the **LeDuc House**, built in 1866 by Andrew Jackson Downing, a rare and virtually untouched historic building. This former home of William

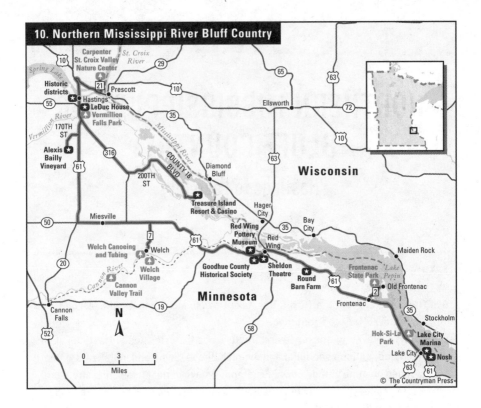

10. Northern Mississippi River Bluff Country

LeDuc—a commissioner of agriculture under President Rutherford Hayes and a Civil War hero—is a delight to visit, but the 4½-acre grounds, which include an apple orchard, are lovely as well.

Also within the city is **Vermillion Falls Park**, an oasis with beautiful waterfalls and trails for hiking and biking, and the Vermillion River is popular with white-water rafters, although its route is fairly short. If you're feeling ambitious, you might try the **Hastings Trail System**, which has a jumping-on point at Vermillion Falls Park, then circles the city in a 15-mile loop. Scenic viewpoints include the Vermillion River, Mississippi River, Lake Isabel, and Lake Rebecca.

To visit the **Carpenter St. Croix Valley Nature Center**, take MN 61 north from Hastings to MN 10; travel east on MN 10 to County Route 21 (CR 21), and then travel north. This small (425 acres) but lavish nature preserve was once a private estate and apple orchard. Today it is a well-maintained natural area, the release site for the University of Minnesota's Raptor Rehabilitation Program, and offers 10 miles of trails, some of which have been adapted for visitors with limited mobility.

When it's time for a meal, stop by the **Onion Grille**, a friendly restaurant where kids are welcome. Open most days for lunch and dinner, house specialties include pizzas, burgers, and classic sandwiches. Another fine option is **Me & Julio,** a Mexican-American eatery with from-scratch cooking. **The Lock and Dam Eatery** offers burgers, Mexican, and Italian foods. An institution in Hastings for more than 50 years, the **Bierstube** serves up generous portions of German specialties along with steaks and burgers. If you're looking for something more upscale, try the **Wiederholt's Supper Club**, a traditional restaurant with a menu focused on standards like steaks and ribs.

Like many of Minnesota's historic river towns, Hastings presents no shortage of shopping opportunities, especially of the antique variety. The streets along the river are home to several good antiques shops, as well as **Briar Patch**, which specializes in clothing, jewelry, and accessories.

For those interested in contemporary accoutrements, the **Scandinavian Marketplace** offers an extensive collection of Scandinavian home and gift items, including hand-painted furniture, tableware, clothing, books, music, and toys; and **Mississippi Clayworks** offers locally made pottery, including custom orders.

If you're in the mood for a little gambling, take MN 316 from Hastings south to 200th Street, then follow 200th for 8 miles to find the **Treasure Island Resort and Casino** in Welch. You'll find slots, blackjack, poker, and bingo in this massive complex, as well as four restaurants, several cocktail bars, and an attached hotel and marina. The hotel features an elaborate indoor pool, fitness center, and child-care center.

Driving south out of Hastings, follow MN 61 to CR 7, or Welch Village Road, to spend some quality winter time on the slopes of **Welch Village**. Welch offers 50 runs of varying difficulty for skiers and snowboarders as well as a terrain park. The Village also provides rustic slopeside rental bunkhouses with shared baths. These accommodations offer the utmost in convenient access for devoted skiers and boarders. You can also rent tubes and

Historic Downtown Hastings

Built during the heyday of river travel, and for a long time the final port reachable year round on the Mississippi, Hastings maintains a strong Victorian sensibility in its architecture. The downtown is a National Register Historic District, known officially as the **East Second Street Commercial Historic District**. Thirty-five buildings constructed before 1900 have retained their beautiful Victorian detailing and Old World charm. A map of the district is available from the Chamber of Commerce or city hall.

In addition to the commercial district, you may wish to explore the **Hastings Second Street Residential District**, comprising homes built prior to 1890. Architectural styles of these homes include Italianate, Greek Revival, and French Second Empire.

Alexis Bailly Vineyard

Head south on MN 61 from Hastings and follow the signs at 170th Street to visit the **Alexis Bailly Vineyard**. Yes, you can grow grapes in Minnesota—it just takes tenacity. Alexis Bailly is Minnesota's first and arguably foremost vineyard. David Bailly planted his first crop of grapes in 1973, against the advice of viticulturists who warned that no grapes could survive a Minnesota winter. By 1978, however, Bailly produced his first vintage. The winery works with classic and new-breed grapes that have been found to withstand extreme cold. In fact, the company's motto is "Where the grapes can suffer." Apparently the suffering works, as Alexis Bailly has won national awards for its wines. Today Bailly's daughter Nan is the winemaker and runs the vineyard, which has an expansive line of wines, including Isis, an ice wine; Voyageur, a blend of French grapes and those developed at the University of Minnesota to withstand winter; and Ratafia, an orange-infused dessert wine. The vineyard is open seasonally for tours and offers numerous special events, including jazz nights and chocolate and cheese tastings. Bring a picnic to enjoy on the grounds, and then enjoy a game of bocce.

canoes in Welch to take out on the Cannon River, and arrange for canoe shuttle services.

The town of Welch is also a juncture for the **Cannon Valley Trail**, a 20-mile paved trail that runs on an old railroad track from Cannon Falls to Red Wing along the Cannon River. The trail winds through shifting terrain that is home to a diverse collection of flora and fauna, including the Minnesota dwarf trout lily, wild turkeys, osprey, pileated woodpeckers, the occasional moose, and the even more rarely seen wood turtle.

Return to MN 61 and travel south to visit Red Wing, which offers innumerable opportunities for outdoor explorations. The drive itself, which veers east to run along the Mississippi River, is part of the Great River Road, a scenic byway that runs from Canada to the Gulf of Mexico. From Red Wing, the Great River Road travels via MN 61 to La Crescent, showcasing 107 miles of river views, forests, small historic river towns and villages, and myriad natural and wildlife experiences.

In Red Wing, learn about local history at the **Goodhue County Historical Society**. This sizable regional museum has extensive collections on numerous aspects of the area's history, spanning archaeology, business, geology, immigration, and agriculture. A clothing exhibition includes sample costumes for kids to try on, and there's a tepee to play in. The society is also in the process of placing signage throughout the county to mark the prior existence of what are now ghost towns.

Near the river, you'll find another interesting experience at the **Red Wing Shoe Museum**. Red Wing Shoes are indeed manufactured in Red Wing, and this small but lively museum in the **Riverfront Centre** features hands-on and historical exhibitions showing how the shoes are made and sold. You'll even get the opportunity to try to build your own shoe.

Another famous local manufacturer has its own museum: the **Red Wing Pottery Museum**, located within the **Pottery Place Historic Center**. Just like the shoes, Red Wing Pottery is made here in Red Wing. Its namesake museum offers displays that illustrate the pottery's manufacturing process and history, as well as an impressive collection of finished objects and historical pieces. The Pottery Place Historic Center itself is worth a visit for its museum, focused on the town's pottery history; and the Pottery Place Mall, located with the Holistic Center in a renovated pottery factory, houses a variety of specialty retailers, including art galleries and stores selling antiques, home furnishings, gifts, and fine chocolates.

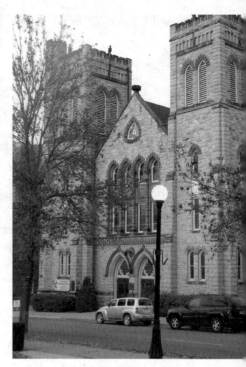

FIRST UNITED METHODIST CHURCH, RED WING

The Sheldon Theatre is named after businessman and former city council member Theodore Sheldon, who donated money to the city to be used in a beneficial but nonsectarian manner. The theater opened in 1904 as an elaborate "jewel box" of a building, full of ornate flourishes in honor of its prominent resident namesake. However, during the Depression, the building was renovated into a movie theater, and much of its architectural grandeur was downscaled. It wasn't until the mid-1980s that the city, with strong support from its residents, decided to restore the Sheldon to its former glory. Today it's host to a wide variety of local, regional, and national arts groups, featuring everything from serious theater to dance to musicals.

Great lodging choices in and around Red Wing are plentiful, but given the town's popularity, it's wise to book ahead. Built in 1875, the **St. James Hotel** offers rooms with a handsome Victorian decor; larger quarters have whirlpools, and two deluxe rooms include spacious seating areas. The **Moondance Inn** is a beautiful stone affair with five spacious guest rooms, all with private bath and fireplaces, and featuring antique furniture and sumptuous decor. **The Candlelight Inn** is a striking Victorian house offering five

CENTRAL PARK BANDSHELL, RED WING

rooms and suites, all with private baths and fireplaces. While each of the rooms is beautifully decorated, the Butternut Suite in particular is a lesson in opulence and luxury. Full breakfast and afternoon appetizers, wine, and lemonade are provided for guests daily. An English Tudor built in 1923 by the former president of the Red Wing Shoe Company, **Golden Lantern Inn** features five lush rooms and suites and several public rooms available to guests. Bedrooms all have private baths, and some offer fireplaces, sitting rooms, and private balconies. Full breakfast is included daily and is available in the dining room or (during warmer months) on the stone patio. During the summer, guests have access to the lavish gardens behind the inn. Another great choice for lodging is the **Pratt-Taber Inn**, a restored 1876 bed-and-breakfast offering four rooms, all with private baths and fireplaces.

THE SHELDON THEATRE, RED WING

Take MN 61 for 4 miles south of Red Wing to Wildwood Lane to find **Round Barn Farm**, built in 1861. Round Barn offers five spacious rooms beautifully decorated in vintage country style, complete with antique furniture, private baths, and fireplaces or Franklin stoves. Breakfast is provided daily in the dining room, which features a massive limestone fireplace. The property, complete with walking trails and a gazebo, is located on 35 acres.

THE ST. JAMES HOTEL, RED WING

Dining options in Red Wing abound. Located in the St. James Hotel, the **Port Restaurant** offers warm and elegant atmosphere alongside steakhouse fare with a few unconventional twists. The food here is excellent, and reservations are strongly recommended. Also located at the St. James Hotel is the **Veranda**, open daily for breakfast and lunch. At the **Staghead Gastropub**, you'll find an ambitious bar menu as well as a wide variety of beers and cocktails. For a more casual meal, you might try **Liberty's,** open daily for breakfast, lunch, and dinner. The menu aims to please with Italian, Mexican, burgers, and steaks; breakfast includes all-you-can-eat pancakes. Not only will Liberty's deliver throughout Red Wing, they also provide free shuttle service to and from boats and hotels. Another good bet is Bev's Café, the oldest restaurant in Red Wing, providing substantial, tasty breakfasts and lunches (and dinners on Fridays).

The small town of Frontenac is a few miles south of Red Wing on MN 61, and nearby is **Old Frontenac,** where trains long ago brought wealthier visitors who built summer homes along Lake Pepin. Today, the whole of Old Frontenac is included on the National Register of Historic Places. In between Frontenac and Old Frontenac is **Frontenac State Park**. If you'd like a more in-depth nature experience, plan for an extended visit. With over 250 species of birds recorded on site, the park is especially beloved by birdwatchers. Plenty of other wildlife make their home in the park, and even buffalo are occasionally spotted. Camping, hiking, and winter sledding are among some of the activities available across the park's prairie, forest, and river bluff settings.

Not far from Frontenac is Lake City, also on the shores of Lake Pepin and home to **Lake City Marina**, the Mississippi's largest recreational marina. A notable piece of Lake City history, waterskiing was invented here by Ralph Samuelson in 1922. The city's main park, **Hok-Si-La Park,** spans 250 lakeside acres, offering impressive views across the lake as well as sandy beaches, tent camping, and a mile-long trail along the Mississippi. Nearby

OLD FRONTENAC

is **Nosh**, a trendy Mediterranean-meets-Midwest restaurant featuring locally sourced ingredients. The main courses are spectacular, but an excellent meal is also made from dining off the restaurant's small plates menu. Save room for dessert.

For casual digs, you can't go wrong with either the **Chickadee Cottage Café** or the **Whistle Stop Café**, both serving up great diner food.

IN THE AREA

Accommodations

THE CANDLELIGHT INN, 818 West 3rd Street, Red Wing. Call 651-388-8034. Website: www.candlelightinn-redwing.com.

THE GOLDEN LANTERN INN, 721 East Avenue, Red Wing. Call 888-288-3315. Website: www.goldenlantern.com.

MOONDANCE INN, 1105 West 4th Street, Red Wing. Call 651-388-8145; 866-388-8145. Website: www.moondanceinn.com/index.html.

PRATT-TABER INN, 706 West 4th Street, Red Wing. Call 651-388-7392. Website: www.pratttaber.com.

ROUND BARN FARM, 28650 Wildwood Lane, Red Wing. Call 651-385-9250. Website: www.roundbarnfarm.com.

THE ST. JAMES HOTEL, 406 Main Street, Red Wing. Call 800-252-1875. Website: www.st-james-hotel.com.

Attractions and Recreation

ALEXIS BAILLY VINEYARD, 18200 Kirby Avenue, Hastings. Call 651-437-1413. Website: www.abvwines.com.

THE BRIAR PATCH, 103 East 2nd Street, Hastings. Call 651-437-4400.

CANNON VALLEY TRAIL, 825 Cannon River Avenue, Cannon Falls. Call 507-263-0508. Website: cannonvalleytrail.com.

CARPENTER ST. CROIX VALLEY NATURE CENTER, 12805 St. Croix Trail South, Hastings. Call 651-437-4359. Website: carpenternaturecenter.org.

THE EMPORIUM, 213 East 2nd Street, Hastings. Call 651-438-5444. Website: www.facebook.com/Emporium-1486422118290934.

FRONTENAC STATE PARK, 29223 CR 28 Boulevard, Frontenac. Call 651-345-3401. Website: www.dnr.state.mn.us/state_parks/frontenac/index.html.

GOODHUE COUNTY HISTORICAL SOCIETY, 1166 Oak Street, Red Wing. Call 651-388-6024. Website: goodhuecountyhistory.org.

HOK-SI-LA-PARK, 2500 North MN 61, Lake City. Call 651-345-3855. Website: www.hoksilapark.org.

LAKE CITY MARINA, 201 South Franklin Street, Lake City. Call 651-345-4211. Website: www.lakecity.org.

THE LEDUC HOUSE, 1629 Vermillion Street, Hastings. Call 651-438-8480. Website: www.dakotahistory.org/LeDuc-historic-estate.

MISSISSIPPI CLAYWORKS, 214 East 2nd Street, Hastings. Website: www.mississippiclayworks.com.

POTTERY PLACE MALL AND ANTIQUES, 2000 Old West Main Street, Red Wing. Call 651-388-7765. Website: www.potteryplaceantiques.com.

RED WING SHOE MUSEUM, 315 Main Street, Red Wing. Call 651-388-6233. Website: www.redwingshoes.com.

SCANDINAVIAN MARKETPLACE, 218 East 2nd Street, Hastings. Call 651-438-9183.

SHELDON THEATRE, 443 West 3rd Street, Red Wing. Call 651-388-8700; 800-899-5759. Website: www.sheldontheatre.org.

TREASURE ISLAND RESORT AND CASINO, 5734 Sturgeon Lake Road, Welch. Call 800-222-7077. Website: www.treasureislandcasino.com.

VERMILLION FALLS PARK, 215 East 21st Street, Hastings. Call 651-480-6175.

WELCH VILLAGE, 26685 CR 7 Boulevard, Welch. Call 651-258-4567. Website: www.welchvillage.com.

Dining

BEV'S CAFÉ, 221 Bush Street, Red Wing. Call 651-388-5227. Great small-town diner food, hearty breakfasts, and hot plates. Website: www.bevscafe.com.

THE BIERSTUBE, 109 West 11th Street, Hastings. Call 651-437-8259. German specialties, steaks, and burgers. Website: www.thebierstube.com.

CHICKADEE COTTAGE CAFÉ, 317 North Lakeshore Drive, Lake City. Call 6551-456-5155. Home-cooked breakfasts and lunches, plus Friday night dinners. Website: www.chickadeecottagecafe.com.

LIBERTY'S, 303 West 3rd Street, Red Wing. Call 651-388-8877. Extensive menu to fit any appetite. Website: www.libertysrestaurant.com.

LOCK AND DAM EATERY, 101 East 2nd Street, Hastings. Call 651-319-0906. Burgers, Italian, and Mexican fare. Website: www.lockanddameatery.com.

ME & JULIO, 350 West 33rd Street, Hastings. Call 651-438-2520. Made-from-scratch Mexican food. Website: www.meandjuliomn.com.

NOSH, 310 ½ South Washington Street, Lake City. Call 651-345-2425. Upscale cuisine with a frequently changing menu. Website: www.nosh restaurant.com.

THE ONION GRILLE, 100 Sibley Street, Hastings. Call 651-437-7577. Gourmet burgers, sandwiches, and pizza. Website: www.theoniongrille.com.

THE PORT RESTAURANT AND THE VERANDA, both in the St. James Hotel, 406 Main Street, Red Wing. Call 800-252-1875. The Port offers fine dining, while the Veranda serves a more casual breakfast and lunch. Website: www.st-james-hotel.com.

STAGHEAD GASTROPUB, 219 Bush Street, Red Wing. Call 651-212-6494. Upscale American fare. Website: www.thestaghead.com.

WHISTLE STOP CAFÉ, 55026 US 63, Lake City. Hearty home-cooked meals. Call 651-345-5800.

WIEDERHOLT'S SUPPER CLUB, 14535 East 240th Street, Hastings. Call 651-437-3528; 507-263-2263. Hearty supper club steaks and ribs. Website: www.wiederholtssupperclub.com.

Other Contacts

HASTINGS AREA CHAMBER OF COMMERCE, 314 Vermillion Street, Suite 100, Hastings. Call 651-437-6775. Website: www.hastingsmn.org.

LAKE CITY CHAMBER OF COMMERCE, 101 West Center Street, Lake City. Call 651-345-4123. Website: www.lakecity.org.

RED WING CONVENTION AND VISITOR BUREAU, 420 Levee Street, Red Wing. Call 651-385-5934. Website: www.redwing.org.

11

LA CRESCENT TO WABASHA
Apple Blossoms and River Towns

ESTIMATED DISTANCE: 200 miles

ESTIMATED TIME: 4 hours

GETTING THERE: From the Twin Cities, take I-494 to MN 55, then take MN 56 to MN 61. Follow MN 61 to La Crescent.

HIGHLIGHTS: The short but lovely Apple Blossom Scenic Drive; the views from Great River Bluff State Park; the Museum of Marine Art in Winona; the National Eagle Center in Wabasha; and the steep (but worthwhile) bluff climb at John A. Latsch State Park. For a longer trip, combine this journey with the Northern Mississippi Bluff Country route (Chapter 10).

The southeastern corner of the state, bordered by the mighty Mississippi to the east, features some of the loveliest terrain in Minnesota: river valleys, rolling hills, woods and wildflowers in season, and one charming small town after another, including some of the oldest in the state featuring intact historic buildings and landmarks. Unlike the state's northern reaches, which were leveled and reconfigured during the last ice age, the bluff country presents a variable landscape that includes both 500-foot limestone escarpments and deep valleys. The climate here is slightly different too, warmer and with more rainfall, leading to vegetation not seen elsewhere in the state, including black walnut trees. The region is also home to Minnesota's only poisonous snakes, the timber rattlesnake and the massasauga, which reside mostly in the bluffs and swampy areas close to the river. These snakes are, however, as timid of humans as we are of them, and are slow to strike.

Bike trails abound, many of which are paved and can be used for cross-country skiing in the winter months. The state parks along the way

LEFT: APPLE BLOSSOM SCENIC DRIVE

offer hiking trails that provide expansive views of the Mississippi and neighboring Wisconsin.

The driving route involves the southeastern Minnesota section of the **Great River Road National Scenic Byway**, a nearly 575-mile route that travels with the Mississippi within the state up to its origins in Itasca State Park. South of Minnesota, of course, the Byway extends all the way to Louisiana. If you were to take the time to follow the entire Minnesota route, you would see a wide variety of scenery as the landscape changes from north to south; within this section, you'll see some of the most striking river bluff scenery in the state.

Starting in La Crescent, you can pick up the **Apple Blossom Scenic Drive** by following County Route 29 (CR 29, also known as North Elm Street) just outside the city center. Shortly after starting the Drive, the road crosses

GREAT RIVER BLUFFS STATE PARK

county lines and becomes CR 1, eventually turning into CR 12 before you arrive in Nodine. Continue north on CR 12 until you reach CR 3, then follow that road back to MN 61 to complete the Drive.

This short (only 17 miles) but lovely route takes you through rolling hills filled with apple orchards. Spring and early summer are great seasons for visiting, when the trees are in full blossom, but don't discount the beauty that fall brings when the leaves change. Fall is also a great time to shop along the Drive, as orchard owners sell not only apples and apple goods like cider and pastries, but pumpkins as well. Even winter is a good time to explore the Drive, with blankets of snow providing a serene backdrop for the arrival of winter birds.

Toward the end of the Apple Blossom Scenic Drive, you'll reach **Great River Bluffs State Park**, the entrance to which is on CR 3. The park is located within the **Richard J. Dorer Memorial Hardwood Forest** and contains acres of red and white pine, maple-basswood, old hickory, and ash, as well as areas of "goat prairie," or dry prairie, a low-moisture grassland

THE PICKWICK MILL

with bedrock beneath it that is inhospitable to trees. The park holds two Scientific Nature Areas, King's and Queen's Bluffs. King's Bluff is a popular hiking trail, especially for birders: the spectacular overlook of the Mississippi is a great spot to watch for eagles and hawks. Hiking in the warmer months and cross-country skiing, snowshoeing, and skate-skiing in the winter keep this park busy year-round.

Follow CR 3 north to MN 61 and continue driving northwest to CR 7. Turning onto CR 7 will bring you to the little town of Pickwick, home of the **Pickwick Mill**. The mill, which operated as both a gristmill and a sawmill, opened shortly before the Civil War and ran 24 hours a day throughout the war before settling into life as a flour mill afterward. Its multiple floors are open to the public, with self-guided tours that explain the function of each floor. The location, right on Big Trout Creek, makes a great stop for a picnic.

Returning to MN 61 and resuming a northern track, take another detour

THE BUNNELL HOUSE, HOMER

LAKE WINONA

south of Winona when you reach US 14. Just off MN 61 is the **Bunnell House**, a Gothic Revival home built in the 1850s by the Bunnells, a pioneer and fur-trading family who enjoyed the natural habitat around them. Its white pine siding has never been painted, giving it a starkly weathered look.

Shortly after leaving the Bunnell House, you'll arrive in Winona. The city of Winona is defined by water: its northern boundary is dictated by the Mississippi River, and its southern boundary is formed by Lake Winona. The city itself rests on a sandbar.

Winona's name came from the Dakota word *wenonah*, or "firstborn daughter." Legend has it that Wenonah was a Dakota girl who, rather than accepting a forced marriage, leapt off a cliff to her death. There is a statue in her honor in the city's center.

Winona's history is rooted in shipping. Founded in 1851, it was already a bustling river town when the railroad arrived in 1862, further enhancing the city's prominence as a center of business and agriculture. By 1900, Winona had more millionaires per capita than any other city in the United States.

Although times have changed and Winona isn't as economically prosperous as it was a century ago, historically it's a treasure trove for visitors. Downtown Winona lists more than 100 buildings on the National Register of Historic Places, with most constructed between 1857 and 1916 in Italianate or Queen Anne style. The best way to take in this large collection of

Victorian commercial buildings (the largest concentration in Minnesota) is on foot. Free walking tour brochures of the district are available from the visitor center on Huff Street, immediately after you turn right off MN 61. Located right on the shores of Lake Winona, the center makes a good spot for a picnic too.

More history can be discovered at the **Winona County History Center**, which underwent an expansion in 2010. A large and fascinating collection of local and regional historic exhibitions, covering the usual (geological history, river trade) as well as the less so (Cold War parking plans in the event of nuclear war). The museum is kid-friendly, with lots of hands-on activities, including a climb-through cave and river steamboat, all in an intriguing and architecturally eclectic building reflecting both Winona's past and present.

The Arches Museum of Pioneer Life is a tribute to the long-lost days of roadside museums. It contains the collection of Walter Rahn, who apparently was fascinated with pioneer life and either collected or built models himself to illustrate their uses. The grounds also have a log cabin and a one-room schoolhouse.

The Polish Cultural Institute pays homage to the point in history when Winona had the largest concentration of Polish immigrants in the United States. The museum reflects that heritage with antiques, folk art, religious items, and displays detailing the immigrants' experience.

One of Winona's prominent employers is J.R. Watkins, the maker of natural home care, remedies, food products, and flavorings. The company has

THE MINNESOTA MARINE ART MUSEUM, WINONA

The Stained-Glass Capital

At the peak of its economic history, Winona was full of millionaires, and those looking to use their discretionary income to build were fond of stained glass. Consequently, Winona has a dozen elaborate buildings, both commercial and religious, that have striking stained-glass collections. Even though most builders no longer use this beautiful (and expensive) architectural adornment, the city remains home to several stained-glass studios with contemporary craftsmen creating and restoring stained-glass around the United States. To see examples of the historical stained glass, you can visit the **J.R. Watkins Company, Merchants National Bank, Winona National Bank** (which also holds the African Safari Museum, collected by the bank's original owner, inside), the **Church of St. Stanislaus Kostka**, and the **Chapel of St. Mary of the Angels**. Two prominent studios working in stained glass today include the **Hauser Art Glass Co.**, the largest stained-glass company in the United States, and **Cathedral Crafts**, both of which offer group tours with advance arrangements. The Winona Visitor Center has a brochure detailing the companies' locations.

been in Winona since 1868, and its history is on display at the **Watkins Museum and Store**, housed in the company's former print shop in its large manufacturing complex.

A newer gem is the **Minnesota Marine Art Museum**. Opened in 2006, this attractive museum, located along the Mississippi, holds an extensive collection of marine art, folk art, photography, maps, and historical displays, all highlighting the diversity of marine life. The permanent collection includes pieces by artists like Homer, Renoir, and Monet. Be sure to slow down as you're driving to and from the museum, so you can enjoy the eclectic groups of houseboats clustered along the river.

Winona has several city parks, some of which are of special interest. Only a city block in size, **Windom Park** is surrounded by several Victorian houses (some of which are listed on the National Register of Historic Places) and features a gazebo and fountain with a sculpture of the legendary Wenonah. **Lake Park**, on the shores of Lake Winona, is a popular city park with an attractive rose garden (**C. A. Rohrer Rose Garden**), fishing piers, and a band shell with weekly live concerts during the summer. Just outside downtown Winona is **Garvin Heights City Park**, nearly 600 feet above the city, offering wide-ranging views of Winona and the river.

Like so many of the river towns in the state, Winona has some lovely historic bed-and-breakfasts. Built in 1886, the **Alexander Mansion Bed & Breakfast** has four elaborately detailed Victorian rooms (all with private bath) and an extensive screened porch for guests to enjoy. Rates include a five-course breakfast and evening hors d'oeuvres. Constructed by lumber baron Conrad Bohn, the **Carriage House Bed & Breakfast** was literally that—it originally housed six carriages and several horses. Today, the renovated house holds four bedrooms, all with private baths, decorated in a cozy Victorian style. Breakfast is included daily, as is the use of single and tandem bicycles and, by prearrangement, a Model A Ford for local touring. The **Windom Park Bed & Breakfast**, located near Windom Park, is a Colonial Revival house built in 1900. Guests can choose among four beautiful rooms in the main house, all with private bath, and two lofts in the nearby carriage house. The lofts have fireplaces and two-person hot tubs. Breakfast is included each day, and guests are encouraged to use the other public rooms, which are impeccably appointed. **The Village House Inn** is nestled into the Mississippi River bluffs and offers four guest rooms, each with private bath, while the **Garvin Crest Guest House** is a single-accommodation rental with a full kitchen and bath, facing west and tucked into pine trees.

Just outside of Winona is **Briggs Farm**, located on 500 acres of farmland and wooded bluffland. The whole-house rental includes three rooms, two bathrooms, and access to 15 miles of trails for hiking and cross-country skiing.

There are plenty of places in Winona to get a good meal. **Signatures** is one of the posher restaurants in the area, along with the **Boat House**. **Betty Jo Byoloski's** is a casual alternative, serving burgers, soups, and chili. Other informal options include the **Jefferson Pub & Grill**, a good spot for soup and hearty sandwiches, and the **Acoustic Café,** offering sandwiches and breakfasts that feature fresh-baked breads.

Just outside downtown Winona is **Garvin Heights Vineyards**, which you can reach by following Huff Street back to and across MN 61, where it turns into CR 44, or Garvin Heights Road. Garvin Heights makes wine from locally grown grapes, including some grown at the vineyard. Besides grapes, the vineyard uses raspberries and cranberries. The Garvin Heights tasting room is open seasonally.

Shortly after departing Winona on MN 61, another side trip is possible at MN 248. Turn left onto the state highway and travel about 3 miles to CR 25, or State Street. You've arrived in the little town of Rollingstone. Turning onto Main Street will bring you to the **Rollingstone Luxembourg Heritage Museum**. The town of Rollingstone was founded by members of Luxembourg's Grand Duchy in the mid-1800s, and at one point it was the largest settlement of Luxembourg emigrants in the country. The Rollingstone Luxembourg Heritage Museum pays tribute to that history in the former city hall and fire station, built in 1900.

A few miles north of the Rollingstone exit on MN 61 is **John A. Latsch State Park**. One of the lesser-visited state parks, it's worth a trip if you're ready for some exercise; there's a ½-mile stairway hike up to the top of bluffs that leads to outstanding views of the Mississippi and surrounding bluffs.

The final leg of this journey brings you through Kellogg and Wabasha, two of the oldest towns on the upper Mississippi, the latter having been founded in 1826 and Kellogg shortly after that. One of Wabasha's claims to fame is as the setting for the movies *Grumpy Old Men* and *Grumpier Old Men*. But it has several other amenities that are equally valuable and entertaining (if not more so), one of which is its population of eagles that can be spotted year round, but particularly in the winter.

THE ROLLINGSTONE LUXEMBOURG HERITAGE MUSEUM, ROLLINGSTONE

River activities are popular in Wabasha. Houseboat and pontoon rentals can be arranged through **Great River Houseboats**, or you can enjoy a sunset or moonlight sail aboard sailboats through **Sail Pepin**.

Fun of a different kind can be found in **Kellogg's Lark Toys**. LARK stands for "Lost Art Revival by Kreofsky," and vintage toys, many made of wood, are produced and sold here, along with children's books. This massive toy complex (more than 30,000 square feet) is more than a store; it's a playground. A working carousel offers rides, and a mini-golf course is available during the warmer months. You'll also find a café on-site.

THE VIEW FROM JOHN A. LATSCH STATE PARK

Just north of Wabasha on MN 61 is the **Wabasha County Historical Museum**. On the second floor of a former schoolhouse, this small museum is a humble affair, but it does have some items of interest to fans of Laura Ingalls Wilder.

Lodging options abound. **Eagles on the River** and **Historic Anderson House Hotel** offers full condos with fireplaces, kitchens, and hot tubs. For bed-and-breakfast enthusiasts, the **River Nest Bed & Breakfast** is a newer construction offering two private suites, both overlooking the river, while **American Eagle Bluff Bed & Breakfast** is in a secluded

THE STAIRS AT JOHN A. LATSCH STATE PARK

The National Eagle Center

The **National Eagle Center**, located on the Mississippi River banks, is a 14,000-square-foot interpretive center with resident eagles, a viewing deck, housing for injured or sick eagles, exhibitions with preserved animals and other artifacts, and demonstration and classroom areas. Five "superstars," or rescued eagles from around the country, are cared for in a sanctuary environment and give visitors a close-up view. The Wabasha area counts more than 100 bald eagles as year-round residents, and thousands more migrate through the region between October and April. Every autumn the NEC holds a special "deck opening" event to mark the arrival of bald eagles for the winter; this area of the Mississippi has one of the largest concentrations of bald eagles in the continental United States.

THE NATIONAL EAGLE CENTER, WABASHA

forest overlooking the Mississippi and Chippewa Rivers, with just two guest suites with private baths. **The Coffee Mill Motel & Suites** offers several rooms and suites with easy access to Wabasha.

Dining presents a number of good options as well. **Slippery's**, which gets mentioned in the *Grumpy Old Men* movies, offers river views and boat-in dining. Burgers, steaks, and Mexican items are served in hearty portions. **The Olde Triangle Pub** is a casual, friendly neighborhood spot with good pub grub, including bangers and mash and Irish stew. **The Town & Country Café** is a classic small-town diner with good home cooking.

IN THE AREA

Accommodations

ALEXANDER MANSION BED & BREAKFAST, 274 East Broadway Street, Winona. Call: 507-474-4224. Website: www.alexandermansionbb.com.

AMERICAN EAGLE BLUFF BED & BREAKFAST, Read's Landing. Call 651-564-0372. Website: www.facebook.com/America-Eagle-Bluff-Bed-and -Breakfast-1950660505535491.

BRIGGS FARM, 27171 CR 9, Winona. Call 507-450-9902. Whole-house rental with three bedrooms and two baths. Website: www.briggsoutdoors .com.

CARRIAGE HOUSE BED & BREAKFAST, 420 Main Street, Winona. Call 507-452-8256. Website: www.chbb.com.

COFFEE MILL MOTEL & SUITES, 90 Coulee Way, Wabasha. Call 651-565-4561; 877-775-1366. Inn with rooms and suites conveniently located near Wabasha. Website: www.coffeemillinnandsuites.com.

EAGLES ON THE RIVER AND HISTORIC ANDERSON HOUSE HOTEL, 152 West Main Street, Wabasha. Call: 651-565-3509; 800-482-8288. Website: www.eaglesontheriver.com.

GARVIN CREST GUEST HOUSE IN THE PINES, 1735 Garvin Heights Road, Winona. Call 507-459-9361. Charming guesthouse tucked into a stand of pine trees. Website: www.garvincrest.com.

THE RIVER NEST BED & BREAKFAST, 20073 CR 77, Reads Landing. Call 651-560-4077. Website: www.therivernest.com.

VILLAGE HOUSE INN, 72 College Road, Winona. Call 507-454-4322. Charming inn with four rooms nestled into the Mississippi River Bluffs. Website: www.villagehouseinn.com.

WINDOM PARK BED & BREAKFAST, 3369 West Broadway, Winona. Call 507-457-9515; 866-737-1719. Website: www.windompark.com.

Attractions and Recreation

ARCHES MUSEUM OF PIONEER LIFE, US 14. Call 507-523-2111. Website: www.winonahistory.org.

BUNNELL HOUSE, 36106 Homer Road, Winona. Call 507-454-2723. Website: www.bunnellfamily.com.

CHAPEL OF ST. MARY OF THE ANGELS, 1155 West Wabasha, Winona. Call 507-453-5550. Website: www.facebook.com/pages/Chapel-of-Saint -Mary-of-the-Angels/144705058883143.

CHURCH OF ST. STANISLAUS KOSTKA, 625 East 4th Street, Winona. Call 507-452-5430. Website: www.ssk-sjn.weconnect.com.

DOWNTOWN NATIONAL REGISTER OF HISTORIC PLACES DISTRICT, Free walking tour brochures available from the Convention and Visitor Bureau, the visitor center at 924 Huff Street, or the **Winona County Historical Society.** Website: visitwinona.com.

GARVIN HEIGHTS CITY PARK, Garvin Heights Road, Winona.

GARVIN HEIGHTS VINEYARDS, 2255 Garvin Heights Road, Winona. Call 507-313-1917. Website: www.ghvwine.com.

GREAT RIVER BLUFFS STATE PARK, 43605 Kipp Drive, Winona. Call 507-643-6849. Website: www.dnr.state.mn.us/state_parks/great_river_bluffs /index.html.

GREAT RIVER HOUSEBOATS, 125 Beach Harbor Road, Alma, Wisconsin. Call 608-685-3333. Website: www.greatriverhouseboats.com.

JOHN A. LATSCH STATE PARK, US 61, Winona. Call 507-312-2300. Website: www.dnr.state.mn.us/state_parks/john_latsch/index.html.

LAKE PARK, 900 Huff Street, Winona.

LARK TOYS, 63604 170th Avenue, Kellogg. Call 507-767-3387. Website: www.larktoys.com.

MERCHANTS NATIONAL BANK, 102 East 3rd Street, Winona. Call 507-457-1100. Website: www.merchantsbank.com.

MINNESOTA MARINE ART MUSEUM, 800 Riverview Drive, Winona. Call 507-474-6626; 866-940-6626. Website: www.mmam.org.

NATIONAL EAGLE CENTER, 50 Pembroke Avenue, Wabasha. Call 651-565-4989; 877-332-4537. Website: www.nationaleaglecenter.org.

PICKWICK MILL, 24813 CR 7, Pickwick. Call 507-457-0499. Website: www.pickwickmill.org.

POLISH MUSEUM OF MINNESOTA, 102 Liberty Street, Winona. Call 507-454-3431. Website: www.polishmuseumwinona.org.

ROLLINGSTONE LUXEMBOURG HERITAGE MUSEUM, 98 Main Street, Rollingstone. Call 507-689-2330; 507-452-8268. Open Sundays May–October.

SAIL PEPIN, 400 First Street, Pepin, WI. Call 715-442-2250. Website: www.sailpepin.com.

WABASHA COUNTY HISTORICAL SOCIETY MUSEUM, 70537 206th Avenue, Reads Landing. Call 651-343-7072. Website: www.wabashacountyhistory.org.

WATKINS MUSEUM AND STORE, East 3rd Street, Winona. Call 507-457-6095.

WINDOM PARK, Huff and West Broadway Street, Winona.

WINONA COUNTY HISTORY CENTER, 160 Johnson Street, Winona. Call 507-454-2723. Website: www.winonahistory.org.

WINONA NATIONAL BANK, 204 Main Street, Winona. Website: www.winonanationalbank.com.

Dining

ACOUSTIC CAFÉ, 77 Lafeyette, Winona. Call 507-453-0394. Sandwiches, soups, treats, and live music. Website: www.acousticcafewinona.com.

BETTY JO BYOLOSKI'S, 66 Center Street, Winona. Call 507-454-2687. Burgers, soups, and daily specials. Website: www.bettyjos.com.

BOAT HOUSE, 2 Johnson Street, Winona. Call 507-474-6550. Seasonal upscale American food. Website: www.boathousewinona.com.

JEFFERSON PUB & GRILL, 58 Center Street, Winona. Hearty pub sandwiches and soups. Call 507-452-2718. Website: www.jeffersonpubandgrill .com.

THE OLDE TRIANGLE PUB, 219 Main Street, Wabasha. Call 651-565-0256. A casual, friendly neighborhood spot with good pub grub, including bangers and mash and Irish stew. Website: www.theoldetrianglepub.com.

SIGNATURES, 22852 CR 17, Winona. Steaks, seafood, and house-made pasta. Call 507-454-3767. Website: www.signatureswinona.com.

SLIPPERY'S, 10 Church Avenue, Wabasha. Call 651-565-4748. Seafood and steaks served in hearty portions in a restaurant with great views of the river. Website: slipperys.com.

TOWN & COUNTRY CAFÉ, 320 East Belvidere Avenue, Kellogg. Call 507-767-4592. Small-town diner with home cooking. Website: www .facebook.com/pages/category/American-Restaurant/Town-Country-Cafe -112306715511308.

Other Contacts

APPLE BLOSSOM SCENIC DRIVE, La Crescent. Website: www.lacrescent mn.com/apple-blossom-scenic-drive.

VISIT WINONA, 924 Huff Street, Winona. Call 800-657-4972. Website: visitwinona.com.

WABASHA KELLOGG CHAMBER OF COMMERCE, 122 Main Street, Wabasha. Call 651-565-4158; 800-565-4158. Website: www.wabashamn.org.

WINONA COUNTY HISTORICAL SOCIETY, 160 Johnson Street, Wabasha. Call 507-454-2723. Website: www.winonahistory.org.

12

FARMLAND AND HISTORIC TOWNS

ESTIMATED DISTANCE: 55 miles

ESTIMATED TIME: 2 hours

GETTING THERE: From the Twin Cities, take MN 62 west to US 212 west. Follow US 212 nearly 10 miles to Jonathan Carver Parkway. Turn left onto Jonathan Carver Parkway, then drive a little over a mile to reach West 6th Street. Turn left onto 6th Street, then drive a little under a mile to Broadway Street, then turn right.

HIGHLIGHTS: Historic Carver; the charming small towns of Chaska, Jordan, and New Prague and the vast farmland between them; the college town of Northfield.

This route could be carried out in reverse before continuing to the Minnesota River Valley Part 1 drive in Chapter 13.

The rich farmland in abundance along the Minnesota River area was once home to many European immigrants, especially those from what was then called Bohemia and later became Czechoslovakia in the late 1800s. In fact, for many decades the town of New Prague had a large mural of Czechoslovakia on a grocery store. Over the decades, small homestead farms grew to become sweeping acreages of corn and soybeans, and dairy and beef cattle ranches. The ancestry of the area, apparent in town names like New Prague (which is pronounced here as "praygue," not "prahgue"), also emerges in popular annual festivals, such as New Prague's Dožínky Festival.

The town of Carver is situated along the Minnesota River, a location which afforded it prominence in the mid-1800s. For many years, Carver served as a key site for cargo transfers among steamboats and barges on

LEFT: FARMHOUSE MARKET, NEW PRAGUE

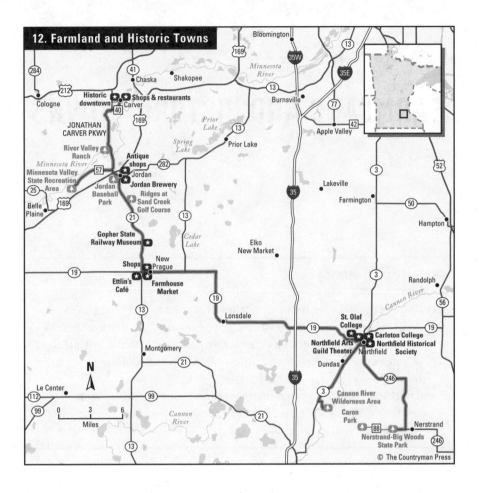

the Minnesota River. However, the arrival of the Minneapolis and St. Louis Railway in 1871 generated a change in the way goods were transported, and Carver's role diminished soon thereafter.

Today nearly all of Carver's downtown, a total of 91 buildings and structures constructed between 1850–1925, is listed on the National Register of Historic Places. Tucked into a series of valleys and hills, Carver is a fun place to park the car and get out and explore. For people who want more than a quick walk, the town is adjacent to a number of interconnected trails that are ideal for walking, running, and biking.

Carver is also home to several "occasional" shops. Often found in smaller towns beyond the metro Twin Cities, these shops have limited hours, open either a few days a week or per month. Hours vary by store, so it's best to check before visiting. But if you catch them open, you may want to drop by **All Things Fabulous**, which sells women's clothes and accessories; and **Sweeter Times**, a vintage candy shop housed in a former gas station.

HISTORIC CARVER

Riverside Art Studio and Gallery, Mustard Moon, the Good Junk Garage, and **Rosehips and Willow,** all purveyors of antiques and vintage, are also worth a browse.

Carver is home to two bar-and-grills serving up hearty sandwiches and entrées: **Harvey's Bar** and **Lisa's Place,** the latter housed in a historic building that was the site of the only known murder in Carver's history.

When leaving Carver, take Broadway Street southeast to West Main Street, also known as CR 40. Turn right and take CR 40 for approximately 1½ miles, then take a left onto Jonathan Carver Parkway. About ½-mile after turning onto Jonathan Carver Parkway, the parkway continues by turning left. Take the left turn and continue a little over 8 miles to Jordan.

Before arriving in Jordan, however, there's an opportunity to visit **River Valley Ranch.** With some preplanning, you can reserve horseback riding and trail rides along the Minnesota River, one of the most scenic areas in this part of the state. The Ranch is open May through October only.

SWEETER TIMES, CARVER

NICOLIN MANSION BED & BREAKFAST, JORDAN

Closer to Jordan is the **Minnesota State Valley Recreation Area**. This area along the Minnesota River offers hiking and horseback riding trails, paved and mountain bike trails, and areas for wildlife spotting. It was also an important location in the US-Dakota War of 1862.

The Recreation Area is just outside of Jordan itself. Founded in 1854 to take advantage of the proximity to the Minnesota River, Jordan's historic part of town is filled with grand old stone buildings tucked into steep river bluffs. Grab a bite for breakfast or lunch at the **Feed Mill** before strolling the small main part of town. There, visitors will find numerous antique shops, including **Treasure Chest Antiques**, **the Jordan Junker**, and **LB Antiques**. There are also two fun women's shops here: **Sassy Kat Boutique** and **Bluff Creek Boutique**, which sell women's clothes and accessories, along with gift items. If you're looking to make a long weekend trip out of this route, consider booking a room at the **Nicolin Mansion Bed & Breakfast**, right on the main street through town and across from the **Roets Jordan Brewery Co**. The front porch of the bed-and-breakfast also has brochures offered by the local history center for self-guided walking tours of Jordan's historic sites.

Behind the Feed Mill is the town's pride and joy, **the Jordan Baseball Park**, known locally as the Mini Met, adjacent to beautiful Sand Creek. Nearby is **Pekarna Meat Market**, a five-generation-family-owned meat shop, a great place to grab some smoked-in-house summer sausage and beef sticks for road food.

Turn south onto MN 21 from Jordan to take a 9-mile drive to New Prague. This part of the state is heavily agricultural, and the drive weaves through rolling fields, which, in season, are full of corn and soybean plants, with wide blue skies above. Right outside of Jordan is the **Ridges at Sand Creek Golf Course**, designed by Joel Goldstrand, and further down the road is the **Gopher State Railway Museum**. Truly a labor of love, this volunteer-run organization doesn't look like much more than a collection of old train cars on a piece of farmland, but if you happen to be around on the first Saturday of the month from May-October, stop by and check out the showpiece: A vintage train car likely to have been the private rail car of none other than

The Jordan Brewery

Just before you leave the historic downtown of Jordan, you'll see a lovely old limestone building on the left side of MN 21, pitched dramatically against the town's steepest bluffs. This is the old **Jordan Brewery**, now listed on the National Register of Historic Places. Originally built around 1868 by local businessman Frank Nicolin, it was used to open a general store and brewery. The hill behind the old brewery is dotted with storage caves that the brewery used to age their products. During Prohibition, the brewery was converted to a hatchery, and eggs were stored in the caves. Eventually it was purchased by the Mankato Brewery, which later closed the facility a few years after a devastating fire. The building went through a long period of decline and changing of hands before the Roets family bought it in 2013, intending to turn it back into a brewery. But an enormous hillslide during heavy rains in 2014 interrupted plans, and the Roets' brewery moved down the street instead. In 2015, the state of Minnesota granted Jordan funds to study what it would take to stabilize the hill and repair the building, and reconstruction began in 2016. Today the building houses both apartments and some retail ventures, including the **Corner Peddler** and the **ReFoundry**.

THE OLD JORDAN BREWERY

railway magnate James J. Hill. As the volunteers continue to fundraise, they hope to build a full museum and include more historically important pieces.

New Prague, as can be guessed from its name, was settled by Czech settlers in the mid-1800s and was first named Praha, then Prague, then New Prague in 1884. The area surrounding the town is primarily agricultural, but industry also developed, which has allowed the town to thrive beyond its initial farm roots.

Take MN 21 until you reach Main Street, also called MN 19. Turn left and enjoy a several-blocks drive through New Prague's historic downtown. Parking is free and abundant, and there are several shops worth visiting, including **Humble Pie Gift Shop, Mainstream Boutique, Merchants on Main, The Refinery Boutique,** and **Vintique Vintage Jewelry,** offering everything from antiques to jewelry to clothing and accessories.

For an experience unique to New Prague, visit the **Farmhouse Market**. This purveyor of local and organic foods and products operates under an unusual business model: The market is only open to the public three hours a day, three days a week. The rest of the time it's accessible to people who purchase an annual membership and have key cards to let themselves in. For a quick visit, it's good idea to plan ahead and stop by on a day when they're open; you'll find a great selection of local items. The owners also have a community garden in the empty space next door during the summer, furnished with places to sit and rest.

ST. WENCESLAUS CATHOLIC CHURCH, NEW PRAGUE

New Prague has some fantastic dining options as well. **Ettlin's Café,** on the outskirts of downtown is open most days for breakfast and lunch, and on a seasonal basis for Friday night dinners. It also frequently offers evening Czech buffets. Food is cooked from scratch, and breakfast is served through the lunch hour. On the other side of town is the **Fish Tale Grill,** a bar and grill with hearty sandwiches and comfort food. In between is **Patty's Place,** a friendly coffee shop and bakery with treats baked in-house.

From New Prague, take MN 19 east nearly 26 miles to Northfield. You'll know you've arrived when you witness the well-known town welcome sign with the city's motto: "Cows, Colleges, and

HISTORIC NORTHFIELD

Contentment." Northfield lies in the heart of agriculture country and is also home to two preeminent colleges, **St. Olaf** and **Carleton**. Both campuses are worth a visit. Carleton College features the **Carleton College Cowling Arboretum,** an 800-acre conservation area dedicated to planting upland forest trees and wildflowers. Also at Carleton is the **Japanese Garden,** designed by a professor who studied for two years with Kinsaku Nakane in Kyoto.

Near Northfield is **Nerstrand-Big Woods State Park,** a 3,000-acre park full of wildflowers (more than 200 varieties) and extensive trails, and home to the remains of a vast oak savanna prairie, with numerous types of trees throughout. One of this park's claims to fame is that it's also the world's only sanctuary for the endangered dwarf trout lily. Just 3 miles away is Caron Park. Carved out of a remnant of the big woods, the 60-acre park is used for both recreation and environmental study.

Northfield began its life along the Cannon River over 150 years ago, and the city has done an exemplary job of maintaining its historic district. It's a highly walkable city with a wide range of activities available. As a river and a college town, Northfield has been able to attract an ongoing slew of creative people, which has led to an extensive arts and culture scene. St. Olaf College is home to internationally renowned musical groups the **St. Olaf Band, St. Olaf Choir**, and **St. Olaf Orchestra**. The annual St. Olaf Choir Christmas

ST. OLAF COLLEGE, NORTHFIELD

concerts are tough tickets to get, so if you're in the area around the holidays, plan accordingly.

The Northfield Arts Guild Theater is a cozy, 118-seat year-round community theater that presents drama, comedy, and musicals. An offshoot of the Northfield Arts Guild, **Northfield Arts Guild Gallery** is a large complex with multiple exhibition spaces and a dance studio. The colleges both have well-regarded art museums as well; St. Olaf has the **Flaten Art Museum,** and Carleton has the **Perlman Teaching Museum**.

Northfield has a more eventful history than many similar small towns; in 1876, the town was under siege by Jesse James and his gang. After robbing a bank, local residents retaliated against them, leading to deaths on both sides. **The Northfield Historical Society** offers permanent exhibitions about this infamous episode, as well as other aspects of Northfield's past.

Northfield's proximity to the river makes possible a considerable number of outdoor recreational opportunities; the **Mill Towns Trail** is an ongoing project that will connect Northfield to Cannon Falls to the northeast and Faribault to the southwest. At press time, there were several miles of trail running through Northfield, allowing trail users a close look at the historic downtown area as well as the Cannon River itself.

Five miles south of Northfield is the **Cannon River Wilderness Area.**

Composed of 850 acres of wooded river valley, it offers hiking and horseback trails along with a canoe launch area to the Cannon River.

Lodging is plentiful here, and a variety of types are available, including bed-and-breakfasts. **The Contented Cottage B&B** is within walking distance to St. Olaf and offers two rooms, both with private bath. The inn serves a three-course breakfast each morning and features a cozy public space with fireplace. You might even get to meet the resident hens the owners keep on the property. **The Magic Door Bed & Breakfast** is a lovely three-story Victorian near downtown with two rooms and a suite, each with private bath and beautiful furnishings. **The Northfield Inn** offers four suites with private baths and not only includes breakfast but delivers it to your room.

The Archer House River Inn is a large, historic building that first opened as a hotel in 1877. Here you'll find 36 impeccably furnished rooms and suites, as well as three restaurants and two shops. **Froggy Bottoms River Suites** is situated on the river, near the waterfalls, and housed within a turn-of-the-century commercial building. There are four suites with kitchens, and some have decks overlooking the river.

Dining choices are plentiful as well. **Spring Creek Grille** at the Northfield Golf Club is an upscale contemporary American restaurant. During the golf season, try to nab a table on the sunset-facing terrace. **Tandem Bagels** prepares bagels from scratch and offers breakfast and lunch sandwiches. For hearty soups and sandwiches, try **Smoqehouse,** and at the Archer House

THE NORTHFIELD HISTORICAL SOCIETY

THE ARCHER HOUSE RIVER INN, NORTHFIELD

River Inn, the **Tavern of Northfield** serves up three meals a day in a quirky historic atmosphere. **The Contented Cow** is a British pub on the bank of the river. There are also a number of independent pizza and pasta houses here, including **B&L Pizza, Basil's Pizza**, and **George's Vineyard**, the latter being home to "Greek pizza." Wherever you eat, leave some room for a trip to **Cake Walk** to satisfy your sweet tooth.

IN THE AREA

Accommodations

ARCHER HOUSE RIVER INN, 212 South Division Street, Northfield. Call 507-645-5661; 800-247-2235. Website: www.archerhouse.com.

CONTENTED COTTAGE, 5 Walden Place, Northfield. Call 507-301-3787. Website: www.contentedcottage.com.

FROGGY BOTTOMS RIVER SUITES, 309 South Water Street, Northfield. Call 507-650-0039. Website: www.froggybottomsriversuites.com.

MAGIC DOOR BED & BREAKFAST, 818 South Division Street, Northfield. Call 507-581-0445. Website: www.magicdoorbb.com.

NICOLIN MANSION BED & BREAKFAST, 221 South Broadway Street, Jordan. Call 952-492-6441. Website: www.nicolinmansion.com.

NORTHFIELD INN, 203 Maple Street, Northfield. Call 507-664-1122. Website: www.northfieldinnmn.com.

Attractions and Recreation

ALL THINGS FABULOUS, 300 Broadway Street, Carver. Call 612-562-6364. Website: www.facebook.com/All-Things-Fabulous-320998281638837.

BLUFF CREEK BOUTIQUE, 232 Broadway Street South, Jordan. Website: bluffcreekboutique.com.

CARLETON COLLEGE, 1 North College Street, Northfield. Website: www.carleton.edu.

CARLETON COLLEGE COWLING ARBORETUM, 1 North College Street, Northfield. Call 507-222-5413. Website: apps.carleton.edu/campus/arb.

CORNER PEDDLER, 415 South Broadway Street, Suite 101, Jordan. Call 952-200-0929. Website: www.cornerpeddler.com.

FARMHOUSE MARKET, 120 West Main Street, New Prague. Website: www.farmhousemarketnp.com.

THE GOOD JUNK GARAGE, 109 1/2 East 3rd Street, Carver. Call 952-212-8454. Website: www.facebook.com/TheGoodJunkGarage.

GOPHER STATE RAILWAY MUSEUM, 25525 Helena Boulevard, New Prague. Call 952-758-8729. Website: www.gsrm.org.

HUMBLE PIE GIFT SHOP, 215 West Main Street, New Prague. Call 952-758-7880. Website: www.humblepiestore.com.

JAPANESE GARDEN, 1 North College Street, Northfield. Website: apps.carleton.edu/campus/japanesegarden.

THE JORDAN JUNKER, 209 Water Street, Jordan. Call 952-358-1970. Website: www.thejordanjunker.com.

LB ANTIQUES, 220 Water Street, Jordan. Call 952-492-3071. Website: www .facebook.com/pages/LB-Antiques/853531804732649.

MAINSTREAM BOUTIQUE, 123 East Main Street, New Prague. Call 952-758-4150. Website: mainstreamboutique.com.

MINNESOTA VALLEY STATE RECREATION AREA, 19825 Park Boulevard, Jordan. Call 651-259-5774. Website: www.dnr.state.mn.us/state_parks/park .html?id=sra00304#homepage.

MUSTARD MOON, 300 Broadway Street, Carver. Website: www.facebook .com/mustardmoonmn.

NERSTRAND-BIG WOODS STATE PARK, 9700 East 170th Street, Nerstrand. Call 507-384-6140. Website: www.dnr.state.mn.us/state_parks /park.html?id=spk00241#homepage.

NORTHFIELD HISTORICAL SOCIETY, 408 South Division Street, Northfield. Call 507-645-9268. Website: www.northfieldhistory.org.

REFINERY BOUTIQUE, 105 East Main Street, New Prague. Website: www .therefinerymn.com.

REFOUNDRY, 415 South Broadway Street, Jordan. Call 812-514-5231. Website: www.therefoundry.com.

RIDGES AT SAND CREEK GOLF COURSE, 21775 Ridges Drive, Jordan. Call 952-492-2644. Website: www.ridgesatsandcreek.com.

RIVER VALLEY RANCH, 16480 Jonathan Carver Parkway, Carver. Call 952-361-3361. Website: www.rivervalleyhorseranch.com.

RIVERSIDE ART STUDIO AND GALLERY, 200-298 Broadway Street, Carver. Call 952-303-5515. Website: www.riversideartcarver.com.

ROSEHIPS AND WILLOW, 308 Broadway Street, Carver. Call 701-739-6909. Website: www.rosehipsandwillow.com.

ST. OLAF COLLEGE, 1520 St. Olaf Avenue, Northfield. Call 507-786-2222. Website: wp.stolaf.edu.

SASSY KAT BOUTIQUE, 219 Water Street, Jordan. Call 612-554-4369. Website: www.facebook.com/sassykatboutiquemn.

SWEETER TIMES, 200 Broadway Street, Carver. Call 651-208-9971. Website: www.facebook.com/Sweeter-Times-244942265714473.

TREASURE CHEST ANTIQUES, 115 East 1st Street, Jordan. Call 952-492-5005. Website: www.treasurechest-antiques.com.

VINTIQUE VINTAGE JEWELRY, 105 West Main Street, New Prague. Call 612-968-4600. Website: www.facebook.com/Vintique-Vintage-Jewelry -Antiques-and-Estate-Items-172421436149765.

Dining

B&L PIZZA, 514 South Division Street, Northfield. Call 507-663-0390. Pizza, subs, wings, and gyros. Website: www.bnlpizza.com.

BASIL'S PIZZA, 301 South Water Street, Northfield. Call 507-663-1248. Pizza, pasta, and luscious desserts. Website: www.basilspizza.net.

CAKE WALK, 303 South Division Street, Northfield. Call 507-786-9255. Decadent cakes, cupcakes, and other pastries. Website: www.cake walknorthfield.com.

THE CONTENTED COW, 302B South Division Street, Northfield. Pub food, including appetizers and sandwiches. Website: www.contentedcow.com.

ETTLIN'S CAFÉ, 208 4th Avenue SW, New Prague. Call 952-758-6772. Breakfast and lunch, and occasional dinners. Excellent breakfasts. Website: www.ettlinscafe.com.

THE FEED MILL, 200 Water Street, Jordan. Call 952-492-3646. Breakfast and lunch with generous portions.

FISH TALE GRILL, 200 CR 37, New Prague. Call 952-758-8000. Hearty bar food. Website: www.fishtalebarandgrill.com.

GEORGE'S VINEYARD, 1160 MN 3, Northfield. Call 507-645-0100. Pasta and an extensive line of specialty pizzas. Website: www.georgesvineyard .com.

HARVEY'S BAR, 220 Broadway Street, Carver. Call 952-448-2289. Great burgers and comfort food specials. Website: www.facebook.com/Harveys -In-Carver-143735642318747.

LISA'S PLACE, 205 North Broadway Street, Carver. Call 952-448-6722. Burgers and pub grub. Website: www.facebook.com/Lisas-Place -172385539482580.

PATTY'S PLACE, 108 East Main Street, New Prague. Call 952-758-5808. Coffee drinks, pastries, sandwiches, and ice cream. Website: www.pattys placenp.com.

PEKARNA MEAT MARKET, 119 Water Street, Jordan. Call 952-492-6101. Great meat snacks, smoked in-house. Website: www.pekarnameats.com.

ROETS JORDAN BREWERY, 230 South Broadway Street, Jordan. Call 952-406-8865. Website: roetsjordanbrewery.com.

SMOQEHOUSE, 212 South Division Street, Northfield. Call 507-664-1008. Casual gourmet fusion food. Website: www.smoqehouse.com.

SPRING CREEK GRILLE, 707 Prairie Street, Northfield. Call 507-645-4026. Upscale contemporary American. Website: www.northfieldgolfclub.com.

TANDEM BAGELS, 317 South Division Street, Northfield. Call 507-786-9977. Bagels and sandwiches, all made in-house. Website: www.tandembagels .com.

TAVERN OF NORTHFIELD, 212 South Division Street, Northfield. Call 507-663-0342. Three meals a day in the Archer House River Inn. Website: www .tavernofnorthfield.com.

Other Contacts

JORDAN CHAMBER OF COMMERCE. Website: www.jordanchamber.org.

MILL TOWNS TRAIL. Website: www.milltownstrail.org.

NEW PRAGUE CHAMBER OF COMMERCE. 101 East Main Street, New Prague. Call 952-758-4360. Website: www.newprague.com.

NORTHFIELD AREA CHAMBER OF COMMERCE, 19 Bridge Square, Northfield. Call 507-645-5604. Website: www.northfieldchamber.com.

SOUTHWEST METRO CHAMBER OF COMMERCE (CARVER), 7925 Stone Creek Drive, #130, Chanhassen. Call 952-474-3233. Website: www.swmetrochamber.com.

13

MINNESOTA RIVER VALLEY, PART 1

Carver to Mankato

ESTIMATED DISTANCE: 55 miles

ESTIMATED TIME: 2 hours

GETTING THERE: From Carver, take County Route 40 (CR 40) to just north of Belle Plaine, then continue on CR 6 to Henderson. CR 6 then becomes MN 93, traveling to Le Sueur, where you can pick up US 169 south to Mankato.

HIGHLIGHTS: The Hooper-Bowler Hillstrom House with its "unique" architectural features; the charming small river town of Henderson; Le Sueur, birthplace of both the founder of the Mayo Clinic and the Jolly Green Giant; Minneopa State Park, with its gorgeous trails and waterfall; and Mankato, home to both literary and sports icons.

This route could be taken in tandem with the Farmland and Historic Towns drive in Chapter 12, if that drive were reversed and ended in Carver.

Leaving the Twin Cities to explore the Minnesota River Valley is a lovely way to spend an afternoon. The Minnesota River was formed by glaciers during the last North American ice age, roughly 10,000 years ago. Today the river flows southeast from Big Stone Lake in the western edge of the state, near the North and South Dakota borders, until it reaches Mankato, where it redirects northeast until it meets the Mississippi near the Twin Cities. The valley is an area full of changing landscape, from closely wooded stretches along rolling riverbanks to wide-open prairie spaces. It's also full of history, perhaps most notably the Dakota Conflict of 1862, numerous Native American sites, and the homes of some iconic Minnesota people and companies, including the founder of the Mayo Clinic and the hometown of the Jolly Green Giant.

LEFT: THE FALLS AT MINNEOPA STATE PARK

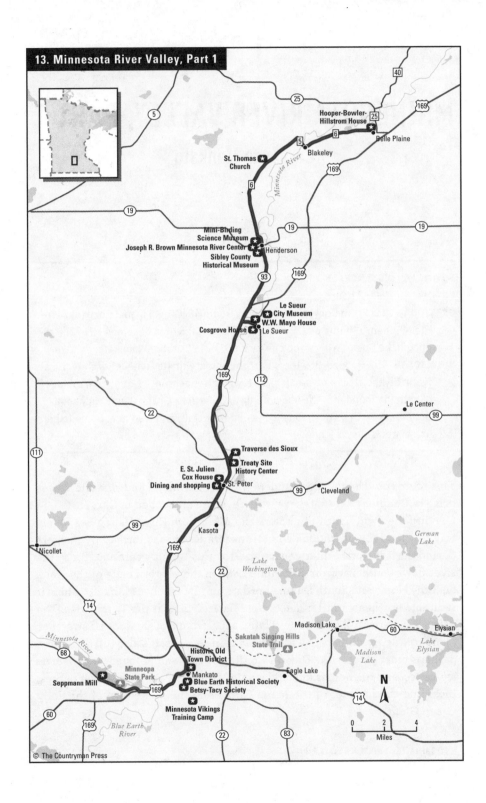

13. Minnesota River Valley, Part 1

St. Thomas Church

Hooper-Bowler-Hillstrom House

Belle Plaine

Blakeley

Mini-Birding Science Museum

Joseph R. Brown Minnesota River Center

Sibley County Historical Museum

Henderson

Le Sueur City Museum

W.W. Mayo House

Cosgrove House

Le Sueur

Le Center

Traverse des Sioux

Treaty Site History Center

E. St. Julien Cox House

Dining and shopping

St. Peter

Cleveland

Kasota

Nicollet

Lake Washington

Madison Lake

Elysian

German Lake

Sakatah Singing Hills State Trail

Lake Elysian

Minnesota River

Historic Old Town District

Minneopa State Park

Mankato

Blue Earth Historical Society

Betsy-Tacy Society

Eagle Lake

Madison Lake

Seppmann Mill

Minnesota Vikings Training Camp

Blue Earth River

N

0   2   4

Miles

© The Countryman Press

The part of the river covered in this trip starts just southwest of the Twin Cities and ends in Mankato, although this route could be combined with the New Ulm to Fort Ridgely leg to make a longer trip. When you look at a map, it appears that taking US 169 from the Twin Cities is the logical choice, as it's the major road heading in that direction. It's faster, that's true, and though scenic in its own way, the parallel county routes recommended here are more rewarding, even if they do force you to slow down. That may be the point!

From Carver, take CR 40 south heading to Belle Plaine. Just before you reach Belle Plaine, the road will turn into CR 6 as you cross a county line. This short stretch of road winds through woods and gently rolling landscape before arriving in Belle Plaine, where you'll turn left onto North Walnut Street. A right turn onto West State Street will bring you to the **Hooper-Bowler-Hillstrom House**. The former home of State Bank founder Samuel Bowler, this home was built in 1871, but its primary claim to fame, besides being an attractive one, is the addition Mr. Bowler added to accommodate his rather large family: a two-story outhouse. A skyway connects the second floor of the "five-holer" to the house; the upstairs facilities are situated farther back, so the waste would land behind the wall of the first floor. Although the home has limited visiting hours, it's worth a stop if it works on your schedule, because the house is packed full of antiques and oddities.

Continue on West State Street, which will merge back onto CR 6. At this point, the road is the journey itself, slow and winding as it follows the curves

THE HOOPER-BOWLER-HILLSTROM HOUSE, BELLE PLAINE

HIGHWAY 6 ROADSIDE GARDEN, BELLE PLAINE

of the Minnesota River. As you approach CR 5, look for its telltale rows of cottonwood trees, known as the Avenue of Trees, which leads east on CR 5 to the Blakely Bridge. The bridge is often the victim of spring floods from the Minnesota River.

Continuing south on CR 6, you'll soon see **St. Thomas Church** on the right. The small, pristine white church, thought to be a marker of the first Irish agrarian settlement in the state, was built in 1870 and is listed on the National Register of Historic Places.

The road winds into Henderson, a small town, reminiscent of one you'd find in New England. At one time, Henderson served as a stopping point for stagecoaches and steamboats; today, shoppers browse for antiques. There is plenty of history to explore; the **Sibley County Historical Museum** displays items immigrants brought with them from Europe, while the **Joseph R. Brown Minnesota River Center** showcases Minnesota River Valley history. A new addition to Main Street is the **Mini-Birding Science Museum**, which educates visitors on a vast number of birds that can be spotted in the area. A complete getaway can be accomplished by booking a stay at the **Henderson House Bed & Breakfast**, on a hill overlooking Main Street. Grab a meal at the **Henderson RoadHaus**, or get a quick sandwich and ice cream at **Toody's Sweet Treats**.

From Henderson, travel on MN 93 south to Le Sueur. Le Sueur is the original home of the Minnesota Canning Company—better known today as Green Giant. The iconic Jolly Green Giant is memorialized on a historic marker at Commerce and Dakota Streets, but the tall green fellow is not the

CHURCH OF ST. THOMAS, JESSENLAND

only person of historical interest in town. The founder of the internationally renowned Mayo Clinic also got his start here. **The W.W. Mayo House**, a little gothic-style house hand-built in 1859 by Dr. Mayo himself, is now open as a museum. Mayo initially set up shop on the second floor. When the Civil War interrupted his practice. he traveled to New Ulm to help wounded veterans while his wife, Louise, remained in the house to shelter 11 refugee families. By 1864, the Mayo family reunited and moved to Rochester, where they founded the Mayo Clinic. The home's story doesn't end there; in the 1870s, the Carson Nesbit Cosgrove family moved into the home. Cosgrove founded the Minnesota Valley Canning Company, which later became Green Giant.

THE MINNESOTA RIVER AT HENDERSON

Additional community history can be explored at the **Le Sueur City Museum**. A small museum in a former schoolhouse, the City Museum has most of what remains of the Green Giant legacy, after Pillsbury bought Green Giant and moved its headquarters out of town. The Green Giant room has a wide variety of memorabilia and antiques. Other displays include an old-time drugstore and an antique doll collection. If you're in the mood for a longer visit, the Cosgrove House is a beautiful, century-old Victorian home with four rooms, all with private bath, and a full breakfast daily.

The next stop is via US 169 south to **Traverse des Sioux**, just a mile north of St. Peter. This shallow river crossing served as a gathering point for Native Americans for centuries, followed by European traders. A treaty signed in 1851 led to a torrent of white settlers, and a town with the Traverse name soon came into being; however, when neighboring St. Peter was named county seat, Traverse des Sioux was all but deserted. A self-guided trail helps visitors navigate the area and explains the culture and history of its past.

Continue south on US 169 to St. Peter. This little river town was the locus of some extreme political maneuvering in 1857, when a bill was introduced to move the state's capitol from St. Paul to St. Peter, which at the time was a more convenient location for remote legislators. However, not all legislators approved of the idea, and money and real estate no doubt played a part. Finally, a rogue senator physically took the bill and hid out in a local hotel, drinking and gambling, until the deadline for signing it into law had passed.

St. Peter has other facets of historical significance too. E. St. Julien Cox, a Civil War officer, attorney, and eventually state senator, built a flamboyant Gothic/Italianate home here in 1871. Filled with 1880s furnishings, the **E. St. Julien Cox House** is open to the public today during the summer, when costumed guides explain the significance of both the home and the family.

Another piece of history worth revisiting is on display at the **Treaty Site History Center**. The center offers permanent and seasonal exhibitions detailing the creation of what is now southern Minnesota, along with Iowa and South Dakota, in the signing of the Traverse des Sioux Treaty in 1851. History aficionados will note that the terms of the treaty were not upheld, leading to the Dakota Conflict several years later. The center doesn't shy away from recounting the uglier aspects of the treaty's story. After the history lesson, if you need something peaceful and soothing, take some time to explore the restored prairie that surrounds the center.

A final historic site worth visiting (and planning ahead for, as it's only open to visitors by appointment) is the **St. Peter Regional Treatment Center**. Built in 1866 to serve as a psychiatric facility, the center has since expanded and is still in operation, but the "old" center is a museum that explores how the mentally ill were diagnosed and treated more than a century ago.

St. Peter is a very walkable city, and it features plenty of good dining and shopping options too. **River Rock Coffee** is more than a coffee shop, offering a small but thoughtful menu of homemade entrées, sandwiches, soups, and don't-miss pastries. The **3rd Street Tavern** serves more substantial plates, with an emphasis on barbecue (and bourbon). **Nicollet Café** is a small-town charmer, with breakfast and lunch and, on most days, dinner.

ANTIQUE SHOPPING, HENDERSON

For shopping, be sure to visit the **St. Peter Woolen Mill** for all kinds of wool items; the **Refinery Boutique** for women's clothing, accessories, and gifts; **Cheese and Pie Mongers** for—well—cheese and pie; and **Cooks & Company** for all things culinary and kitchen.

Mankato, the county seat and fourth-largest city in the state, is the next stop as you continue south on US 169. The city's name is derived from the Dakota phrase Makato Osa Watapa, or "river where blue earth is gathered." The Blue Earth River runs through the city, where it joins the Minnesota River.

The city's history is open for exploration at the **Blue Earth Historical Society**. The museum of the Blue Earth County Historical Society has wide-ranging exhibitions covering local historic events, including a Maud Hart Lovelace exhibition, displays featuring Native American artifacts, remnants from the region's early days of farming and milling, and a diorama of old Mankato.

The settlement, like many others in the region, had rocky relationships with indigenous people. In 1862, 38 Dakota Indians were hanged in Mankato. Near that site is now a six-foot, two-ton statue of a Dakota Warrior, part of 1987's "Year of Reconciliation" as mandated by then-governor Rudy Perpich.

Some famous Minnesota authors have lived here as well. Well-loved Maud Hart Lovelace, author of the popular Betsy-Tacy-Tib books, grew up in Mankato and based the books on her childhood. **The Betsy-Tacy Society** gives fans of the series the opportunity to visit the sites of the fictional Deep Valley. The house Tacy's home was based on is open for tours; and the model for Betsy's house is around the corner. The society has also produced a brochure detailing 55 important stops in Mankato for Betsy-Tacy fans; the map was created in part by Lovelace herself. Check the society's website for a detailed walking map, and call ahead for driving directions. Another notable author, Nobel Prize–winning Sinclair Lewis, owned a summer home in town. While not open to the public, fans can view the exterior at 315 South Broad Street.

Sports fans converge on Mankato each summer, just in time for the **Minnesota Vikings Training Camp**. When the Vikings begin to gear up for the season in July, they start out in Mankato. Attending a practice is free, while admission is charged for scrimmages and games. Get tickets in advance from the Vikings ticket office or from the Mankato Chamber of Commerce (listed at the end of this chapter).

For anyone wanting to spend time outdoors, Mankato has some wonderful options. The **Sakatah Singing Hills State Trail** is a 39-mile paved

MINNEOPA STATE PARK

trail utilizing a former railroad bed that winds from Mankato to Faribault through farmland and woods. From Mankato, take MN 22 north to access public parking. The trail is multiuse and open to all forms of recreation (with the exception of snowmobiles with studded tracks—regular snowmobiles are welcome). A secondary trail is available for horseback riders only.

Just west of Mankato on MN 68 is **Minneopa State Park**. In the Dakota language, Minneopa means "water falling twice," a perfect name for this park, home to Minnesota's largest waterfall. A winding trail leads to and around the falls, with a limestone stairway descending into the valley, and out into native prairie grasses. **Seppmann Mill**, a wind-driven gristmill made of stone and wood, is no longer functional but continues to draw admirers. At one time there was a town here as well, but three consecutive years of grasshopper plagues in the 1870s drove residents away. Tourists, however, continue to flock to this popular park, for its waterfalls, trails, and bird-watching. Campsites and one cabin are available for rental.

Mankato also has opportunities for some fine dining. **The Wine Café** offers tasty dishes, but its main draw is a full bar menu that includes 70 wines by the glass and a comparable number of beers. At **Charley's,** you'll find the focus is on steaks, chicken, and seafood, while **Number 4 American Bar** has a hearty menu of grilled meats and pasta dishes. For something more casual, **Blue Bricks Bar and Eatery** offers sandwiches and steaks, while Bradley's on Stadium has burgers and pizzas (and breakfast on weekends). **La Terraza,** meanwhile, serves up plates of authentic homemade Mexican food. Another option is **Friesen's Bakery and Bistro** for homemade baked goods and a small but first-rate lunch menu.

If staying in Mankato, the **Hilton Garden Inn,** near the Minnesota River downtown, or the **Mankato City Center Hotel** or **River Hills Hotel** are all good choices.

IN THE AREA

Accommodations

COSGROVE HOUSE, 228 South 2nd Street, Le Sueur. Call 507-665-2500.

HENDERSON HOUSE BED & BREAKFAST, 104 North 8th Street, Henderson. Call 507-248-3356.

HILTON GARDEN INN, 20 Civic Center Plaza, Mankato. Call 507-344-1111. Website: www.hiltongardeninn3.hilton.com.

MANKATO CITY CENTER HOTEL, 101 East Main Street, Mankato. Call 507-345-1234; 877-345-5577. Website: www.mankatomnhotel.com.

RIVER HILLS HOTEL, 1000 Raintree Road, Mankato. Call 507-388-8688. Website: riverhillshotel.com.

Attractions and Recreation

BETSY-TACY HOUSES, 332-333 Center Street, Mankato. Call 507-345-9777. Website: www.betsy-tacysociety.org.

BLUE EARTH HISTORICAL SOCIETY, 424 Warren Street, Mankato. Call 507-345-5566. Website: www.bechshistory.com.

BROAD STREET ANTIQUES, 1434 North Broad Street, Mankato. Call 507-291-5529. Website: www.facebook.com/broadstreetantiquesmankato.com.

CHEESE AND PIE MONGERS, 317 South Minnesota Avenue, St. Peter. Call 507-934-9066. Website: www.cheeseandpie.com.

COOKS & COMPANY, 316 South Minnesota Avenue, St. Peter. Call 507-934-1172. Website: www.cooksandcompany.com.

DAKOTA WARRIOR, 100 East Main Street, Mankato.

E. ST. JULIEN COX HOME, 500 North Washington Avenue, St. Peter. Call 507-934-2160. Website: www.nchsmn.org/sites/e-st-julien-cox-house.

HOOPER-BOWLER-HILLSTROM HOUSE, 405 North Chestnut Street, Belle Plaine. Call 952-873-6109. Website: www.belleplainemn.com/node/5.

JOSEPH R. BROWN MINNESOTA RIVER CENTER, 600 Main Street, Henderson. Call 507-248-3234. Website: www.joebrownrivercenter.org.

LE SUEUR CITY MUSEUM, 709 North 2nd Street, Le Sueur. Call 507-655-2050.

LITTLE RED SHED, 601 North Riverfront Drive, Mankato. Call 507-345-7433.

MINI-BIRDING SCIENCE MUSEUM, 526 Main Street, Henderson. Website: www.hendersonfeathers.org/mini-science-museum.

MINNEOPA STATE PARK, 54497 Gadwall Road, Mankato. Call 507-386-3910. Website: www.dnr.state.mn.us/state_parks/minneopa/index.html.

MINNESOTA VIKINGS TRAINING CAMP, Blakeslee Field, Minnesota State University. Call 507-389-3000. Website: www.vikings.com.

POND ROAD ANTIQUES, 111 Butterworth Street, Mankato. Call 507-386-7663.

THE REFINERY BOUTIQUE, 216 South Minnesota Avenue, St. Peter. Call 507-931-1198. Website: www.therefinerymn.com.

ST. PETER REGIONAL TREATMENT CENTER, 1851 North Minnesota Avenue, St. Peter. Call 507-931-7270.

ST. PETER WOOLEN MILL, 101 West Broadway, St. Peter. Call 507-934-3734; 800-208-9821. Website: www.woolenmill.com.

SIBLEY COUNTY HISTORICAL MUSEUM, 700 Main Street, Henderson. Call 507-248-3434. Website: www.sibleycountyhistoricalmuseum.com.

TRAVERSE DES SIOUX, US 169, 1 mile north of St. Peter. Call 507-934-2160. Website: www.sites.mnhs.org/historic-sites/traverse-des-sioux.

TREATY SITE HISTORY CENTER, 1851 North Minnesota Avenue, St. Peter. Call 507-934-2160. Website: www.nchsmn.org/sites/treaty-site-history -center.

VINTAGE MALL ANTIQUES, 1247 Range Street, Mankato. Call 507-388-6016. Website: www.vintagemallantiques.com.

W.W. MAYO HOUSE, 118 North Main Street, Le Sueur. Call 507-665-3250. Website: www.sites.mnhs.org/historic-sites/ww-mayo-house.

Dining

3RD STREET TAVERN, 408 South 3rd Street, St. Peter. Call 507-934-3314. Steakhouse and barbecue eats. Website: www.3rdstreettavern.com.

BLUE BRICKS BAR AND EATERY, 424 South Front Street, Mankato. Call 507-386-1700. Hearty bar food and steaks. Website: www.bluebricksmankato .com.

BRADLEY'S ON STADIUM, 1600 Warren Street, Suite 17, Mankato. Call 507-388-5005. Burgers and pizza, and breakfast on weekends. Website: www.bradleysonstadium.com.

CHARLEY'S RESTAURANT AND LOUNGE, 920 East Madison Avenue, Mankato. Call 507-388-6845. Steakhouse offerings. Website: www .charleysrestaurant.com.

FRIESEN'S FAMILY BAKER & BISTRO, 515 North Riverfront Drive, Mankato. Call 507-345-4114. Bakery and lunch café. Website: www .mankatobakery.com.

HENDERSON ROADHAUS, 510-518 Main Street, Henderson. Call 507-248-3691. Substantial home-cooked fare. Website: www.facebook.com /hendersonroadhaus.

LA TERRAZA, 1404 Madison Avenue, Mankato. Call 507-344-0607. Authentic, homemade Mexican cuisine. Website: laterrazamankato.com.

NICOLLET CAFÉ, 402 South 3rd Street, St. Peter. Call 507-934-0056. Casual American food and coffee. Website: www.facebook.com/nicolletcafe.

NUMBER 4 AMERICAN BAR, 124 East Walnut Street, Mankato. Call 507-344-1444. Upscale American cuisine. Website: www.number4mankato.com.

RIVER ROCK COFFEE, 301 South Minnesota Avenue, St. Peter. Call 507-931-1540. Bakery and café with homemade sandwiches and soups, as well as inventive coffee and tea drinks. Website: www.rrcoffee.com.

TOODY'S SWEET TREATS, 417 Main Street, Henderson. Call 507-248-3326. Ice cream, sundaes, sandwiches. Website: www.facebook.com/Toodys -Sweet-Treats-272228436285606.

WINE CAFÉ, 301 North Riverfront, Mankato. Call 507-345-1516. A charming bistro with a wine shop and an extensive wine list. Website: www .winecafebar.com.

Other Contacts

BELLE PLAINE CHAMBER OF COMMERCE, 204 North Meridian Street, Belle Plaine. Call 952-873-4295. Website: www.belleplainemn.com.

GREATER MANKATO CONVENTION & VISITOR BUREAU, 12 Civic Center Plaza, Suite 1645, Mankato. Call 507-385-6660. Website: www .visitgreatermankato.com.

HENDERSON, MN. Call 507-248-3234. Website: www.hendersonmn.com.

LE SUEUR CHAMBER OF COMMERCE, 500 North Main Street, Le Sueur. Call 507-665-2501. Website: www.lesueurchamber.org.

ST. PETER AREA CHAMBER OF COMMERCE, 101 South Front Street, St. Peter. Call 507-934-3400. Website: www.stpeterchamber.com.

14

MINNESOTA RIVER VALLEY, PART 2
Mankato to Fairfax

ESTIMATED DISTANCE: 35 miles

ESTIMATED TIME: 1 hour

GETTING THERE: From the Twin Cities, take MN 5 west to Gaylord, where the high-way number changes to MN 19. Follow MN 19 to Fairfax, then travel south on County Route 74 (CR 74) to the Fairfax Historical Depot Museum.

HIGHLIGHTS: Historical highlights: Fort Ridgely State Park, the Brown County Historical Museum, the Harkin Store, and the John Lind House. Scenic high-lights: the lovely drive along the Minnesota River and the beautiful historic town of New Ulm, which includes the gardens at Schell's Brewery and Flan-drau State Park.

This is a short but both scenically and historically rich route, and it ends in a river town well worth exploring. You could lengthen the experience by com-bining it with the Pioneer Trails (Chapter 17) and/or the Carver to Mankato route (Chapter 13).

The scenery in this area, replete with winding, hilly roads around the Minnesota River, benefits from having been formed during the last ice age, which left it full of lakes and wetlands. It's also rich in Native American and pioneer history, not all of it joyful—various sites throughout this region were involved in the Dakota Conflict of 1862, when the Dakota people struck out against white settlers in protest of treaty violations and the hunger and deprivation resulting from misdirected or stolen annuities by Indian agents. In the end, innocent people on both sides were killed, and the aftermath of the conflict reverberated throughout the area for decades. This route visits another important historical site in that war.

LEFT: THE WANDA GAG HOUSE, NEW ULM

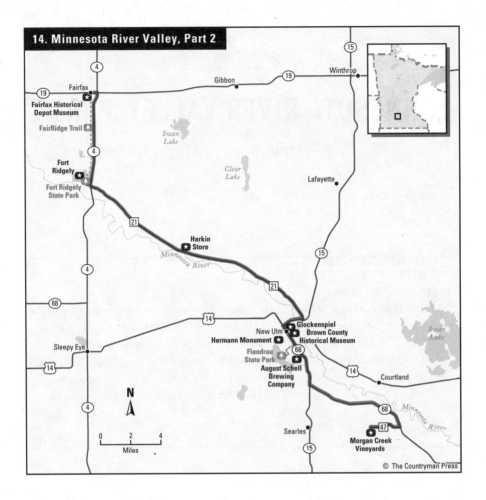

The journey begins with a historic site in the small town of Fairfax. The **Fairfax Historical Depot Museum** is a restored railroad depot in Depot Park, full of remnants of Fairfax's rail past as well as pieces of the town's history. Depot Park serves as the beginning of the **FairRidge Trail**, a paved hiking and biking trail that meanders through woodlands and hills before ending at Fort Ridgely State Park. Part of the trail has a horseback riding path running adjacent to it.

From Fort Ridgely, travel southeast on CR 21. This is a winding, hilly stretch of road that at points hugs the Minnesota River and at other times twists and turns throughout narrow, tree-lined stretches. Through the trees you might see the winding river, glimpses of farmland tucked into the valleys, or wetlands. Take your time—around every corner is another beautiful view. If you want to pull over for a closer look or to take a snapshot, park carefully—there are many blind curves. The road is beautiful any time of year, but it especially shines in the fall, when the colors change.

Fort Ridgely State Park

At a little over 1,000 acres, **Fort Ridgely State Park** isn't one of the state's largest parks, but it's packed with things to do. In its small space are hiking and horseback riding trails, campsites, fishable waters, a hill appropriately sized for some excellent winter sledding, and a nine-hole golf course. History buffs will want to wander around the remains of Fort Ridgely, which was completed in 1855 and housed 300 people during its time (the fort closed in 1872). Its primary purpose was to be not so much a military outpost as a police station, keeping order and protecting the newly arrived white settlers. It was attacked twice during the Dakota Conflict. Today, one of the fort's buildings has been restored and is available for tours, or visitors can wander on their own through the remnants of the other fort buildings. Comprehensive interpretive signs explain what each building was and its significance to the fort. Nearby is a historic cemetery, with gravestones and monuments revealing additional information about the people who lived, fought, and died in the fort. Recent excavations have also uncovered Indian burial mounds and signs of settlements that may date back centuries.

FORT RIDGELY STATE PARK

THE MINNESOTA RIVER NEAR NEW ULM

Continuing on CR 21, you'll find the **Harkin Store**, a piece of history still vibrant today. The Harkin Store was a community general store until the day the railroad decided to bypass it. The store was forced to close, and today much of the merchandise on display is exactly where it was left the day the store shuttered its doors. Costumed guides provide historical background and explain what some of the products, common in their day, were for. The Harkin Store provides a rare opportunity to see what a general store was really like more than 100 years ago.

At the intersection of CR 21, CR 15, and US 14, follow US 14 west to New Ulm. This charming river city was conceived by German settlers who, after arriving in Chicago in 1853, built their own community in Minnesota. Besides its river location, which made the city an important one in the early days of commerce and trading, New Ulm served as a valuable refuge for people trying to escape the Dakota Conflict. In the 1920s, the town acquired another claim to fame, as resident Whoopee John Wilfahrt and his musical magic gave New Ulm the reputation of "polka capital of the nation."

New Ulm's German heritage is still apparent today, in the architecture, landmarks, and festivals and celebrations that take place each year. One example is the **Glockenspiel**. New Ulm is home to one of the world's few freestanding carillons. The 45-foot glockenspiel puts on its show three times a day, and more frequently during festivals; when the bells chime, three-foot-tall polka figures come dancing out, except at Christmas, when a nativity scene appears instead.

In the town, you'll also find the **Hermann Monument**, built in 1897 in honor of Hermann of Cherusci, who is recognized for liberating Germany from Rome in 9 AD and is considered the liberator of the German people. The monument was built through the efforts of several chapters of the Sons of Hermann, a fraternal order of German Americans. The memorial stands 102 feet tall and, for those willing to climb the stairs, provides an excellent view of greater New Ulm. Bring a picnic lunch to enjoy in the park grounds.

New Ulm's history is on full display at the **Brown County Historical Museum**. Housed in a 1910 post office, the museum is a surprisingly diverse and comprehensive collection of historic and cultural artifacts. German heritage (including items donated by the German city of Ulm), Native American history, and the economic mainstays of the area (known as "beer, brats, and bricks") are all detailed in various exhibitions. The Dakota Conflict is especially well covered. The building is beautiful and is itself worth a visit.

Nearby is the **John Lind House**. Built in 1887, this Victorian beauty served as both home and venue for state functions for Governor John Lind. The house had fallen into serious disrepair before being listed on the National Register and purchased by the newly formed Lind House Association, which restored it and operates it today. While tours are available, the building remains in use, home to the local chapter of the United Way.

THE HARKIN GENERAL STORE, NEW ULM

THE GLOCKENSPIEL, NEW ULM

A more whimsical display of New Ulm's history may be encountered on the **Heritage Tree**, a fanciful tree decorated with historic figures from New Ulm's past.

A piece of religious history lies just outside the historic city center. Built in 1904, **The Way of the Cross** is composed of 14 stations along a path climbing a hill (of moderate height) depicting the trial and crucifixion of Jesus, cresting at the top in a chapel dedicated to the Mother of Sorrows. The Way of the Cross was renovated in 2004 and offers a lovely bit of nature and history tucked into more mundane urban surroundings.

Literary history is on view in New Ulm at the **Wanda Gag House,** where children's author and illustrator Wanda Gag, notable for such classics as

Millions of Cats, was born and raised. The compact home with turrets and skylights makes for an interesting afternoon's exploration.

For an oasis in the city, visit **Flandrau State Park**. At only 800 acres, this is a smaller park, but popular nonetheless, due in no small part to the fact that it's within walking distance of downtown New Ulm. The sand-bottomed swimming pond and extensive campgrounds are a big draw here, as are the

August Schell Brewing Company

Oktoberfest comes to town every year, due in no small part to the **August Schell Brewing Company**. Founded in 1860, Schell's is the second-oldest family brewing company in the United States. Having offered hospitality to visiting Dakota, the brewery was largely left alone during the Dakota Conflict. It also remained operational by producing "near beer" and root beer during Prohibition (it still produces a root beer called 1919, named for the year the 18th Amendment was passed). Today the brewery is open for tours seasonally; kids are welcome—while the adults enjoy a beer tasting, minors and nondrinkers can sample the 1919 root beer. There's also a small museum and gift shop. Another reason to visit the brewery is its grounds and gardens. Stop in the spring for the arrival of the bulbs, or in midsummer to see the rest of the garden in full bloom. You might even see some wildlife in the adjacent deer park.

THE GARDENS AT THE AUGUST SCHELL BREWING COMPANY

hiking trails. The trails are groomed for cross-country skiing in the winter, and ski and snowshoe rentals are available.

Beer is not the only adult beverage produced in the New Ulm area. Take MN 68 to CR 47 south, then 101 South. The first farm on the left is **Morgan Creek Vineyards**, part of the **Three Rivers Wine Trail**. Morgan Creek is the only Minnesota vineyard with an underground winery. Stop by during their regular business hours for tours and tastings, or check their website for one of their numerous special events.

As befits a historic river town, New Ulm has some lovely bed-and-breakfasts available for lodging, many of which are more than 100 years old. Good choices include the **Deutsche Strasse** and **Bingham Hall**.

There are several choices for dining. For a meal reflecting the town's heritage, stop by **Veigel's Kaiserhoff**, New Ulm's oldest German restaurant, and try the ribs. **Turner Hall** is New Ulm's oldest bar, in existence for over 160 years and located in a building listed on the National Register of Historic Places. It offers an extensive bar menu to go with its drinks. **George's Fine Steaks and Spirits** is a congenial steakhouse in a pretty building, and one of the best choices for a more upscale meal. If cozy and casual is what you're looking for, check out the **Ulmer Café**, a local diner with plentiful breakfasts and lunches. Contemporary American food and a full line of coffee drinks can be found at **Lola American Bistro**. Another good choice is the **Backerei and Coffee Shop**, a longtime local bakery with excellent pastries and reasonable prices.

Shopping options abound, and there are retailers that reflect New Ulm's

THE BROWN COUNTY HISTORICAL SOCIETY, NEW ULM

NEW ULM

German heritage. **Domeier's German Store** is packed full of German imports, from the kitschy to the classic. The **Guten Tag Haus** is an importer of German gifts, including a large array of Christmas items.

Those searching for antiques should stop by **Antiques Plus**, which houses more than 25 antiques dealers selling a wide variety of items.

IN THE AREA

Accommodations

BINGHAM HALL BED & BREAKFAST, 500 South German Street, New Ulm. Call 507-276-5070. Website: www.bingham-hall.com.

DEUTSCHE STRASSE BED & BREAKFAST, 404 South German Street, New Ulm. Call 507-354-2005. Website: www.deutschestrasse.com.

Attractions and Recreation

ANTIQUES PLUS, 28 North Minnesota Street, New Ulm. Call 507-359-1090. Website: www.facebook.com/pages/category/Antique-Store-Antiques-Plus -of-New-Ulm-2027801927250281.

AUGUST SCHELL BREWERY, 1860 Schell's Road, New Ulm. Call 507-354-5528; 800-770-5020. Website: www.schellsbrewery.com.

BROWN COUNTY HISTORICAL MUSEUM, 2 North Broadway Street, New Ulm. Call 507-233-2616. Website: www.browncountyhistorymnusa.org.

DOMEIER'S GERMAN STORE, 1020 South Minnesota Street, New Ulm. Call 507-354-4231. Website: www.facebook.com/pages/Domeiers-German -Store/116877278372011.

FAIRFAX HISTORICAL DEPOT MUSEUM, 200 South Park Street, Fairfax. Call 507-426-7919. Website: fairfax-mn.gov.

FAIRRIDGE TRAIL, Fairfax. Website: fairfax-mn.gov.

FLANDRAU STATE PARK, 1300 Summit Avenue, New Ulm. Call 507-233-9800. Website: www.dnr.state.mn.us/state_parks/flandrau/index.html.

FORT RIDGELY STATE PARK, 72158 CR 30, Fairfax. Call 507-426-7840. Website: www.dnr.state.mn.us/state_parks/fort_ridgely/index.html.

GLOCKENSPIEL, 327 North Minnesota Street, New Ulm.

GUTEN TAG HAUS, 127 North Minnesota Street, New Ulm. Call 507-233-4287. Website: www.gutentaghaus.com.

HARKIN STORE, CR 21, New Ulm. Call 507-354-8666. Website: www.mnhs .org/places/sites/hs.

HERITAGE TREE, 101 South Minnesota Street, New Ulm.

HERMANN MONUMENT, Center Street and Monument Street, New Ulm. Website: www.hermannmonument.com.

JOHN LIND HOUSE, 622 Center Street, New Ulm. Call 507-354-8802. Website: www.lindhouse.org.

MORGAN CREEK VINEYARDS, 23707 478th Avenue, New Ulm. Call 507-947-3547. Website: www.morgancreekvineyards.com.

WANDA GAG HOUSE, 226 North Washington Street, New Ulm. Call 507-359-2632. Website: www.wandagaghouse.org.

WAY OF THE CROSS, 1500 5th Street North, New Ulm.

Dining

BACKEREI AND COFFEE SHOP, 27 South Minnesota Street. Call 507-354-6011. Coffee, breads, and pastries. Website: www.backereinewulm.com.

GEORGE'S FINE STEAKS AND SPIRITS, 301 North Minnesota Street, New Ulm. Call 507-354-7440. Steakhouse fare. Website: www.georgessteaks.biz.

LOLA AMERICAN BISTRO, 16 North Minnesota Street, New Ulm. Call 507-359-2500. Three meals a day featuring upscale American cuisine. Website: www.lolaamericanbistro.com.

PLAZA GARIBALDI, 1707 North Broadway, New Ulm. Call 507-359-7073. Authentic Mexican. Website: plazagaribaldinewulm.com.

TURNER HALL, 102 South State Street, New Ulm. Call 507-354-4916. Sandwiches, burgers, and salads. Website: www.newulmturnerhall.org.

ULMER CAFÉ, 115 North Minnesota Street. Call 507-354-8122. Sandwiches, soups, coffee, and desserts. Website: www.facebook.com/ulmercafe.

VEIGEL'S KAISERHOFF, 221 North Minnesota Street. Call 507-359-2071. Steakhouse items and German specialties. Website: www.kaiserhoff.org.

Other Contacts

CITY OF FAIRFAX, 112 SE 1st Street, Fairfax. Call 507-426-7255. Website: fairfax-mn.gov.

NEW ULM CONVENTION & VISITOR BUREAU, 1 North Minnesota Street, New Ulm. Call 888-463-9856. Website: www.newulm.com.

15

RIVER BLUFFS AND AMISH COUNTRY

ESTIMATED DISTANCE: 85 miles

ESTIMATED TIME: 2 hours

GETTING THERE: From the Twin Cities or Rochester, take US 52 south to Preston.

HIGHLIGHTS: Visit the Root River Valley towns of Preston and Lanesboro; shop in the Amish town of Harmony; explore the Root River Trail; tour Amish Country. This is a great area for fall colors.

This stretch of southeastern Minnesota along the Iowa border is unlike many of its northern counterparts in that its dramatic topography is not the direct result of the last round of glaciers (the Wisconsin glaciation from about 75,000 years ago). Instead, the geologic area is referred to as driftless, with spots of karst topography—an area, in this case, built of limestone and characterized by caves and sinkholes. That's good news for travelers interested in caving and for those who want to soak in dramatic scenery. While the area is an easy day trip from the Twin Cities, many people make a weekend of it in order to have plenty of time to explore. A word to the wise: plan well in advance if you want to book one of the area's popular bed-and-breakfasts for summer and fall weekend visits. They can book up months in advance, and there's little in the way of traditional hotels to handle drop-in visitors.

The town of Fountain is the gateway to the Root River bluff country, and it's the starting point for the **Root River Trail**. This 60-mile paved trail winds eastward, along the Root River and through rolling landscapes that include 300-foot-high bluffs, concluding in Houston, not far from the Wisconsin border. The scenery is spectacular, and it offers both level trails (along a former railroad grade) and more challenging inclines that lead to gorgeous vistas.

LEFT: EAGLE BLUFF ENVIRONMENTAL LEARNING CENTER

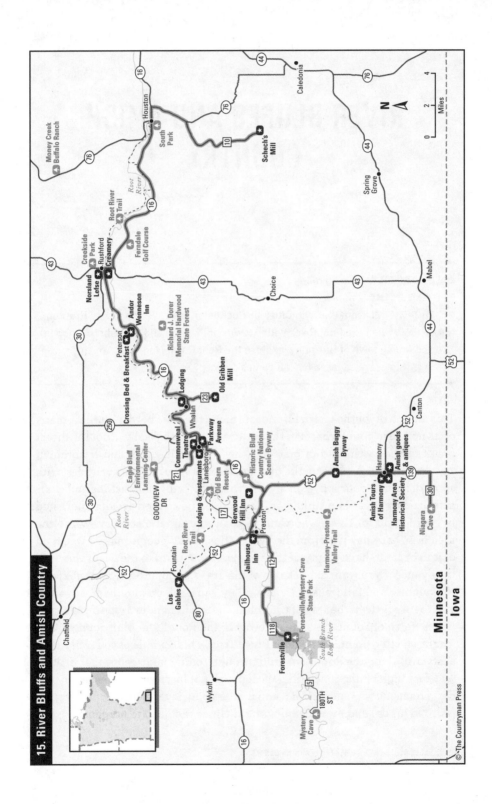

15. River Bluffs and Amish Country

Minnesota

Iowa

Money Creek Buffalo Ranch

Houston

South Park

Schech's Mill

Caledonia

Spring Grove

Mabel

Root River Trail

Creekside Park
Rushford
Creamery

Ferndale Golf Course

Choice

Norsland Lefse

Andor Wenneson Inn

Peterson
Crossing Bed & Breakfast

Richard J. Dorer Memorial Hardwood State Forest

Canton

Lodging

Old Gribben Mill

Whalan

Eagle Bluff Environmental Learning Center

GOODVIEW DR

Commonweal Theatre

Parkway Avenue

Lanesboro

Lodging & restaurants

Old Barn Resort

Historic Bluff Country National Scenic Byway

Amish Buggy Byway

Harmony

Amish goods & antiques

Amish Tours of Harmony

Harmony Area Historical Society

Berwood Hill Inn

Preston

Harmony-Preston Valley Trail

Niagara Cave

Fountain

Root River Trail

Los Gables

Jailhouse Inn

Forestville/Mystery Cave State Park

Chatfield

Wykoff

Forestville

180TH ST

Mystery Cave

South Branch Root River

N

0   2   4
Miles

© The Countryman Press

240 | BACKROADS & BYWAYS OF MINNESOTA

Those adventurous enough to bike the entire trail will be rewarded with changing scenery including wooded areas, rivers and bluffs, and diverse wildlife. The trails are open for cross-country skiers in the winter (seasonal fees apply). You can kick off your stop here with lunch at **Los Gables**, an authentic Mexican restaurant where you'd least expect it.

The trail first travels south to the town of Preston, the county seat. Like many of the small towns in this region, Preston was built in the mid-1800s and took advantage of its river proximity to establish traffic corridors for milling operations. Preston is a crossroads of sorts, with the Root River Trail continuing northeast and a second branch, the **Harmony-Preston Valley Trail**, extending south to the Amish community of Harmony. Preston is also on the **Historic Bluff Country National Scenic Byway**, an 88-mile stretch of MN 16 that runs from La Crescent in the east to Dexter in the west, covering miles of rivers, bluffs, sprawling farmland, and forests, including the **Richard J. Dorer Memorial Hardwood State Forest**. The Historic Bluff Country National Scenic Byway is dotted with small towns, many of which were built during the milling boom years. None of these towns has more than 3,000 residents today, and most have done an exemplary job of maintaining the buildings and natural environs. The presence of acres of deciduous trees, including several varieties of maples, elms, and birches, gives this area spectacular spring and fall views.

You can overnight in Preston at the **Jailhouse Inn**, the former county jail and sheriff's residence. Ten themed rooms pay homage to the inn's past, including the Drunk Tank and the Cell Block (and, in an odd twist, the Amish Room). Before you set off to explore the bluff country, you can stop at the **Old Barn Resort** to play a round of riverside golf, followed by a hearty meal at the restaurant. Old Barn also has campsites available and hostel accommodations as well.

West of Preston is **Forestville/Mystery Cave State Park**. This park has something for everyone: Mystery Cave takes visitors to underground pools and geologic cave formations; aboveground, hikers and horse riders can experience 15 miles of trails that wind through the bluff areas and wildflowers (in spring). Skiers and snowmobilers are welcome in winter. Forestville is a trip back in time to a once-functioning town that declined after the railroad bypassed it. Today, visitors cross the Carnegie Steel Bridge to visit the General Store, where costumed guides lead tours and demonstrate activities from the store's past, giving tourists the chance to work with the farm laborers in the garden.

At this point, you can deviate slightly by traveling south on US 52 to Harmony. This, of course, is home to the other end of the Harmony-Preston Valley Trail. It's also the center point for the Amish community in Minnesota, with Amish farms and businesses surrounding it. Consequently, it's not unusual to see the black Amish buggies on the roads, so drive with extra

THE GOLF COURSE AT OLD BARN RESORT

caution. The stretch of US 52 between Preston and Prosper (southeast of Harmony) is known as the **Amish Buggy Byway**, and the highway has widened shoulders for use by the buggies.

The area's geologic forms are explained and on display at the **Harmony Area Historical Society**, which has exhibitions about karst topography and a new interpretive site on the topic of sinkholes. Karst is responsible for another popular attraction: **Niagara Cave**. Here, a one-hour guided tour is available; bring a jacket to fully enjoy the 60-foot underground waterfall and crystal wedding chapel.

There are several restaurants serving home-style meals. **Harmony House** is open for breakfast and lunch, serving omelets, cinnamon rolls, burgers, sandwiches, and a daily lunch special with homemade mashed potatoes. **On the Crunchy Side** presents a typical restaurant menu of steaks, pizzas, salads, burgers, and sandwiches. **Village Square of Harmony** is a quintessential family restaurant, with a cheery red-and-white awning and a menu packed with pizza and sandwiches.

Amish goods and antiques figure heavily in the retail landscape. **The Amish Connection** and the **Village Depot and School** specialize in Amish goods, including furniture and quilts, while a wide variety of antiques can be found at **Old Crow Antiques** and the **New Generations of Harmony Antique Mall**.

Lodging choices are surprisingly diverse here. **Asahi Loft** has a distinctly Japanese feel to it, thanks to the years the owners spent in Japan and the decorating sensibility they brought back with them. **The Country Lodge Inn** offers one of the few traditional hotel-style lodgings in the area, but it is still small, with only 25 rooms.

Following MN 16 east will bring you to Lanesboro. Preston may be the county seat, but Lanesboro is tourism headquarters for the bluff country. The town itself is a gem, set gently into a valley with soaring bluffs along its northern edges. Lanesboro began as a resort town, with a dam built to create a lake, but its proximity to the Root River also made it attractive for mill owners. The natural beauty of the area drew residents and farmers, including a doctor whose pastime of bird-watching left behind highly detailed records still in use today. Red-shouldered hawks, bald eagles, wild turkeys, screech owls, and the tufted titmouse are just a few of the more than 300 types of birds that have been identified around the bluff country. To learn more about the birds in the area, and to find high-quality bird feed to take home, stop by **Avian Acres**.

Besides the Root River and Harmony-Preston Valley Trails, one of the best ways to explore nature is to spend time at the **Eagle Bluff Environmental Learning Center**, one of only seven such centers in the state and the only one south of the Twin Cities. Eagle Bluff sits on 80 acres of land surrounded by 1,000 acres of state forest, with hiking trails winding throughout and a scenic overlook from the top of a bluff over a deeply forested valley. The center offers residential programs for kids, adults, and families, including a challenging but popular ropes course. Course offerings run the gamut from canoeing to hiking, learning to make maple syrup, stargazing, archery, fishing, orienteering, geocaching, and compass training.

ROOT RIVER OUTFITTERS, LANESBORO

Of course, you can manage your outdoor adventures yourself by bringing your transportation mode of choice with you. But if that's not practical, Lanesboro has several outfitters that can rent canoes, kayaks, inner tubes, and bikes. **Root River Outfitters** rents all of the above, and offers guided fishing trips. **River Rats Outfitters** rents canoes and kayaks, and owner Ken Soiney is a native of the area, so you can expect him to answer your questions, especially those related to fishing and camping. **Little River General Store** provides canoes, kayaks, and bikes, and it also has a bike repair service if you've brought your own and run into trouble. All outfitters can arrange shuttle service.

Although easily explored on a day trip, Lanesboro is a popular overnight or long weekend destination, and with good reason. Besides biking, hiking, canoeing, kayaking, and tubing, the town of Lanesboro has plenty to offer. Drive down **Parkway Avenue**, Lanesboro's main street, and visit the business district, which is listed on the National Register of Historic Places. The northern end of the town concludes with steep wooded bluffs, and the business district begins there. Windy Mesa Jewelry and Art showcases Navajo, Hopi, and Zuni art.

The arts community is alive and well in Lanesboro, too. **Commonweal Theatre** (see sidebar) is a pillar of the community, supporting not only their own work but the efforts of nearby **Lanesboro Art Center**. The art center arranges exhibitions and juried gallery exhibitions of local artists, as well as an annual Art in the Park event. They also arrange events and concerts at the **St. Mane Theatre**.

Dining in Lanesboro is a casual affair. That doesn't mean you can't find a gourmet meal, but it does mean you can dress casually and stay relaxed. If you're seeking an imaginative menu with locally sourced foods featured in seasonal dishes, try the **Old Village Hall Restaurant & Pub**. Specialties

Guided Tours

Along the Minnesota–Iowa border is a small but thriving Amish community. Here you'll find tour companies offering rides through the area as well as stops at selected farms and shops. Amish country tours operate Monday through Saturday in-season. For religious reasons, tours aren't available on Sunday. If you'd like to take pictures of Amish farms and buggies, that's fine, but please respect the beliefs of some orders of Amish that prohibit taking photographs of people.

Amish Tours of Harmony offers tours Monday through Saturday, April through November. Discounts are given if you use your own vehicle. **Bluffscape Amish Tours** operates Monday through Saturday, May through October. If you'd prefer a self-directed tour, an audio CD called Amish Backroads Tour is available from several Lanesboro retailers.

For a more adventurous ride, **Bluff Country Jeep Tours** provides daily tours (weather permitting) from April through October. Tours take on rough terrain, venturing up into the hills and bluffs overlooking the river, and last about an hour; think twice if you get carsick easily.

include grilled beef filet with tarragon butter and horseradish mashed potatoes, and salt cod cakes on black pepper biscuits with roasted pepper remoulade. For more standard supper club fare, try **Riverside at the Root**, which has an excellent patio and serves up steak and pasta dishes. For an inexpensive meal, stop by the **Pedal Pushers' Café**, open for breakfast, lunch, and dinner, and using local sources for their burgers, chicken sandwiches, and homemade pies. **The High Court Pub** offers several craft beers along with an extensive bar menu, while the **Spud Boy Diner** serves hearty breakfasts in vintage style. Open seasonally, **Another Time Ice Cream Parlor & Chocolates** features Bridgeman's Ice Cream,

COMMONWEAL THEATRE, LANESBORO

Caribou Coffee and espresso drinks, and Minnesota-based family-owned Abdallah Chocolates, among other treats. If you're looking for pizza and sandwiches, check out **The Bite**.

If you've succumbed to the lure of Lanesboro and want to stay longer, there are several options. Keep in mind that most of the local lodgings are

LANESBORO

THE OLD VILLAGE HALL RESTAURANT AND PUB, LANESBORO

small bed-and-breakfasts that, while lovely, are not always kid-friendly and may have limited rooms available.

There's a cluster of Victorian homes serving as bed-and-breakfasts in the southern end of Lanesboro. On Parkway Avenue South, you'll find the **Historic Scanlan House** and **O'Leary's**. Running parallel to Parkway is Fillmore Avenue, home to **Anna V's, Fillmore House**, and **Habberstad House**. Also nearby is **Grandma's Inn**, built in 1895.

In the business district, check out **Stone Mill Suites**, reconstructed from a former mill, or the **Cottage House Inn**, or the **Coffee Street Inn**, located right across from the Root River Bike Trail. Or you can try the **Art Loft Lodging**, for a suite (or apartment) with a full kitchen in the historic Lanesboro Art Galleries building, a beautiful accommodation with exposed brick and tall windows. Another unique option is **A Guest Hus Motel & Historic Knotty Pine Cabins**. Not a motel in the traditional sense, this is a lodging with five rooms in a historic 1900 house, along with two vintage cabins, all with private baths. **Mrs. B's Historic Lanesboro Inn** has nine rooms in a

Nationally Known Commonweal Theatre

The **Commonweal Theatre** opened its doors in 1989, then again in 2007 in a new building that allowed for larger audiences and more theatrical flexibility. It's tempting to think of the playhouse as a tourist attraction, but with a season running from April through December, the theater depends on local audiences as well, and is nationally known for its productions of the works of Henrik Ibsen and annual Ibsen Festival. The festival has received international acclaim, as well as a grant from the Norwegian government to continue exploring Ibsen's work. Besides Ibsen, Commonweal produces at least four other plays each year, sponsors readings of new works, and produces a live radio show every summer. The new building's lobby was decorated by a local artist, who made creative use of local artifacts, offering yet another reason to visit.

historic limestone building adjacent to the Root River. Feeling brave? The inn continues to undergo studies by After Hours Paranormal Investigations.

Just a few miles outside Lanesboro is a particularly beautiful and scenic option for your stay. On a hillside overlooking miles of trees and farmland is **Berwood Hill Inn**, which provides charming Victorian rooms and Adirondack chairs along the hillside, so you can spend time admiring the view.

BERWOOD HILL INN, LANESBORO

Four miles outside Lanesboro on County Route 16 (CR 16) is Whalan, a small town on the Root River Trail. Here you'll find the **Cedar Valley Resort**, composed of several large log cabins perfectly designed for families, with volleyball and horseshoe courts, fire pits, and lawn swings, just steps from the trail. Canoes, kayaks, and bikes are available for rent. On the other side of Whalan but also right on the trail is the **Cyclin-Up Inn**, a three-bedroom whole-house rental. It's likewise conveniently located on the grounds of the **Gator Greens Mini Golf**, and if you're visiting at the right time of the summer season, there are opportunities to pick your own produce, including strawberries. Whalan is also home to a well-loved local institution: the **Aroma Pie Shop**. The name says it all, and the pies are made from scratch on-site. Lunch items are also available.

Head south out of Whalan on CR 23 onto a gravel road that winds through dense tree cover, and you'll suddenly turn a corner and find the **Old Gribben Mill**. The remnants of this former milling operation, now deserted, with its stone construction crumbling and greenery growing over it, may convince you you're somewhere in Europe instead of southern Minnesota. Take a walk around the ruins (good shoes and long pants are recommended, especially during tick season), and bring a picnic basket. If you explore the area behind the ruins, you'll find waterfalls near the bluffs.

Continuing east on CR 16 from Whalan brings you to the community of

THE OLD GRIBBEN MILL, WHALEN

Peterson, which has two bed-and-breakfasts near the Root River Trail that are worth a visit: **Crossing Bed & Breakfast** and the **Andor Wenneson Inn**. Both are near a mill operation. While not as scenic as some of the Lanesboro properties, the inns are comfortable and literally only steps from the trail.

Further east is Rushford, where at **Norsland Lefse** you can not only sample some of the Scandinavian delicacy known as lefse, you can learn how it's made (hint: rolling pins are crucial). Sweets of another kind are sold at the **Creamery**, which boasts 36 flavors of ice cream. Take your cone next door to **Nordic Lanes** if the weather isn't cooperating and bowl a few frames. When the weather improves, enjoy a little golf at the nine-hole **Ferndale Golf Course**. Younger travelers will want to visit **Creekside Park**, an elaborate playground park built in 2009 to replace an older one destroyed by flooding in 2008. The bed-and-breakfast of choice here is **Meadows Inn**, recently built and lavishly appointed.

Before continuing east, take a detour south on MN 43 to Choice, home of a unique land formation known as **Cabbage Rocks**, an outcropping that strongly resembles heads of cabbage.

The last eastward leg of the trip heads back to MN 16 and on to Houston. Here you can get up close and personal with a buffalo at **Money Creek Buffalo Ranch**. While visiting, plan on taking a hike at **South Park**, which has trails that wind their way through valleys and up bluffs, where you will find striking rock formations.

Take MN 76 south out of Houston to find **Schech's Mill** for a tour of the only remaining water-powered flour mill in Minnesota. The milling history of this region is deep-rooted, and the opportunity to see it in action is well worth the time.

IN THE AREA

Accommodations

A GUEST HUS MOTEL & HISTORIC KNOTTY PINE CABINS, 610 Parkway Avenue South, Lanesboro. Call 507-438-5272. Not a motel in the traditional sense, but five rooms in a restored historic home along with two vintage cabins, all with private bath. Website: www.aguesthus.com.

ANDOR WENNESON INN, 425 Prospect Street, Peterson. Call 507-875-2587. Nine rooms, all with private bath, are offered between the main house and the carriage house. Rooms are named for their color schemes, and all have period furniture and decor. The inn is a short walk from the Root River Trail. Breakfast served only on weekends. Website: andorwennesoninn.com.

ANNA V'S BED & BREAKFAST, 507 Fillmore Avenue South, Lanesboro. Call 507-467-2686. Another of the Victorian clusters on the south end of Lanesboro, this property has three guest rooms with private bath and full multicourse breakfast each day. Website: www.annavbb.com.

ART LOFT LODGING, 103 Parkway Avenue North, Lanesboro. Call 507-467-2446. Website: lanesboroarts.org/art-lofts-lodging.

ASAHI LOFT OF HARMONY, 255 5th Street SE, Harmony. Call 507-226-3735. A large suite with Japanese-themed amenities. Website: www.asahiloft.com.

BERWOOD HILL INN, 22139 Hickory Road, Lanesboro. Call 612-867-3614. Five miles from downtown Lanesboro and one of the most romantic inns in the area. Website: www.berwood.com.

CEDAR VALLEY RESORT, 905 Bench Street, Whalan. Call 507-467-9000. A family-friendly resort, just steps from the Root River Trail. This family-friendly resort, just steps from the Root River Trail and along the Root River, offers large cabins suitable for large families or family reunions. Canoes, kayaks, inner tubes, and cross country skis are available for rent on-site. Website: www.cedarvalleyresort.com.

COFFEE STREET INN, 305 Coffee Street East, Lanesboro. Call 507-467-2674. Located across from the Root River Bike Trail, offering seven rooms and two suites, all with private bath. Website: www.coffeestreetinn.com.

COTTAGE HOUSE INN, 209 Parkway Avenue North, Lanesboro. Call 507-467-2577. A historic inn offering 14 rooms and one suite, all with private bath. Website: www.cottagehouseinn.com.

COUNTRY LODGE INN, 525 Main Avenue North, Harmony. Call 507-886-2515. A traditional hotel with 25 rooms and typical hotel amenities, including cable TV, ice machines, and wifi. Website: www.countrylodgeinnharmonymn.com.

CROSSING BED & BREAKFAST, 427 Prospect Street, Peterson. Call 507-875-2725. A Victorian-themed inn offering four rooms and two suites, with an enhanced continental breakfast extending beyond a simple pastry daily and free passes to the Ferndale Country Club on weekdays. Website: www.thecrossingbb.com.

CYCLIN-UP INN, 920 Bench Street, Whalan. Call 507-251-5101. A whole-house rental located a few yards from the Root River Trail and next to Gators Greens Mini Golf. Website: www.cyclin-inn.com.

GRANDMA'S INN, 100 Elmwood Street East, Lanesboro. Call 507-467-2144. Built in 1895, a lovely home with eight rooms and two suites, with breakfast available April through August. Website: www.grandmasmn.com.

HABBERSTAD HOUSE, 706 Fillmore Avenue South, Lanesboro. Call 507-467-3560. Six beautiful rooms and suites tucked inside a restored Victorian home, surrounded by lush gardens and sitting areas. Website: www .habberstadhouse.com.

HISTORIC SCANLAN HOUSE B&B, 708 Parkway Avenue South, Lanesboro. Call 507-467-2158; 800-944-2158. A striking 1889 Queen Anne mansion with seven elaborately furnished and romantic rooms and suites, all with private bath. Website: www.scanlanhouse.com.

JAILHOUSE INN, 109 Houston Street Northwest, Preston. Call 507-765-2181. Website: www.jailhouseinn.com.

JAMES A. THOMPSON HOUSE, 401 Parkway Avenue South, Lanesboro. Call 507-467-2253. A bed-and-breakfast overlooking the Root River and offering four guest rooms. Website: www.jamesathompsonhouse.com.

MEADOWS INN BED & BREAKFAST, 900 Pine Meadows Lane, Rushford. Call 507-864-2378. Five rooms with private bath, plus extensive gardens and a sizable patio. Children allowed with parents. Website: www.facebook .com/Meadows-Inn-Bed-and-Breakfast-16322343595974.

MRS. B'S HISTORIC LANESBORO INN, 101 Parkway Avenue North, Lanesboro. Call 507-467-2154. Nine rooms with private bath, warmly decorated with color and quilts. Website: www.mrsbsinn.com.

O'LEARY'S BED & BREAKFAST, 707 Parkway Avenue South, Lanesboro. Call 507-467-3737. Five rooms, all with private bath, located in the cluster of Victorian homes in south Lanesboro. Website: www.olearysbandb.com.

OLD BARN RESORT & RIVERS' BEND GOLF, 24461 Heron Road, Preston. Call 507-467-2512. Website: www.barnresort.com.

SCANDINAVIAN INN, 701 Kenilworth Avenue South, Lanesboro. Call 507-467-4500. Five rooms with private bath, plus a rooftop gazebo and large front porch. Website: www.scandinavianinn.com.

SELVIG HOUSE BED & BREAKFAST, 140 East Center Street, Harmony. Call 507-886-2200. Website: www.selvighousebb.com.

STONE MILL SUITES, 100 Beacon Street East, Lanesboro. Call 507-467-8663. Ten rooms and suites named and decorated after an aspect of the region, including the Amish Room, the Grain Room, and the Egg Jacuzzi Suite. Kids are welcome here. Website: www.stonemillsuites.com.

Attractions and Recreation

AMISH CONNECTION STORE, 90 2nd Street NW, Harmony. Call 507-886-2409. Website: www.village-depot.com/amishconnection.php.

AMISH TOURS OF HARMONY, Harmony. April through November. Call 507-886-2303; 800-752-6474. Website: www.amish-tours.com.

AVIAN ACRES, 32637 Grit Road, Lanesboro. Call 5007-467-2996; 800-867-2473. Open Tuesday through Saturday, from 9 a.m. to 6 p.m., and occasionally on Monday. Website: www.avianacres.com.

BLUFF COUNTRY JEEP TOURS, 439 Half Street, Lanesboro. Call 507-272-2149. April through October daily (weather permitting), $60 per ride (three people maximum). Website: www.wegoplaces/com.

BLUFFSCAPE AMISH TOURS, 102 East Beacon Street, Lanesboro. May through October, Monday through Saturday. Call 507-467-3070. Website: www.bluffscape.com.

COMMONWEAL THEATRE, 208 Parkway Avenue North, Lanesboro. Call 507-467-2525; 800-657-7025. Season runs April through December. Website: www.commonwealtheatre.org.

EAGLE BLUFF ENVIRONMENTAL LEARNING CENTER, 28097 Goodview Drive, Lanesboro. Call 507-467-2437. Website: www.eagle-bluff.org.

FERNDALE COUNTRY CLUB, 23239 MN 16, Rushford. Call 507-864-7626. Website: www.ferndalegolfcourse.com.

FORESTVILLE/MYSTERY CAVE STATE PARK, 21071 CR 118, Preston. Call 507-352-5111. Hours limited in winter months, call for information. Website: www.dnr.state.mn.us/state_parks/forestville_mystery_cave/index.html.

GATOR GREENS MINI GOLF, 439 Half Street, Lanesboro. Call 507-467-3000. Website: www.cyclin-inn.com/gatorgreehm.html.

HARMONY AREA HISTORICAL SOCIETY, 15 2nd Street NW, Harmony. Website: www.harmonymnhistory.org.

LANESBORO ARTS CENTER, 103 Parkway Avenue North, Lanesboro. Call 507-467-2446. Art gallery exhibiting and selling works by local and national artists. Website: lanesboroarts.org.

LITTLE RIVER GENERAL STORE, 105 East Coffee Street, Lanesboro. Call 507-467-2943. Website: lrgeneralstore.net.

MONEY CREEK BUFFALO RANCH, 32488 Cody Drive, Houston. Call 507-896-2345. Website: www.buffalogal.com.

NEW GENERATIONS OF HARMONY ANTIQUE MALL, 50 Industrial Boulevard NE, Harmony. Call 507-886-6660. Website: www.generationsof harmony.com.

NIAGARA CAVE, 29842 CR 30, Harmony. Call 800-886-6606. Open daily in May through October, and on weekends in April. Website: www.niagara cave.com.

NORSLAND LEFSE, 210 West Jessie Street, Rushford. Call 507-864-2323. Website: www.norslandlefse.com.

OLD CROW ANTIQUES, 101 US 52, Canton. Call 563-379-5112. Website: www.oldcrowantiques.blogspot.com.

ROOT RIVER AND HARMONY-PRESTON VALLEY TRAILS. Website: www.rootrivertrail.org.

RIVER RATS OUTFITTERS, Parkway Avenue and Ashburn, Lanesboro. Call 507-429-7202. Website: www.riverratsoutfitters.com.

ROOT RIVER OUTFITTERS, 109 Parkway Avenue South, Lanesboro. Call 507-467-3400. Website: www.rootriveroutfitters.com.

SCENIC VALLEY WINERY, 103 East Coffee Street, Lanesboro. Call 888-965-0250. Open April through October, Monday through Saturday 10 a.m. to 5 p.m., and Sunday 1 to 5 p.m. Call for appointment the rest of the year. Website: www.scenivvalleywinery.com.

SCHECH'S MILL, West Beaver Road, Caledonia. Call 507-896-3481. Open for public tours mid-May through October. Website: www.schechsmill.com.

WINDY MESA INDIAN JEWELRY, 102 Parkway Avenue North, Lanesboro. Call 507-467-2198. Website: www.facebook.com/Windy-Mesa-14549 8078927992.

Dining

ANOTHER TIME ICE CREAM PARLOR & CHOCOLATES, 100 Parkway Avenue North, Lanesboro. Call 507-467-3556. Seasonal ice cream and candy parlor. Website: www.facebook.com/Another-Time-Ice-Cream-Parlor -Chocolates-LLC-422445987775516.

THE AROMA PIE SHOP, 618 Main Street, Whalan. Call 507-467-2623. Seasonal shop serving sandwiches, soups, hot dogs, brats—and of course, homemade pie. Website: www.thearomapieshop.com.

THE BITE, 111 Parkway Avenue North, Lanesboro. Call 507-467-2200. Pizza and sandwiches. Website: www.facebook.com/TheBiteofLanesboro.

BRANDING IRON SUPPER CLUB, 1100 Circle Heights Drive, Preston. Call (507) 765-3388. Steak and other hearty foods. Website: www .brandingironmn.com.

HARMONY HOUSE RESTAURANT, 57 Main Avenue North, Harmony. Call 507-886-4612. Home cooking with an Amish bent. Website: www.facebook .com/pages/Harmony-House-Restaurant/108071652567834.

HIGH COURT PUB, 109 Parkway Avenue North, Lanesboro. Call 507-467-2782. Craft beers and pub fare. Website: www.highcourtpub.com.

LOS GABLES, US 52 and MN 80, Fountain. Call 507-268-1020. Owned and operated by the Gomez family, using family recipes on the menu. Website: www.losgables.com.

OLD VILLAGE HALL RESTAURANT & PUB, 111 Coffee Street, Lanesboro. Call 507-467-2962. Menu changes seasonally, taking advantage of local foods, including herbs from the restaurant's own garden. Website: www .oldvillagehall.com.

ON THE CRUNCHY SIDE, 31 Main Avenue North, Harmony. Call 507-886-5560. Website: www.facebook.com/onthecrunchyside.

PEDAL PUSHERS CAFÉ, 121 Parkway Avenue North, Lanesboro. Call 507-467-1050. A '50s-style restaurant with hearty breakfasts, sandwiches and burgers for lunch, and comfort food like chicken pot pie and meat loaf for dinner, as well as daily blue plate specials. Website: www.pedalpusherscafe .com.

RIVER TRAIL PICNIC BASKET, 100 Parkway Avenue North, Lanesboro. Call 507-467-3556. Ice cream, coffee drinks, sandwiches.

RIVERSIDE AT THE ROOT, 109 Parkway Avenue South, Lanesboro. Call 507-467-3663. Located on the Root River, serving standard steakhouse fare, along with pizza and pasta, and occasionally wild game (elk). Website: riversideontheroot.com.

SPUD BOY DINER, 105 3/4 Parkway Avenue North, Lanesboro. Call 563-419-0272. Vintage diner serving hearty breakfasts. Website: www.spud .nydiners.com.

Other Contacts

HISTORIC BLUFF COUNTRY. Call 844-452-0409. Website: www.bluff country.com.

LANESBORO CHAMBER OF COMMERCE, 100 Milwaukee Road, Lanesboro. Call 507-467-2696. Website: www.lanesboro.com.

ROOT RIVER TRAIL. Website: www.rootrivertrail.org.

16

PIONEER TRAILS, DIFFERENT ERAS

ESTIMATED DISTANCE: 170 miles

ESTIMATED TIME: 4 hours

GETTING THERE: From the Twin Cities, take US 169 south to Henderson, where you'll pick up MN 19 west to Morton. This trip could easily be combined with Chapter 14, the Minnesota River Valley, Part 2: Mankato to Fairfax.

HIGHLIGHTS: A journey through the history of both Native Americans and the pioneers who were sometimes at odds with them: the Birch Coulee and Loyal Indian Monuments; the Lower Sioux Agency; the Laura Ingalls Wilder Museum and the Ingalls Dugout; the Sod House on the Prairie in Sanborn; and the Jeffers Petroglyphs.

This somewhat circular trip serves the purpose of both introducing you to the prairie lands of southwest Minnesota (see Chapter 17, Prairie Country, for more of this area) and exploring various facets of Minnesota's Native American and pioneer history, which are entwined for better and for worse.

The landscape changes significantly over the course of this trip. Beginning at the Minnesota River, with its rolling, wooded hills, you'll move on to more level terrain and wide-open spaces. There's still water to be found, and trees, but you'll also experience the beauty of distant horizons and miles of flowing farmland. While much of the original native prairie disappeared under agricultural plantings years ago, some patches remain, and efforts are being made to restore some of this land to its original state. When you stumble upon actual prairie grasses and wildflowers, take the time to appreciate them (especially in midsummer, when the wildflowers are at their most

LEFT: LAKE SHETEK STATE PARK

colorful). Places like the Jeffers Petroglyphs offer hiking options through prairie fields, which are well worth the extra time.

Please be aware that many of the sites listed here have limited visiting hours, and some are open only in the summer. Check the site's website (listed at the end of this chapter) or call for current information.

The first stop is the **Birch Coulee Battlefield**, just north of Morton at the junction of County Route 2 (CR 2) and CR 8. One of the worst battles of the US–Dakota war took place here on September 2, 1862. This war has also been described as the Minnesota Civil War, and it had devastating effects on both sides in terms of casualties and cultural/psychological impact. Today the site is a restored prairie area, with trails leading to various notable points that have detailed interpretive signs. Returning to Morton and traveling east on MN 19, the **Birch Coulee and Loyal Indian Monuments** are in view. The Birch Coulee Monument was built in 1892 to honor the soldiers involved

in the Birch Coulee battle, and the Loyal Indian Monument followed in 1899 to honor six Dakota who saved the lives of white settlers. Southeast of Morton on County Road 2, the **Lower Sioux Agency**, an administrative center created in 1853 for the Dakota reservation, has a history center focused on life around the time of the Dakota War, a war in which 20 people were killed and more were captured in an attempt to force the white settlers to abandon the Minnesota River Valley. The Lower Sioux Agency exhibitions examine the causes of the war and demonstrate other facets of life for the Sioux during this time period.

After visiting the Lower Sioux Agency, go west on CR 2 for 1 mile, then turn south on CR 13 and travel about 4 miles to reach the **Gilfillan Estate**. The estate was built by Charles Duncan Gilfillan, who raised livestock for export to Great Britain and was very successful. His son eventually donated the home to the Redwood County Historical Society and funded construction of several buildings in the nearby city of Redwood Falls, including city offices and a library. The Gilfillan home itself is fully furnished with antiques, and you can choose between a tour of just the house or one that includes the farm as well.

Continue south on CR 13 until you turn right to head west on US 14, also known as Laura Ingalls Wilder Historic Highway. The highway stretches from Pepin, Wisconsin (home of *Little House in the Big Woods*) to De Smet, South Dakota (*By the Shores of Silver Lake*). When you reach **Walnut Grove**, you've arrived at the location of *On the Banks of Plum Creek*. The Ingalls family arrived in Walnut Grove in 1874 and stayed two years, then returned in 1877 for two more years. There are few actual traces of their lives there; a school Wilder attended and a hotel where she worked still exist, but they are now private homes not open to the public. **The Laura Ingalls Wilder Museum** itself is a collection of vintage and re-created pioneer buildings, none of which has a direct association with Wilder, but the main Depot Building has a collection of items including a number of pieces once owned by Wilder, including a quilt she made and needlework supplies. Fans of the TV show will also enjoy stopping here, as a room is devoted to memorabilia from the show, and in the summer cast members sometimes make public appearances. For hard-core history buffs, this may not be worth a stop, but if you like general pioneer history and/or have kids traveling with you, it's definitely worth a visit.

Just 1½ miles north on CR 5, however, is an artifact more directly linked to the Ingalls family. Along the banks of Plum Creek is a **dugout home** where the Ingalls family lived from 1874 to 1876 before selling it after several crop failures and moving to Iowa. The family's ownership was discovered by the illustrator of Wilder's books, Garth Williams, who informed the current owners of the historic nature of their property. Although the dugout itself is not much more than a hollow in the ground, it's surprisingly moving, especially

THE LAURA INGALLS WILDER MUSEUM, WALNUT GROVE

when you look down to Plum Creek (you can also walk down to it and enjoy some time wading in it). The site is scenic, and picnic tables are available to make for a pleasant stop.

There are a couple of dining options in Walnut Grove, including **Nellie's Café**, open daily for lunch and breakfast, and the **Walnut Grove Bar & Grill**, a supper-club-style restaurant open every day but Sunday for lunch and dinner.

Take CR 5 south back to US 14 and continue west to Tracy, where you can find lodging at the **Wilder Inn Motel** or the **Valentine Inn Bed & Breakfast**. On US 14 is the **Wheels Across the Prairie Museum**. Wheels Across the Prairie is a pioneer village filled with several genuine buildings and artifacts from the 1800s, as well as a 1915 locomotive, an 1890 town hall, and a log cabin from 1866.

From the museum, head south on CR 38 toward Currie. Continue west on CR 37 to **Lake Shetek State Park**. Besides being a lovely park with a fishing pier (Lake Shetek is the largest lake in southwest Minnesota), swimming beach, 14 miles of hiking trails, and 6 miles of paved biking trails, Lake Shetek State Park is home to the Koch Cabin, built in 1857 and thought to be the oldest building in the county. There is also the Shetek Monument, which memorializes the 15 settlers who were killed in the Dakota Conflict of 1862.

From the park, take CR 37 east to CR 38 south into Currie to visit the **End-O-Line Railroad Park and Museum**. Among the many exhibitions is a manually operated railroad turntable, still functional and in its original location, a piece of equipment that's on the National Register of Historic Places.

THE INGALLS DUGOUT SITE, WALNUT GROVE

Other sights include a restored 1875 steam locomotive, an interpretive center with a wide variety of memorabilia, and an exhibition about hobos, bums, and tramps. There are several historic buildings to visit, including an original general store, school, courthouse, and church buildings, and a Lakota teepee. Here you'll also find a paved bike trail that connects End-O-Line with Lake Shetek State Park.

HISTORIC CABIN AT LAKE SHETEK STATE PARK

To find another historical site related to the Dakota Conflict of 1862, travel south on CR 38 from Currie, then turn east on MN 30, which leads to CR 11. Travel north on 225th Avenue to the **Slaughter Slough WPA (Waterfowl Production Area)**. The parking lot is near the corner of 225th Avenue and 161st Street. In the Slough is a monument paying tribute to three separate groups who were involved in and lost lives during

THE END O' LINE MUSEUM, CURRIE

the Dakota Conflict: the Dakota, the white settlers, and the Fool Soldiers, young Lakota men who negotiated for the release of captives and were later shunned by other Lakota for their work. The Slough is also a great location for bird- and wildlife watching.

THE JEFFERS PETROGLYPHS

Resume driving east on MN 30, heading for Jeffers. Past the little town of Jeffers itself, take US 71 north to CR 10. Turn east onto CR 10, then south onto CR 2 to reach the **Jeffers Petroglyphs**. Thought to date from 3,000 BC to possibly as recently as the mid-1700s, these islands of rock that appear throughout the prairie grasses hold over 2,000 Native American carvings. Two separate trails visit the glyphs, both starting at the visitor center, 1½-mile roundtrip, the other slightly over a mile. Interpreters are available to explain the significance of the glyphs, which have a wide range of subject matter and meaning: humans, arrows, elk, buffalo, deer, and turtles are just some of the identifiable figures. The glyphs detail the history of the region and the people, identifying significant events and sacred ceremonies. Native Americans still come today for religious visits.

But it's not just the historic or spiritual aspects that make the area a worthwhile visit. The landscape here is striking: pink quartzite, prickly pear cactus, and dozens of wildflowers. The Jeffers site has areas of original prairie, a rarity, and just over half of the site is part of the state's first prairie re-cultivation effort. In the northern reaches, areas of buffalo rubs can be seen, where migrating bison would stop to rub their coats against the rocks, eventually leaving them with a glossy surface. After visiting the glyphs, take some time to admire the rest of the scenery and hike the full trails.

The best time to visit is either morning or late afternoon, when the sunlight is less harsh, making the glyphs easier to read. But even in the middle of the day, there are glyphs that can be recognized, and guides can work with mirrors to help you see the less defined designs.

Heading back to US 71 and traveling north, you'll come full circle to US 14. Travel east on US 14 for about 1 mile, until you see the sign for **Sod House on the Prairie**. A personal project of owner Stan McCone, Sod House is actually several sod buildings, constructed meticulously at the size and with the materials the original pioneers used to build their first homes. The replica home site includes a sod home, dugout, and log cabin; the "soddie" was built

SOD HOUSE ON THE PRAIRIE, SANBORN

SOD HOUSE ON THE PRAIRIE, SANBORN

in the style of Laura Ingalls Wilder's day, with two-foot-thick walls and a lumber roof and floor, as opposed to the dugout, which has a dirt floor and roof. In previous years, the soddie was available as a bed-and-breakfast, but for now only tours are offered. There are pioneer costumes available for both kids and adults, and the area around the sod homes is undergoing restoration to prairie lands, with a short trail running throughout. They may not be original sod houses, but they're historically accurate (enough so to be included in a History Channel documentary) and offer visitors a strong sense of what living in one was like.

Finally, if your journeys through pioneer trails have left you hungry, continue east to Springfield, a city running alongside the Big Cottonwood River. The historic downtown is charming and walkable, and there are more dining choices here than in most of the other communities in the region. Nicer fare in a sit-down restaurant is available at **Tommy's Central Street Steakhouse**, or you can combine dining with bowling at the **Springfield Lanes and The Garage**.

IN THE AREA

Accommodations

VALENTINE INN BED & BREAKFAST, 385 Emory Street, Tracy. Call 507-629-3827. Four rooms, all with private bath, in a Victorian home that began its life as a hospital. Two rooms have walkout porches. Rates start at $85. Website: www.facebook.com/pages/Valentine-Inn-Bed-Breakfast /115624915134193.

WILDER INN MOTEL, 1000 Craig Avenue, Tracy. Call 507-629-3350. A small motel a few miles from Walnut Grove, basic in amenities but well tended.

Attractions and Recreation

BIRCH COULEE AND LOYAL INDIAN MONUMENTS, MN 19, Morton.

BIRCH COULEE BATTLEFIELD, CR 2 and CR 18, Morton. Call 800-657-3773. Website: www.sites.mnhs.org/historic-sites/birch-coulee-battlefield.

SHEEP FARM, SPRINGFIELD

END-O-LINE RAILROAD PARK & MUSEUM, 440 North Mill Street, Currie. Call 507-763-3708. Website: www.endoline.com.

GILFILLAN ESTATE, 28269 MN 67, Morgan. Call 507-249-3451. Website: www.redwoodcountyhistoricalsociety.com/gilfillan-estate.

INGALLS DUGOUT, 13001 CR 5, Walnut Grove. Website: www.walnutgrove .org/ingalls-dugout-site.html.

JEFFERS PETROGLYPHS, 27160 CR 2, Jeffers. Call 507-628-5591. Website: www.sites.mnhs.org/historic-sites/jeffers-petroglyphs.

LAKE SHETEK STATE PARK, 163 State Park Road, Currie. Call 507-763-3256. Website: www.dnr.state.mn.us/state_parks/lake_shetek/index.html.

LAURA INGALLS WILDER MUSEUM, 330 8th Street, Walnut Grove. Call 507-859-2358; 800-528-7280. Website: www.walnutgrove.org/museum .html.

LOWER SIOUX AGENCY, 32469 County Highway 2, Morton. Call 507-697-6321. Website: www.sites.mnhs.org/historic-sites/lower-sioux-agency.

SOD HOUSE ON THE PRAIRIE, 12598 Magnolia Avenue, Sanborn. Call 507-723-5138. Website: www.sodhouse.org.

WHEELS ACROSS THE PRAIRIE, 3297 US 14, Tracy. Call 507-626-1949. Website: www.wheelsacrosstheprairie.org.

Dining

NELLIE'S CAFÉ, 550 US 14, Walnut Grove. Call 507-859-2384. Open daily for breakfast and lunch, Monday through Friday for dinner. Diner fare. Website: www.facebook.com/pages/Nellies-Cafe/223807654315812.

SPRINGFIELD LANES AND THE GARAGE, 3 North Cass Avenue, Springfield. Call 507-723-6000. Bowling alley with pizza, pasta, and burgers. Website: www.thelanesandgarage.com.

TOMMY'S CENTRAL STREET STEAKHOUSE, 8 West Central Street, Springfield. Call 507-723-9191. Steak, ribs, chicken, and sandwiches. Website: www.facebook.com/Tommys-Central-Street-Steakhouse-123417321027065.

WALNUT GROVE BAR & GRILL, 651 Main Street, Walnut Grove. Call 507-859-2399. American cuisine. Website: www.facebook.com/Walnut-Grove -Bar-Grill-121170667932076.

Other Contacts

SPRINGFIELD CHAMBER OF COMMERCE, 33 South Cass Avenue, Springfield. Call 507-723-3508. Website: www.springfieldmnchamber.org.

TRACY CHAMBER OF COMMERCE, 372 Morgan Street, Tracy. Call 507-629-4021. Website: www.tracymn.org.

WALNUT GROVE. Website: www.walnutgrove.org.

17

PRAIRIE COUNTRY

ESTIMATED DISTANCE: 45 miles

ESTIMATED TIME: 1 hour

GETTING THERE: From Rochester, head south on US 52, then take I-90 west before following US 75 north to Luverne. From Mankato, take MN 60 south to west I-90, then US 75 north to Luverne.

HIGHLIGHTS: The quintessential small town of Luverne; Blue Mounds State Park with its swimming beach and hiking trails through prairie grasses; the historic town of Pipestone and the adjacent Pipestone National Monument; and the town (and wind power center) of Lake Benton.

When people think of Minnesota, the images that are most likely to come to mind are, of course, lakes and acres of forests. That's not an inaccurate portrayal, especially in the northeast and north-central parts of the state, but it's not the only scenery to be found.

Along the border between Minnesota and South Dakota, from the Iowa border north, is an area known as the Coteau des Prairie. It's the remnant of many glacial movements and retreats. The highest part of the Coteau in Minnesota is known as Buffalo Ridge, an area around Lake Benton and Pipestone with bedrock of shale, sandstone, and clay that have settled over Sioux quartzite before being covered with layers of glacial drift. As opposed to other parts of Minnesota, featuring dramatic hills and valleys covered with trees, the Coteau des Prairie has long, sloping hills that were once covered with tallgrass prairie. Today most of that natural prairie growth has given way to agricultural endeavors, with long stretches of soybean and corn fields.

LEFT: PIPESTONE NATIONAL MONUMENT

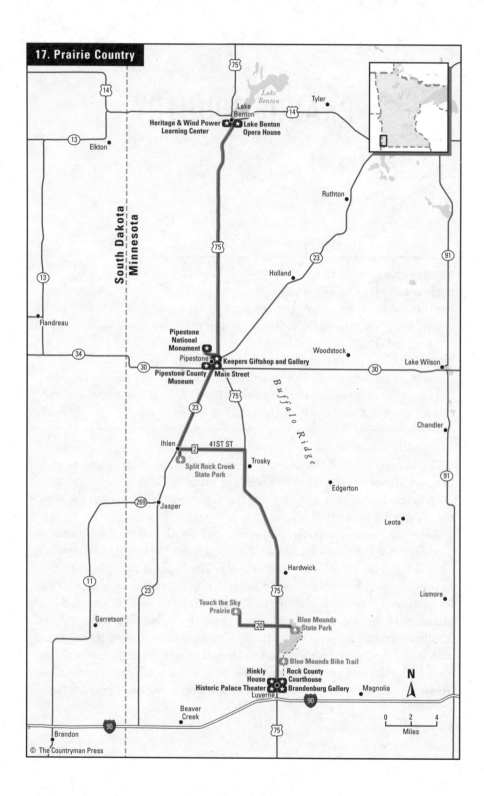

17. Prairie Country

South Dakota
Minnesota

75
14
13
Elkton
13
Lake Benton
Tyler
14
Heritage & Wind Power Learning Center
Lake Benton Opera House
Ruthton
91
75
23
Holland
Flandreau
34
30
Pipestone National Monument
Pipestone
Keepers Giftshop and Gallery
Pipestone County Museum
Main Street
Woodstock
Lake Wilson
30
75
Buffalo Ridge
Chandler
23
Ihlen
2
41ST ST
Split Rock Creek State Park
Trosky
91
269
Jasper
Edgerton
Leota
11
23
Hardwick
75
Lismore
Touch the Sky Prairie
Garretson
20
Blue Mounds State Park
Blue Mounds Bike Trail
Hinkly House
Rock County Courthouse
Historic Palace Theater
Brandenburg Gallery
Luverne
Magnolia
90
Beaver Creek
Brandon
90
75

N

0 2 4
Miles

© The Countryman Press

However, in the farthest southwest, there are still some natural prairie areas remaining, or in the process of being cultivated again. It's a unique kind of beauty. As Minnesota poet and essayist Bill Holm put it in his essay "Horizontal Grandeur": "A woods man looks at 20 miles of prairie and sees nothing but grass, but a prairie man looks at a square foot and sees a universe; 10 or 20 flowers and grasses, heights, heads, colors, shades, configurations, bearded, rough, smooth, simple, elegant. When a cloud passes over the sun, colors shift, like a child's kaleidoscope." Taking the time to explore this part of the state, less traveled than other areas, is a richly rewarding experience full of natural beauty, wide-open skies, wildlife, rivers, Native American sites, and the slowly returning prairie.

When making plans to visit this area of the state, check ahead for restaurant open and close times. Many restaurants are closed on Sundays, and some are closed Mondays as well.

Shortly after you leave I-90 for US 75 north, the town of Luverne comes into view. This community of about 4,600 people is the county seat for Rock County. From a tourist's perspective, though, it's representative of what some people dream of when they envision small-town America: a walkable downtown with historic buildings, quiet residential streets with charming Victorian homes and cottages, with a pride of place and history. Perhaps its biggest claim to fame is being one of the four towns profiled in Ken Burns's landmark documentary *The War*. Several residents of Luverne, all World War II veterans, were interviewed for the documentary, including fighter pilot Quentin Aanenson, for whom the local airport is named. The community's respect for these veterans is on view at the **Rock County Veterans Memorial**, on the grounds of the beautiful **Rock County Courthouse**. The courthouse, built in 1888 of Sioux quartzite, is on the National Register of Historic Places.

More history is offered at the **Rock County Historical Society**, which offers limited hours in the summer for visitors to peruse its holdings. The building itself, a former Unitarian Church built in 1899, is worth a stop.

Nearby is the **Hinkly House**, another lovely Sioux quartzite building from 1892, originally built by the town's mayor. Also on the National Register of Historic Places, the Hinkly House is open for tours during select hours in the summer, or by appointment off-season.

The downtown area of Luverne along Main Street is dotted with century-old buildings, many constructed of Sioux quartzite. Of particular note is the **Historic Palace Theater**, which has been showing movies since 1915. Recent renovations have modernized its operations, but with its large pipe organ still intact, it's as far from a modern multiplex as you can get. The theater hosted the premiere of Burns's documentary.

History and art intersect at the **Brandenburg Gallery**, housed at the Rock County Veterans Memorial Building. Internationally renowned *National*

HINKLY HOUSE MUSEUM, LUVERNE

Geographic nature photographer Jim Brandenburg, a Luverne native, has a gallery of his works for viewing and for sale, with a focus on the prairie lands around Luverne. Brandenburg is also one of the founders of the Brandenburg Prairie Foundation, which works to restore and expand native prairie grasses and flowers. (Brandenburg also has a gallery in Ely; see Chapter 3, Western Boundary Waters, for more information.) You can visit the work in progress at the **Touch the Sky Prairie**, an 800-acre tract of pristine prairie land just outside Luverne. Take US 75 north 4 miles to County Route 20 (CR 20). Drive 3 miles west on CR 20, then turn right and drive for another mile. At the T intersection is the prairie, and there is a parking area at the top of the hill to the west. Visitors are welcome to explore the area.

The next stop north out of Luverne is **Blue Mounds State Park**. The park can be accessed by bike or foot, taking the **Blue Mounds Bike Trail** from Blue Mound Avenue in Luverne, or by taking US 75 north by car to CR 20 (the same road that travels to the Touch the Sky Prairie). Go west on CR 20 for 1 mile to reach the park entrance. This 1,800-acre park sits above surrounding farmland by virtue of a natural pedestal of Sioux quartzite. The Blue Mounds were named for the way they looked to westward-moving settlers; this stretch of rock 1,250 feet long that runs in an east–west direction, corresponding to the rising and setting of the sun, is thought to have been placed by early Dakota. Interesting fact about the rock: each year at the

BLUE MOUNDS STATE PARK

spring and autumn solstice, the sunrise happens exactly on the east end and the sunset exactly on the west end. Deer, coyote, numerous birds, and even bison live here and can be seen by visitors.

The park is an excellent place to immerse yourself in the loveliness of the prairie, especially midsummer, when the wildflowers are in full bloom. The 13 miles of hiking trails wander deep into the prairie, and in some of the lower stretches hikers will find themselves threading a narrow path surrounded by wildflowers nearly six feet tall on either side. Bikers have access to 2 miles of paved trails as well. Rock climbing is available, as is swimming and camping. Don't miss the bison-viewing stand—the park is home to a herd of bison that peacefully roam within a large, fenced space.

The drive from Luverne to Pipestone along US 75 is a quiet one, full of rolling farmlands and prairie remnants. Staying on US 75 will take you directly to Pipestone, but if you have time, a slight detour to **Split Rock Creek State Park** is worthwhile. About 18 miles north of Luverne, take a left onto CR 2 (41st Street) and follow it 5 miles to CR 20 (Bertha Avenue South). Turn

PRAIRIE LANDS AT BLUE MOUNDS STATE PARK

left onto CR 20 and follow it nearly a mile to the park entrance. Once at the park, visit the dam built of Sioux quartzite, constructed in 1938 by the WPA to develop a lake in a part of the state that has few. The park has hiking and horseback riding trails, as well as a swimming area.

When leaving the state park for Pipestone, turn right on CR 20 and follow it back to CR 2, then turn left. Less than a quarter of a mile later, turn right onto MN 23 and follow it 8 miles to Pipestone.

Pipestone, a town rich in Native American and quarrying history, is named after the red stone called pipestone, or catlinite after the artist and writer George Catlin, who visited the area first in 1836, sketching it and recording its local tales. The community was further memorialized by poet Henry Wadsworth Longfellow's "Song of Hiawatha," although Longfellow never actually traveled to Pipestone. The pipestone was, and still is, central to Native American ceremonial rites. They quarried it to create pipes, an activity recorded by Lewis and Clark in the early 1800s. (See the Pipestone National Monument sidebar for more details.)

Pipestone's downtown is so packed full of historic quartzite buildings that the entire **Main Street** area is listed on the National Register of Historic Places, one of the largest such districts in the state. An easy walk of about 12 blocks, mostly along Main Street and North Hiawatha Avenue, will take you past towering stone buildings, each with its year of construction at the top, and sometimes the name of the original owner. The buildings are striking not just for their bygone architectural style, but for the distinctive red stone used to build them. On East Main Street are a series of buildings with whimsical gargoyles above the entrances, carved by sculptor Leon Moore (hence the building's name: the Moore Block). At the junction of Main and Hiawatha is the **Historic Calumet Inn**, built in 1888 and still in operation as a hotel, restaurant, and bar. A good option for overnighting in the area, it's hard to beat getting up in the morning and stepping right out into the historic district. Be sure to take a stroll around the **Pipestone County Courthouse** and the **Carnegie Library. The Episcopal Church** nearby was built in 1892 and is one of the oldest churches still standing in Pipestone. Finally, a visit to the **Pipestone County Museum**, housed in the **Old City Hall**, gives you not only a look at the inside of one of the historic buildings, but also at the history of the area overall.

Just a few blocks east of the historic district is the **Concrete Water Tower** in a rest area near US 75. The 132-foot concrete structure was built in 1920 and served the city until 1976. It's one of very few concrete water towers still in existence, and it is also on the National Register of Historic Places.

On the edge of the town is the **Keepers Giftshop and Gallery,** near the entrance to the Pipestone National Monument. The Keepers shop is full of pipes and Indian art crafts. The shop is run by the Keepers of the Sacred Tradition of Pipemakers, a nonprofit formed by local Native Americans and

HISTORIC DOWNTOWN PIPESTONE

tribal leaders to protect the nearby pipestone quarries and to educate the public about their history and importance.

Across from the Pipestone National Monument entrance is **Fort Pipestone Trading Post and Museum**. This replica of a stockade from the 1862 Sioux uprising is a little kitschy and more entertaining to kids than to adults in search of serious history, but if you have young ones with you and are willing to browse the souvenirs, it's not a bad stop.

As mentioned previously, the Historic Calumet Inn is a good choice for really soaking up the atmosphere of this town. There are other options as well, including the **GrandStay Pipestone**, which offers a variety of suites, daily breakfast, and a large indoor pool.

Dining at the Calumet is also worthwhile, but make time to eat at the very popular **Lange's Café and Bakery** on US 75. Lange's earned national attention when Roadfood writers Jane and Michael Stern highlighted its sour

Pipestone National Monument

Just outside Pipestone is one of two national monuments in Minnesota (the other is Grand Portage National Monument in the northeast corner of the state). **Pipestone National Monument** is a significant historic and cultural site. The red pipestone, so-called because its primary use is to be carved into ceremonial pipe bowls, has been quarried by Native Americans since at least the seventeenth century, and the quarry is viewed as a sacred site. The pipes from this quarry were highly acclaimed across the United States, and the land that produced it was, for the most part, neutral territory for different tribes because of the symbolic power of the site.

Today, the only quarrying allowed is by Native Americans, a right they retained when they sold the land to the US government in 1937. A comprehensive visitor center details the significance and history of the area, and there are locally made pipestone products in the gift shop. During the summer months, visitors can watch as quarrying takes place. The site also houses the Pipestone Indian Shrine Association, a nonprofit that continues the ancient Indian art form of pipemaking.

Take time to hike the Circle Trail, a ¾-mile walk from the visitor center, which provides beautiful views of quartzite, native prairie grasses and wildflowers, and Winnewissa Falls and the Oracle, a naturally occurring stone "face" that Native Americans believed to be a sentient being. Also of interest at the monument's entrance are the large granite boulders known as Three Maidens. The boulders were once one massive boulder that landed at this spot thanks to glaciers; many legends have sprung up about their meaning today.

cream raisin pie as a don't-miss dessert. (The stuffed hash browns at break-fast are worth considering, too.)

Like many communities, Pipestone has several annual events, but one of the biggest is Civil War Days, which takes place each year in August. The festival includes Civil War reenactments, reconstructed military camps, vis-its from Abe and Mary Lincoln, and other historical events and activities.

You could end the drive in Pipestone and feel like you've seen a lot, but a quiet closing trip is just a few more miles north on US 75. Lake Benton is located on the shores of Lake Benton (appropriately enough) and is in the valley of the Buffalo Ridge. Nearby you'll see a number of wind turbines, which take advantage of the rolling prairie land, relatively unobstructed by forest, to collect and harness wind power. There are more than 70 of these turbines in operation, generating enough power to provide electricity to 125 homes. To learn more about the process, visit the **Heritage and Wind Power Learning Center**. The center, opened in 2001, offers changing exhibitions that illustrate how the wind power is collected and how it's used.

Lake Benton is also home to the highly active **Lake Benton Opera House**, offering a variety of Broadway musicals and seasonal and children's pro-ductions. The opera house was first opened in 1896 but fell into disuse and disrepair in the late 1950s. In 1970, a group of local residents launched a campaign to save and restore the building, a process that took nearly 30 years because of the efforts to restore rather than replace.

WIND POWER FARM NEAR PIPESTONE

THE BENTON HOUSE BED & BREAKFAST, LAKE BENTON

If you're looking for a cozy, romantic escape, the **Benton House Bed & Breakfast** on the edge of town offers three charming rooms. Just outside the city is the **Wooden Diamond Bed & Breakfast**, which doesn't have any Victorian charm but rather a fantastic location on the shores of Lake Benton. Dining runs heavily toward supper club or bar fare; check out the **Knotty Pine Supper Club** (a few miles west of Lake Benton, near Elkton, South Dakota) or **the Country House Supper Club** for hearty meals.

IN THE AREA

Accommodations

BENTON HOUSE BED & BREAKFAST, 211 West Benton Street, Lake Benton. Call 507-368-9484.

GRANDSTAY PIPESTONE, 915 7th Street SE, Pipestone. Call 855-455-7829. Website: www.grandstayhospitality.com.

HISTORIC CALUMET INN, 104 West Main, Pipestone. Call 507-825-5871. In the heart of historic downtown Pipestone, a historic inn with small but charming rooms, restaurant, bar, and access to a recreation center across the street. Website: www.calumetinn.com.

WOODEN DIAMOND BED & BREAKFAST, 1593 Shady Shore Drive, Lake Benton. Call 507-368-4305. Website: www.facebook.com/BandJVollmer.

Attractions and Recreation

BLUE MOUNDS STATE PARK, 1410 161st Street, Luverne. Call 507-283-6050. Website: www.dnr.state.mn.us/state_parks/blue_mounds/index.html.

BRANDENBURG GALLERY/ROCK COUNTY VETERANS MEMORIAL BUILDING, 213 East Luverne Street, Luverne. Call 507-283-1884. Website: www.jimbrandenburg.com.

FORT PIPESTONE TRADING POST, 104 9th Street NE, Pipestone. Call 507-825-4474.

HERITAGE AND WIND POWER LEARNING CENTER, 110 South Center Street, Lake Benton. Call 507-368-9577, ext. 6. Website: www.facebook.com /pages/Fort-Pipestone/156560231050184.

HINKLY HOUSE, 217 North Freeman, Luverne. Call 507-283-9476. Website: www.rockcountyhistorical.com/hinkly-house.html.

HISTORIC DISTRICT, Pipestone. Call 507-825-3316; 800-336-6125. Website: www.pipestoneminnesota.com.

HISTORIC PALACE THEATRE, 104 East Main Street, Luverne. Call 507-283-4339. Website: www.palacetheatre.us.

KEEPERS GIFT SHOP AND GALLERY, 400 North Hiawatha Avenue, Pipestone. Call 507-825-3734. Website: www.pipekeepers.org.

PIPESTONE COUNTY MUSEUM, 113 South Hiawatha Avenue, Pipestone. Call 507-825-2563. Website: www.pipestoneminnesota.com/museum.

PIPESTONE NATIONAL MONUMENT, US 75, Pipestone. Call 507-825-5464. Website: www.nps.gov/pipe.

ROCK COUNTY COURTHOUSE/VETERANS MEMORIAL, 204 East Brown Street, Luverne. Website: www.co.rock.mn.us.

ROCK COUNTY HISTORICAL SOCIETY, 312 East Main Street, Luverne. Call 507-283-2122. Website: www.rockcountyhistorical.com.

SPLIT ROCK CREEK STATE PARK, 336 50th Avenue, Jasper. Call 507-283-6050. Website: www.dnr.state.mn.us/state_parks/park.html?id=spk00267 #homepage.

Dining

COUNTRY HOUSE SUPPER CLUB, 405 East Benton Street, Lake Benton. Call 507-368-4223. American cuisine. Website: www.facebook.com/Country -House-Supper-Club-5918585109051891.

GLASS HOUSE RESTAURANT, 102 Waldo Avenue South, Ihlen. Call 507-348-7651. Steakhouse menu, including seafood and chicken, and a Sunday smorgasbord.

HISTORIC CALUMET INN, 104 West Main, Pipestone. Call 507-825-5871. American food, full bar. Website: www.calumetinn.com.

KNOTTY PINE SUPPER CLUB, 1014 County Highway 10, Elkton, South Dakota. Call 507-548-3781. American cuisine. Website: www .theknottypinesupperclub.com.

LANGE'S CAFÉ AND BAKERY, 110 8th Avenue SE, Pipestone. Call 507-825-4488. Open 24/7, serving home-cooked meals including the usual sandwiches and soups as well as some more inventive pastas and meat dishes. Be sure to have the pie for dessert. Website: www.facebook.com/Langes-Cafe -1086864997001.

Other Contacts

LAKE BENTON CHAMBER OF COMMERCE, 108 South Center Street, Lake Benton. Call 507-368-9577. Website: www.lakebenton.us.

LUVERNE AREA CHAMBER OF COMMERCE, 213 East Luverne Street, Luverne. Call 507-283-4061. Website: www.luvernechamber.com.

PIPESTONE CHAMBER OF COMMERCE, 117 8th Avenue SE, Pipestone. Call 507-825-3316. Website: www.pipestoneminnesota.com.

Index